Impact maths 3R

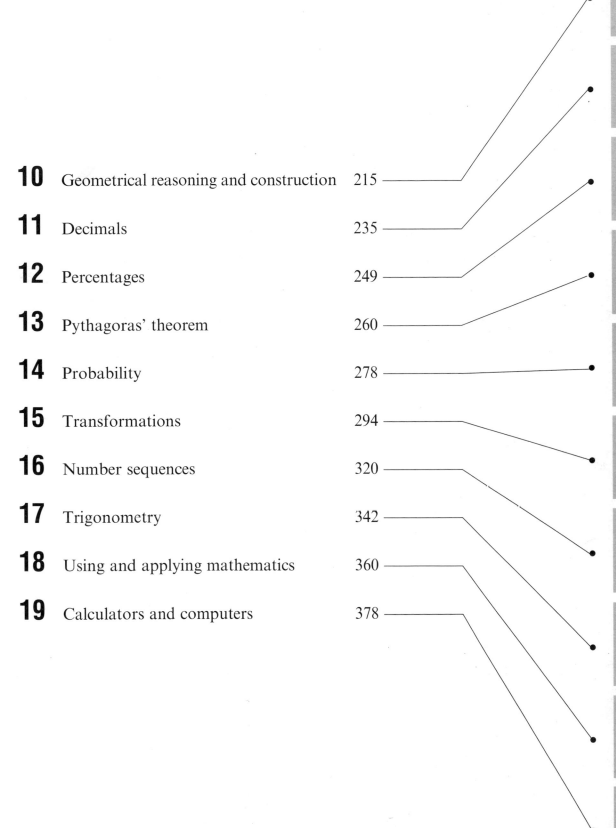

10

11

12

13

14

15

16

17

18

19

About this book

Impact maths provides a complete course to help you achieve your best in your Key Stage 3 mathematics course. This book will help you understand and remember mathematical ideas, solve mathematical problems with and without the help of a calculator and develop your mental maths skills.

Exercises you should try without the help of a calculator are marked with this symbol:

Extension

Extension sections at the end of the unit are marked **E**. These sections contain more challenging work. You should attempt them once you are confident with the rest of the work in that unit.

Remembering key ideas

We have provided clear explanations of the key ideas you need throughout the book with **worked examples** showing you how to answer questions. **Key points** you need to remember look like this:

■ **The probabilities of all the possible outcomes of an event add up to 1.**

and are listed in a **summary** at the end of each unit.

Investigations and information technology

Two units focus on particular skills you need for your course:
- **Using and applying mathematics** (unit 18) – shows you some ways of investigating mathematical problems.
- **Calculators and computers** (unit 19) – shows you some ways of using calculators and computers and will help with mental maths practice.

Internet links

All the internet links used in this book can be found at www.heinemann.co.uk/hotlinks. Express codes in the textbook help you find the webpages you need quickly and easily.

Heinemann Educational Publishers
Halley Court, Jordan Hill, Oxford, OX2 8EJ
a division of Reed Educational & Professional Publishing Ltd
Heinemann is a registered trademark of Reed Educational & Professional Publishing Ltd

OXFORD MELBOURNE AUCKLAND
JOHANNESBURG BLANTYRE GABORONE
IBADAN PORTSMOUTH NH (USA) CHICAGO

First published 2002

ISBN 0 435 01833 7

05 04 03 02
10 9 8 7 6 5 4 3 2

Designed and typeset by Tech-Set Ltd, Gateshead, Tyne and Wear
Illustrated by Barry Atkinson, Barking Dog and Tech-Set
Cover design by Miller, Craig and Cocking
Printed and bound by Edelvives, Spain

Acknowledgements

The authors and publishers would like to thank the following for permission to use photographs:

P1: Science Photo Library/Space Telescope Institute/NASA. P22: Still Pictures/Jorgen Schytte. P40: Robert Harding Picture Library/Vanderharst. P56: Q.A. Photos/Eurotunnel. P61: Quadrant Picture Library. P81: HMV. P89: Robert Harding Picture Library/ Michael DeYoung. P92: Science Photo Library/Peter Aprahamian. P96: MG Rover Group Communications. P102: Science Photo Library/NASA. P123: Science Photo Library/David Nunuk. P171 (top): Robert Harding Picture Library. P171 (bottom): Sally & Richard Greenhill/Sally Greenhill. P174: Empics/Mike Egerton. P178: Bruce Coleman Collection. P179: Robert Harding Picture Library. P193: Photodisc. P195: Science Photo Library/David Parker. P197: Impact/David Reed. P203: Science Photo Library/Dept. of Clinical Radiology, Salisbury District Hospital. P221: Science Photo Library/David Parker. P227: Science Photo Library. P231: Science Photo Library/Frank Close. P238: Science Photo Library/Space Telescope Science Institute/NASA. P244 (top): Science Photo Library/Martin Bond. P244 (bottom): Science Photo Library/European Space Agency. P249: Robert Harding Picture Library/Simon Harris. P251: Science Photo Library/Renee Lynn. P260: Ancient Art and Architecture. P302 (top): Photodisc. P302 (middle): Rupert Horrox. P302 (bottom): Digital Stock. P305: Rupert Horrox. P307: Chris Honeywell. P320: Science Photo/Library/Mehau Kulyk.

Cover Photo by Getty Images.

Publishing team

Editorial
Sue Bennett
Lauren Bourque
Philip Ellaway
Maggie Rumble
Nick Sample
Harry Smith
Isabel Thomas
Sue Glover
Katherine Pate

Design
Phil Richards
Colette Jacquelin
Mags Robertson

Production
David Lawrence
Jason Wyatt

Author team
David Benjamin
Sue Bright
Tony Clough
Gareth Cole
Diana DeBrida
Ray Fraser
Trevor Johnson
Peter Jolly
David Kent

Gina Marquess
Christine Medlow
Graham Newman
Sheila Nolan
Keith Pledger
Ian Roper
Mike Smith
John Sylvester

Tel: 01865 888058 www.heinemann.co.uk

Contents

National Curriculum cross-references in italics refer to the KS4 Higher programme of study.

4   Averages and spread

5   Formulae, equations and inequalities

16　Number sequences

E 17　Trigonometry

18　Using and applying mathematics

19   Calculators and computers

1 Number

For cosmologists numbers describe the universe we live in: how it was born and what will happen to it in the distant future.

1.1 Significant figures

26 MILLION PEOPLE PLAY THE LOTTERY EACH WEEK

You sometimes have to round to a given number of significant figures.

- **To round to a given number of significant figures look at the next significant figure:**
  - **If it is less than 5, round down.**
  - **If it is 5 or more, round up.**

Example 1

Round 4075 to

(a) 1 significant figure **(b)** 2 significant figures
(c) 3 significant figures

(a) The second significant figure is 0 so round down:
$$4075 = 4000 \text{ to 1 s.f.}$$

1st significant figure	2nd significant figure	3rd significant figure	4th significant figure
4	0	7	5

(b) The third significant figure is 7 so round up:

4075 = 4100 to 2 s.f.

(c) The fourth significant figure is 5 so round up:

4075 = 4080 to 3 s.f. ——————————————

You must always write down how accurate your answer is.

Exercise 1A

1 Round each number to
- 1 significant figure
- 2 significant figures
- 3 significant figures

(a) 5306   **(b)** 7528   **(c)** 4784   **(d)** 2954

(e) 8796   **(f)** 9843   **(g)** 84 709   **(h)** 89 983

2 To how many significant figures has each number been rounded?

(a) 426 = 430 to ☐ s.f.   **(b)** 8045 = 8050 to ☐ s.f.

(c) 6473 = 6470 to ☐ s.f.   **(d)** 35 874 = 36 000 to ☐ s.f.

(e) 74 589 = 74 590 to ☐ s.f.   **(f)** 498 = 500 to ☐ s.f. ——————

(g) 7396 = 7400 to ☐ s.f.   **(h)** 6998 = 7000 to ☐ s.f.

Hint: there are two possible answers to this question.

3 Match each number in the cloud to a statement in the box:

(a)

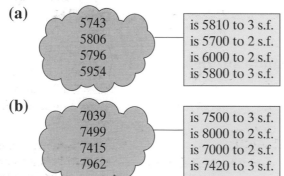

5743
5806
5796
5954

is 5810 to 3 s.f.
is 5700 to 2 s.f.
is 6000 to 2 s.f.
is 5800 to 3 s.f.

(b)

7039
7499
7415
7962

is 7500 to 3 s.f.
is 8000 to 2 s.f.
is 7000 to 2 s.f.
is 7420 to 3 s.f.

4 True or false:

(a) 473 = 480 to 2 s.f.   **(b)** 635 = 630 to 2 s.f.

(c) 749 = 700 to 1 s.f.   **(d)** 489 = 500 to 2 s.f.

(e) 1476 = 1500 to 2 s.f.   **(f)** 5448 = 5450 to 3 s.f.

(g) 4995 = 4900 to 3 s.f.   **(h)** 986 = 100 to 1 s.f.

1.2 Upper and lower bounds

When you have a number which has been rounded to a given number of significant figures, you may need to know the largest and smallest values the original number might have been. These values are called the **least upper bound** and **greatest lower bound** of the number.

Example 2

The population of the Falkland Islands is 2300 to 2 s.f. What are the least upper bound and greatest lower bound for the population?

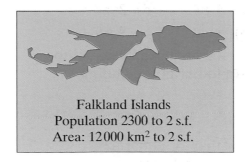

Falkland Islands
Population 2300 to 2 s.f.
Area: 12 000 km² to 2 s.f.

Population can only take a whole number value. You cannot have fractions of a person!

The smallest number that rounds up to 2300 is 2250.

The largest number that rounds down to 2300 is 2349.

2200   2250   2300   2350   2400

The greatest lower bound for the population is 2250.
The least upper bound is 2349.
So the population is between 2250 and 2349.
The population can be equal either to the greatest lower bound, or to the least upper bound, or to any whole number value in between these bounds.

This can be written as $2250 \leqslant \text{population} \leqslant 2349$
It is read as

'The population is greater than or equal to 2250 but less than or equal to 2349.'

Population is a **discrete variable**. The values of a discrete variable can always be counted separately.

Any number less than 2250 is also a lower bound for the population.

Any number greater than 2349 is also an upper bound for the population.

It is important to use the words **greatest** and **least** to describe your bounds.

Example 3

The area of the Falkland Islands is $12\,000\,\text{km}^2$ to 2 s.f.
What are the upper and lower bounds for the area?

Area does not need to take whole number values.
For example, the area of the Falkland Islands could be
$12\,499.284\,\text{km}^2$, or $12\,499\frac{3}{4}\,\text{km}^2$, or $12\,499.999\,996\,\text{km}^2$.

Area is a **continuous variable**. A continuous variable can take the value of any whole number, or any value between whole numbers.

The smallest number that rounds up to $12\,000$ is $11\,500$.

Any number bigger than $12\,000$ but less than $12\,500$ would round down to $12\,000$.

$11\,000$	$11\,500$	$12\,000$	$12\,500$	$13\,000$

The greatest lower bound for the area is $11\,500$.
The least upper bound is $12\,500$.
So the area is between $11\,500$ and $12\,500$.
Because it is a continuous variable, the area can be equal to
the lower bound, or to any value up to but not including
the upper bound.

This can be written as $\quad 11\,500\,\text{km}^2 \leqslant \text{area} < 12\,500\,\text{km}^2$

It is read as $\quad$ 'The area is greater than or equal to
$11\,500\,\text{km}^2$ but less than $12\,500\,\text{km}^2$.'

Exercise 1B

1 Which are discrete variables and which are continuous
variables?
(a) the number of pupils in a class
(b) the height of a person
(c) the length of a river
(d) the capacity of a bottle
(e) the number of sweets in a bag
(f) the price in pennies of a bar of chocolate
(g) the time you take to brush your teeth
(h) the price in pounds of a book

2 How would you read each of these sets of bounds?
(a) $265\,\text{m} \leqslant \text{perimeter of a garden} < 275\,\text{m}$
(b) $175 \leqslant \text{pupils in Year 7} \leqslant 184$
(c) $1750\,\text{m.p.h.} \leqslant \text{speed of a plane} < 1850\,\text{m.p.h.}$
(d) $1250 \leqslant \text{pupils in school} \leqslant 1349$

■ **When you remove brackets from expressions like $(4^3)^2$ you multiply the indices.**

e.g. $(4^3)^2 = 4^{3 \times 2} = 4^6$

Example 10

Evaluate $(2^5)^2 \div (2^3)^2$

First simplify the expression.

Remove the brackets:	$(2^5)^2 \div (2^3)^2 = 2^{10} \div 2^6$
Subtract the indices:	$= 2^4$
Then evaluate:	$= 16$
so	$(2^5)^2 \div (2^3)^2 = 16$

Example 11

Write 8^5 as a power of 2

Write 8 as a power of 2:	$8^5 = (2^3)^5$
Remove the brackets:	$= 2^{15}$
so	$8^5 = 2^{15}$

Exercise 1G

1 Simplify

  (a) $(2^5)^2$ (b) $(4^3)^4$ (c) $(3^2)^5$

  (d) $(7^4)^3$ (e) $(6^2)^2$ (f) $(5^3)^3$

  (g) $(3^4)^2 \times (3^2)^3$ (h) $(2^3)^7 \div (2^5)^2$ (i) $(6^3)^5 \div (6^4)^2$

  (j) $(4^4)^2 \times (4^3)^3$ (k) $(5^4)^3 \times (5^5)^2$ (l) $(2^4)^6 \div (2^5)^3$

2 Evaluate

  (a) $(2^5)^2 \div (2^3)^2$ (b) $(4^3)^4 \div (4^5)^2$ (c) $(3^8)^2 \div (3^4)^4$

  (d) $(7^5)^2 \div (7^2)^4$ (e) $(6^3)^3 \div (6^3)^2$ (f) $(5^7)^3 \div (5^2)^9$

  (g) $(3^9)^2 \div (3^6)^3$ (h) $(2^5)^7 \div (2^8)^4$ (i) $(10^4)^5 \div (10^5)^3$

3 Write as a power of 2:

  (a) 4^3 (b) 8^4 (c) 16^3 (d) 64^2

  (e) 32^3 (f) $4^3 \times 8^2$ (g) $8^3 \div 16^2$ (h) $64^2 \div 32^2$

4 Write as a power of 3:

  (a) 9^4 (b) 9^6 (c) 27^2 (d) 81^2

  (e) 243^2 (f) $9^3 \times 27^2$ (g) $81^3 \div 27^2$ (h) $243^2 \div 81^2$

5 Which of these expressions have a value of 1?

$27^4 \div 9^6$ $16^3 \div 64^2$ $32^3 \div 8^4$ $81^5 \div 9^{10}$

$27^3 \div 81^2$ $8^8 \div 16^6$ $125^6 \div 25^9$

6 Investigate the relationship between a and b if

(a) $(2^a)^b = 2^{a+b}$ (b) $(3^a)^b = 3^{a+b}$

7 Investigate the relationship between a, b, c and d if

(a) $2^a \times 2^b = 4^c \div 4^d$ (b) $3^a \times 3^b = 9^c \div 9^d$
(c) $2^a \times 2^b = 8^c \div 8^d$ (d) $10^a \times 10^b = 1000^c \div 1000^d$

1.6 Square roots and cube roots

A **root** is the opposite of a power.

$4^2 = 16$ so a square root of 16 is 4.
$(-4)^2 = 16$ so another square root of 16 is -4.

The symbol $\sqrt{}$ is the positive root so
$$\sqrt{16} = 4$$
You can write $\pm\sqrt{16}$ to refer to both square roots.

■ **Every positive number, n, has two square roots, one positive and one negative. They are written as $\pm\sqrt{n}$.**

So $\pm\sqrt{16}$ refers to both 4 and -4.

$4^3 = 64$ so the cube root of 64 is 4.

$(-4)^3 = -64$ so the cube root of -64 is -4.

■ **Every integer has just one cube root.**
The cube root of a positive number is positive.
The cube root of a negative number is negative.
The cube root of a number, n, is written as $\sqrt[3]{n}$.

Remember: **Integers** are positive or negative whole numbers.

For example: $\sqrt[3]{64} = 4$
$$\sqrt[3]{(-64)} = -4$$

Consider: $\sqrt{4} \times \sqrt{9} = 2 \times 3 = 6$

But $\sqrt{(4 \times 9)} = \sqrt{36} = 6$

so $\sqrt{4} \times \sqrt{9} = \sqrt{(4 \times 9)}$

■ **The product of two square roots is the same as the square root of the product:** $\sqrt{a} \times \sqrt{b} = \sqrt{(a \times b)}$.

For example: $\sqrt{4} \times \sqrt{9} = \sqrt{(4 \times 9)}$

Consider: $\sqrt{36} \div \sqrt{9} = 6 \div 3 = 2$

But $\sqrt{(36 \div 9)} = \sqrt{4} = 2$

so $\sqrt{36} \div \sqrt{9} = \sqrt{(36 \div 9)}$

■ **The quotient of two square roots is the same as the square root of the quotient:** $\sqrt{a} \div \sqrt{b} = \sqrt{(a \div b)}$.

This can also be written as $\dfrac{\sqrt{a}}{\sqrt{b}} = \sqrt{\dfrac{a}{b}}$.

For example: $\sqrt{36} \div \sqrt{9} = \sqrt{(36 \div 9)}$.

Example 12

Simplify then evaluate

(a) $\dfrac{\sqrt{108}}{\sqrt{3}}$

(b) $\sqrt{5} \times \sqrt{80}$

(a) Using the quotient rule: $\dfrac{\sqrt{108}}{\sqrt{3}} = \sqrt{\dfrac{108}{3}}$

Simplify the fraction: $= \sqrt{36}$

Evaluate the square root: $= 6$

(b) Using the product rule: $\sqrt{5} \times \sqrt{80} = \sqrt{(5 \times 80)}$

Work out the multiplication: $= \sqrt{400}$

Evaluate the square root: $= 20$

Example 13

Evaluate $\sqrt{5}(\sqrt{125} - \sqrt{5})$

Multiply out the brackets: $\sqrt{5}(\sqrt{125} - \sqrt{5}) = \sqrt{5}\sqrt{125} - \sqrt{5}\sqrt{5}$

Use the product rule: $\qquad\qquad\qquad = \sqrt{(5 \times 125)} - \sqrt{(5 \times 5)}$

Work out the multiplications: $\qquad = \sqrt{625} - \sqrt{25}$

Evaluate the square roots: $\qquad\quad = 25 - 5$

$\qquad\qquad\qquad\qquad\qquad\qquad\quad = 20$

Exercise 1H

1 Simplify then evaluate

   (a) $\dfrac{\sqrt{18}}{\sqrt{2}}$ **(b)** $\dfrac{\sqrt{72}}{\sqrt{2}}$ **(c)** $\dfrac{\sqrt{28}}{\sqrt{7}}$ **(d)** $\dfrac{\sqrt{45}}{\sqrt{5}}$

   (e) $\sqrt{2} \times \sqrt{8}$ **(f)** $\sqrt{3} \times \sqrt{12}$ **(g)** $\sqrt{5} \times \sqrt{20}$ **(h)** $\sqrt{6} \times \sqrt{24}$

   (i) $\dfrac{\sqrt{54}}{\sqrt{6}}$ **(j)** $\dfrac{\sqrt{48}}{\sqrt{3}}$ **(k)** $\dfrac{\sqrt{125}}{\sqrt{5}}$ **(l)** $\dfrac{\sqrt{64}}{\sqrt{16}}$

   (m) $\sqrt{3} \times \sqrt{27}$ **(n)** $\sqrt{2} \times \sqrt{18}$ **(o)** $\sqrt{32} \times \sqrt{2}$ **(p)** $\sqrt{8} \times \sqrt{18}$

2 Multiply out the brackets, simplify, then evaluate

   (a) $\sqrt{3}(\sqrt{3} + \sqrt{27})$ **(b)** $\sqrt{2}(\sqrt{8} + \sqrt{32})$ **(c)** $\sqrt{5}(\sqrt{20} - \sqrt{5})$

   (d) $\sqrt{2}(\sqrt{18} + \sqrt{8})$ **(e)** $\sqrt{2}(\sqrt{8} - \sqrt{2})$ **(f)** $\sqrt{3}(\sqrt{27} - \sqrt{12})$

   (g) $\sqrt{6}(\sqrt{24} + \sqrt{6})$ **(h)** $\sqrt{3}(\sqrt{12} + \sqrt{48})$ **(i)** $\sqrt{8}(\sqrt{18} - \sqrt{2})$

3 Mo wrote this down in her homework book:

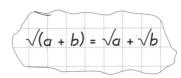

$$\sqrt{(a + b)} = \sqrt{a} + \sqrt{b}$$

Substitute values for *a* and *b* into this expression to show that Mo is wrong.

E 1.7 Surds

Look at the table of square roots and their decimal equivalents. Only the square numbers have square roots that can be written exactly using decimals.

The square roots of other numbers have decimal equivalents that go on for ever and never repeat themselves.

These are called **surds**.

Square root	Decimal equivalent
$\sqrt{2}$	1.414 2135 ...
$\sqrt{3}$	1.732 0508 ...
$\sqrt{4}$	2
$\sqrt{5}$	2.236 0679 ...
$\sqrt{6}$	2.449 4897 ...
$\sqrt{7}$	2.645 7513 ...
$\sqrt{8}$	2.828 4271 ...
$\sqrt{9}$	3
$\sqrt{10}$	3.162 2776 ...
$\sqrt{11}$	3.316 6247 ...
$\sqrt{12}$	3.464 1016 ...
$\sqrt{13}$	3.605 5512 ...
$\sqrt{14}$	3.741 6573 ...
$\sqrt{15}$	3.872 9833 ...
$\sqrt{16}$	4
$\sqrt{17}$	4.123 1056 ...

■ **A surd is the square root of any number which is not a square number. A surd cannot be written exactly as a decimal.**

$\sqrt{2}$, $\sqrt{3}$, $\sqrt{5}$, $\sqrt{6}$, $\sqrt{7}$, $\sqrt{8}$, $\sqrt{10}$, $\sqrt{11}$, $\sqrt{12}$, $\sqrt{13}$, $\sqrt{14}$, $\sqrt{15}$, $\sqrt{17}$ ... are all surds.

$\sqrt{1}$, $\sqrt{4}$, $\sqrt{9}$, $\sqrt{16}$, $\sqrt{25}$ ... are not surds.

Surds often appear when solving mathematical problems, for example when using Pythagoras' theorem. In order to get the most accurate answer to a problem, you should not convert them to decimals until you have the final solution. This is one reason why you need to learn to manipulate square roots.

Example 14

Write $\sqrt{63}$ in terms of the simplest possible surd.

Look for a square number that is a factor of 63:   9 is a factor of 63

Write 63 as a multiple of 9: $\sqrt{63} = \sqrt{(9 \times 7)}$

Use the product rule: $= \sqrt{9} \times \sqrt{7}$

Evaluate $\sqrt{9}$: $= 3\sqrt{7}$

Exercise 1I

1 Write in terms of the simplest possible surd:
   (a) $\sqrt{8}$ (b) $\sqrt{12}$ (c) $\sqrt{27}$ (d) $\sqrt{18}$
   (e) $\sqrt{28}$ (f) $\sqrt{75}$ (g) $\sqrt{80}$ (h) $\sqrt{20}$
   (i) $\sqrt{48}$ (j) $\sqrt{45}$ (k) $\sqrt{125}$ (l) $\sqrt{99}$

2 Multiply out the brackets and write the expression in
   terms of the simplest possible surds, collecting like
   terms where possible:
   (a) $\sqrt{21}(\sqrt{12} + \sqrt{2})$ (b) $\sqrt{6}(\sqrt{8} + \sqrt{10})$
   (c) $\sqrt{32}(\sqrt{9} + \sqrt{27})$ (d) $\sqrt{44}(\sqrt{28} + \sqrt{11})$
   (e) $\sqrt{3}(\sqrt{18} + \sqrt{27} + \sqrt{45})$ (f) $\sqrt{8}(\sqrt{7} + \sqrt{24} + \sqrt{3})$

3 A circle has an area of $27\pi \, \text{cm}^2$. Work out its diameter,
   giving your answer in terms of the simplest possible surd.

E 1.8 Indices and roots

By the laws of indices: $64^{\frac{1}{3}} \times 64^{\frac{1}{3}} \times 64^{\frac{1}{3}} = 64^1$

But also: $\sqrt[3]{64} \times \sqrt[3]{64} \times \sqrt[3]{64} = 64$

So $64^{\frac{1}{3}} = \sqrt[3]{64}$

Remember:
$64^1 = 64$

■ **The nth root of a number is the same as the number
   raised to the power of $\frac{1}{n}$**

   $$\sqrt[n]{x} = x^{\frac{1}{n}}$$

   For example: $\sqrt[3]{64} = 64^{\frac{1}{3}}$, $\sqrt[2]{16} = 16^{\frac{1}{2}}$,
   $\sqrt[5]{100\,000} = 100\,000^{\frac{1}{5}}$

Example 15

Evaluate
(a) $125^{\frac{1}{3}}$ (b) $16^{\frac{3}{2}}$

(a) $125^{\frac{1}{3}} = \sqrt[3]{125}$ (b) $16^{\frac{3}{2}} = (16^{\frac{1}{2}})^3$
         $= 5$ $= 4^3$
                                 $= 64$

Example 16

(a) $5^{\frac{15}{4}} \div 5^{\frac{3}{4}}$

(b) $\left(\dfrac{125}{216}\right)^{\frac{2}{3}}$

(a) $5^{\frac{15}{4}} \div 5^{\frac{3}{4}} = 5^{\frac{15}{4} - \frac{3}{4}}$

$\qquad = 5^{\frac{12}{4}}$

$\qquad = 5^3$

$\qquad = 125$

(b) $\left(\dfrac{125}{216}\right)^{\frac{2}{3}} = \left(\left(\dfrac{125}{216}\right)^{\frac{1}{3}}\right)^2$

$\qquad = \left(\dfrac{125^{\frac{1}{3}}}{216^{\frac{1}{3}}}\right)^2$

$\qquad = \left(\dfrac{5}{6}\right)^2$

$\qquad = \dfrac{25}{36}$

Exercise 1J

1 What is the value of

(a) $8^{\frac{1}{3}}$ (b) $36^{\frac{1}{2}}$ (c) $81^{\frac{1}{4}}$ (d) $32^{\frac{1}{5}}$

(e) $16^{\frac{1}{2}}$ (f) $16^{\frac{1}{4}}$ (g) $1000^{\frac{1}{3}}$ (h) $64^{\frac{1}{6}}$

2 Evaluate

(a) $25^{\frac{3}{2}}$ (b) $27^{\frac{2}{3}}$ (c) $4^{\frac{5}{2}}$ (d) $64^{\frac{5}{6}}$

(e) $81^{\frac{3}{4}}$ (f) $100^{\frac{5}{2}}$ (g) $125^{\frac{2}{3}}$ (h) $36^{\frac{3}{2}}$

3 Simplify then evaluate

(a) $5^{\frac{3}{2}} \times 5^{\frac{1}{2}}$ (b) $6^{\frac{2}{3}} \times 6^{\frac{4}{3}}$ (c) $4^{\frac{9}{4}} \times 4^{\frac{3}{4}}$

(d) $3^{\frac{5}{2}} \div 3^{\frac{1}{2}}$ (e) $5^{\frac{9}{4}} \div 5^{\frac{1}{4}}$ (f) $3^{\frac{5}{3}} \times 3^{\frac{7}{3}}$

(g) $10^{\frac{11}{2}} \div 10^{\frac{3}{2}}$ (h) $6^{\frac{5}{2}} \times 6^{\frac{1}{2}}$ (i) $6^{\frac{13}{4}} \div 6^{\frac{1}{4}}$

4 Evaluate

(a) $\left(\dfrac{4}{25}\right)^{\frac{1}{2}}$ (b) $\left(\dfrac{9}{4}\right)^{\frac{1}{2}}$ (c) $\left(\dfrac{16}{9}\right)^{\frac{1}{2}}$ (d) $\left(\dfrac{25}{49}\right)^{\frac{1}{2}}$

(e) $\left(\dfrac{27}{8}\right)^{\frac{1}{3}}$ (f) $\left(\dfrac{125}{27}\right)^{\frac{1}{3}}$ (g) $\left(\dfrac{64}{125}\right)^{\frac{1}{3}}$ (h) $\left(\dfrac{8}{64}\right)^{\frac{1}{3}}$

5 Evaluate

(a) $\left(\dfrac{27}{64}\right)^{\frac{2}{3}}$ (b) $\left(\dfrac{8}{27}\right)^{\frac{2}{3}}$ (c) $\left(\dfrac{4}{9}\right)^{\frac{3}{2}}$ (d) $\left(\dfrac{8}{125}\right)^{\frac{2}{3}}$

(e) $\left(\dfrac{16}{25}\right)^{\frac{3}{2}}$ (f) $\left(\dfrac{125}{8}\right)^{\frac{4}{3}}$ (g) $\left(\dfrac{27}{8}\right)^{\frac{4}{3}}$ (h) $\left(\dfrac{81}{16}\right)^{\frac{3}{4}}$

Summary of key points

1st significant figure	2nd significant figure	3rd significant figure	4th significant figure
4	0	7	5

1 To round to a given number of significant figures, look at the next significant figure:
- If it is less than 5, round down.
- If it is 5 or more, round up.

2 You can check that a calculator answer is in the right region by rounding each number to 1 s.f. and then estimating the answer.

3 To check that a calculator answer is correct, you can use the inverse number machine. This is called using inverse operations.

4 When multiplying powers of the same number, you add the indices.
$$4^2 \times 4^3 = 4^{2+3} = 4^5$$

> Remember: 'indices' is another word for 'powers'.

5 When dividing powers of the same number, you subtract the indices.
$$4^5 \div 4^3 = 4^{5-3} = 4^2$$

6 Any number (other than 0) raised to the power of zero equals 1.
$$2^0 = 3^0 = 4^0 = (5.4)^0 = (7\tfrac{1}{2})^0 = 1$$

7 When you remove brackets from expressions like $(4^3)^2$ you multiply the indices.
$$(4^3)^2 = 4^{3 \times 2} = 4^6$$

8 Every positive number, n, has two square roots, one positive and one negative. They are written as $\pm\sqrt{n}$.

So $\pm\sqrt{16}$ refers to both 4 and -4.

> The symbol $\sqrt{}$ is the positive root so
> $$\sqrt{16} = 4$$
> You can write $\pm\sqrt{16}$ to refer to both square roots.

9 Every integer has just one cube root.
The cube root of a positive number is positive.
The cube root of a negative number is negative.
The cube root of a number, n, is written as $\sqrt[3]{n}$.

So $\qquad \sqrt[3]{64} = 4$
and $\qquad \sqrt[3]{(-64)} = -4$

10 The product of two square roots is the same as the square root of the product: $\sqrt{a} \times \sqrt{b} = \sqrt{(a \times b)}$.
For example: $\sqrt{4} \times \sqrt{9} = \sqrt{(4 \times 9)}$

11 The quotient of two square roots is the same as the square root of the quotient: $\sqrt{a} \div \sqrt{b} = \sqrt{(a \div b)}$.

This can also be written as $\dfrac{\sqrt{a}}{\sqrt{b}} = \sqrt{\dfrac{a}{b}}$.

For example: $\sqrt{36} \div \sqrt{9} = \sqrt{(36 \div 9)}$

E A surd is the square root of any number which is not a square number. A surd cannot be written exactly as a decimal.
$\sqrt{2}, \sqrt{3}, \sqrt{5}, \sqrt{6}, \sqrt{7}, \sqrt{8}, \sqrt{10}, \sqrt{11}, \sqrt{12}, \sqrt{13}, \sqrt{14}, \sqrt{15}, \sqrt{17} \ldots$ are all surds.
$\sqrt{1}, \sqrt{4}, \sqrt{9}, \sqrt{16}, \sqrt{25} \ldots$ are not surds.

E The nth root of a number is the same as the number raised to the power of $\dfrac{1}{n}$.

$$\sqrt[n]{x} = x^{\frac{1}{n}}$$

For example: $\sqrt[3]{64} = 64^{\frac{1}{3}}, \sqrt[2]{16} = 16^{\frac{1}{2}}, \sqrt[5]{100\,000} = 100\,000^{\frac{1}{5}}$.

2 Working with algebra

Algebra is a universal language. Mathematicians from around the world use algebra to explain their ideas to each other.

To solve many problems in mathematics, you need to be able to work with algebra confidently.

Revision

- **In algebra a collection of letters and numbers is called a *term*.**
  For example: $5y$ is a term in y;
  $\qquad\qquad$ $8mn$ is a term in m and n.

- **A collection of terms is called an *expression*.**
  For example: $5p + 6q$ is an algebraic expression which has two terms: $5p$ and $6q$.

- **Terms that contain exactly the same letters are called *like terms*.**
  For example: $3rs$ and $7rs$ are like terms because they both contain only rs.

2.1 Multiplying and dividing powers

In chapter 1 you saw how to multiply powers of numbers:
$$5^3 \times 5^5 = (5 \times 5 \times 5) \times (5 \times 5 \times 5 \times 5 \times 5)$$
$$= 5^{3+5}$$
$$= 5^8$$

You need to be able to multiply powers of letters:
$$p^3 \times p^2 = (p \times p \times p) \times (p \times p)$$
$$= p^{3+2}$$
$$= p^5$$

- **To multiply powers of numbers or letters, add the indices together:**
  $$x^a \times x^b = x^{a+b}$$

The expression
$$x^a \times x^b = x^{a+b}$$
is true for all values of a, b and x. An expression that is true for all values of the variables is called an **identity**. You can write an identity using the symbol $\equiv$, which means 'is identically equal to'. For example:
$$x^a \times x^b \equiv x^{a+b}$$

You also need to be able to divide powers of letters.
For example:

$$t^5 \div t^3 = \frac{t \times t \times \cancel{t} \times \cancel{t} \times \cancel{t}}{\cancel{t} \times \cancel{t} \times \cancel{t}}$$

$$= t \times t \quad\text{————} \quad \text{Cancelling } t \times t \times t$$
$$\text{top and bottom}$$
$$= t^2$$

$$t^5 \div t^3 = t^{5-3} = t^2$$

■ **To divide powers of numbers or letters, subtract the indices:**
$$x^a \div x^b = x^{a-b}$$

Sometimes you need to find a power of a power.
For example:

$$(q^2)^3 = q^2 \times q^2 \times q^2$$
$$= (q \times q) \times (q \times q) \times (q \times q)$$
$$= q^6$$

■ **To find a power of a power multiply the indices:**
$$(x^a)^b = x^{ab}$$

■ **Any letter raised to the power of zero is equal to one.**
$$x^0 = 1$$

Example 1

Simplify
(a) $x^3 \times x^4$ (b) $x^7 \times x$ (c) $y^{10} \div y^3$ (d) $x^6 \div x$

(e) $y^2 \times y^3 \times y^4$ (f) $\dfrac{x^3 \times x^5}{x^2}$ (g) $4x^3 \times 5x^2$

(a) $x^3 \times x^4 = x^{3+4} = x^7$

(b) $x^7 \times x = x^{7+1} = x^8$ Remember: $x = x^1$

(c) $y^{10} \div y^3 = y^{10-3} = y^7$

(d) $x^6 \div x = x^{6-1} = x^5$

(e) $y^2 \times y^3 \times y^4 = y^{2+3+4} = y^9$

(f) $\dfrac{x^3 \times x^5}{x^2} = x^{3+5} \div x^2 = x^8 \div x^2 = x^{8-2} = x^6$

(g) $4x^3 \times 5x^2 = 4 \times 5 \times x^3 \times x^2 = 20x^{3+2} = 20x^5$

Exercise 2A

Simplify these expressions:

1 $b^3 \times b^2$

2 $d^4 \times d$

3 $p^4 \times p^7$

4 $r \times r^6$

5 $x^2 \times x^2$

6 $y^3 \times y^9$

7 $t^3 \div t^2$

8 $s^6 \div s^3$

9 $m^9 \div m^2$

10 $n^5 \div n^4$

11 $(b^3)^4$

12 $(c^2)^8$

13 $(x^5)^5 \times x^2$

14 $(z^3)^2 \times (z^4)^2$

15 $c^4 \times c^2 \times c^5$

16 $f^{11} \times f^2 \times (f^5)^2$

17 $(g^2)^2 \times g \times g^3$

18 $w^4 \times w^4 \times w^4$

19 $x^3 \div x^3$

20 $y^2 \times y^5 \times y^2$

21 $\dfrac{a^2 \times a^3}{a^4}$

22 $\dfrac{r^6 \times r^2}{r^3}$

23 $\dfrac{m^2 \times m^7}{m^3}$

24 $\dfrac{x^3 \times x^2}{x^5}$

25 $\dfrac{y^2 \times y^7}{y^9}$

26 $\dfrac{x^3 \times x^2}{x}$

27 $\dfrac{x^{19}}{x^2 \times x^8 \times x^7}$

28 $\dfrac{t^3 \times t^9}{t^4}$

29 $\dfrac{b^3 \times b^4 \times b^5}{b^2 \times b^7}$

30 $\dfrac{a^3 \times a^2 \times a^5}{a^2 \times a^3}$

31 $5x^2 \times 4x^3$

32 $3a^4 \times 2a^5$

33 $3t^3 \times 7t^5$

34 $8r^3 \times 3r^6$

35 $3x^2 \times 2x^3 \times 5x^3$

36 $5y^2 \times 3y^3 \times y^5$

37 $4(y^2)^3 \times 2y^6 \times (y^4)^2$

38 $2h^2 \times (h^3)^3 \times 9(h^2)^2$

39 $\dfrac{2(y^3)^2 \times y^4}{(y^3)^3}$

40 $\dfrac{6m^4 \times (m^2)^2 \times m^3}{3(m^3)^2}$

2.2 Adding and subtracting expressions with brackets

You can simplify expressions with brackets by expanding the brackets and collecting like terms.

Example 2

Simplify $2(3x + 2y) - 3(x - 2y)$

Expand the brackets: $2 \times 3x + 2 \times 2y - 3 \times x - 3 \times -2y$

$$= 6x + 4y - 3x + 6y$$

Collect like terms: $6x - 3x + 4y + 6y$

$$= 3x + 10y$$

Remember:
$- \times - = +$

Example 3

Simplify $7(3x - 2y) - (2x + y)$

Expand the brackets: $21x - 14y - 2x - y$

Collect like terms: $21x - 2x - 14y - y$

$$= 19x - 15y$$

Remember:
$-(2x + y)$ means
$-1(2x + y)$

Example 4

Simplify $m^2(m^3 - 2) + m^3(m^2 + 3)$

Expand the brackets:

$$m^2 \times m^3 - 2 \times m^2 + m^3 \times m^2 + 3 \times m^3$$
$$= m^{2+3} - 2m^2 + m^{3+2} + 3m^3$$
$$= m^5 - 2m^2 + m^5 + 3m^3$$

Collect like terms:

$$m^5 + m^5 + 3m^3 - 2m^2$$
$$= 2m^5 + 3m^3 - 2m^2$$

Remember:
like terms must
contain exactly the
same letters. m^3 and
m^2 are not like
terms.

Exercise 2B

Simplify these expressions:

1 $2(x + y) + 3(2x + y)$
2 $5(2m + n) + 3(3m + 2n)$

3 $4(3s + 2t) + 3(s - t)$
4 $7(3a - 2b) + 5(a - 3b)$

5　$3(c - d) + 4(c + d)$　　　**6**　$5(2p - 5q) + 2(p + 2q)$

7　$6(4 - 2x) + 3(2x - 4)$　　　**8**　$4(3e + 5f) + 3(2e - 7f)$

9　$5(2x + 3y) - 2(x + 2y)$　　　**10**　$3(3x + 2y) - 4(x + 3y)$

11　$7(3c - 2d) - 5(2c - 3d)$　　**12**　$3(m - n) - 3(m + n)$

13　$3(r + 2s) - (r + s)$　　　　**14**　$2(3p - 2q) - 3(2p - 7q)$

15　$2(3x - 5y) - 3(2x - y)$　　　**16**　$4(3g + 2h) - (5g - 2h)$

17　$4(3a - 4b) - 3(2a + 5b)$　　**18**　$7(2x + y) - 5(x - 2y)$

19　$3(2c - 3d) - 3(3c - 2d)$　　**20**　$(3m - 7n) - (2m + 3n)$

21　$(6w - 3y) - (3w - 4y)$　　　**22**　$3(3x + 2y) - 4(3x - 2y)$

23　$4(3x - 4y) - 2(2x - 7y)$　　**24**　$x(3x - 2y) + y(3x - 4y)$

25　$a(3a - 4b) + 2a(a - b)$　　**26**　$11t^2(t^3 - 5) - (2t^5 - 11t^2)$

27　$5p^2(p + 3) + 3p(p^2 - 7)$　**28**　$3y(5y^2 + 3) + 2y(3y^2 + 1)$

29　$2x(3x + 2) - x(5x + 1)$　　**30**　$a^3(a^2 - 1) - a^2(a^3 - 3)$

2.3 Factorising simple expressions

■　**Factorising is the reverse process to removing brackets.**

Factorising lets you write algebraic expressions in a shorter form using brackets. It also helps you to solve algebra problems.

Example 5

Factorise the expression $5x + 10$

Look for the highest common factor of the terms $5x$ and 10.

Factors of $5x$ are:

　$\underline{1}, \underline{5}, x, 5x$

Factors of 10 are:

　$\underline{1}, 2, \underline{5}, 10$

The common factors are 1 and 5 so the highest common factor is 5.

You can write the 5 outside a bracket:

　$5x + 10 = 5(x + 2)$

The common factors are underlined.

Example 6

Factorise $12x - 18y$

Look for the highest common factor of the terms $12x$ and $18y$. 6 is the highest common factor.
So 6 can be taken outside a bracket:
$$12x - 18y = 6(2x - 3y)$$

Example 7

Factorise the expression $4x^2 + 12x$

Look for the highest common factor of the terms $4x^2$ and $12x$.
Factors of $4x^2$ are:
$$1, 2, 4, x, 2x, 4x, x^2, 2x^2, 4x^2$$
Factors of $12x$ are:
$$1, 2, 3, 4, 6, 12, x, 2x, 3x, 4x, 6x, 12x$$

The common factors are $1, 2, 4, x, 2x$ and $4x$ so the highest common factor is $4x$.

You can write $4x$ outside a bracket:
$$4x^2 + 12x = 4x(x + 3)$$

Example 8

Factorise $6xy - 8y$

The highest common factor is $2y$.
So: $\qquad 6xy - 8y = 2y(3x - 4)$

Exercise 2C

1 **(a)** Write out the factors of $9x^2$.
   (b) Write out the factors of $6x$.
   (c) Underline the common factors.
   (d) Factorise $9x^2 + 6x$.

2 Factorise these expressions:
   (a) $4a + 16$
   (b) $8r + 24$
   (c) $6x + 9$
   (d) $6y - 12$
   (e) $10y - 15$
   (f) $4p + 6q$
   (g) $8r - 12s$
   (h) $12x - 30y$
   (i) $15w - 3z$

3 Factorise these expressions:

(a) $3y^2 + 9y$ (b) $3b + 4b^2$ (c) $6e^2 + 15e$

(d) $60ab + 45a$ (e) $15y^2 - 6y$ (f) $4b^2 + 6b$

(g) $3x^2 - 2x$ (h) $8ab + 4b$ (i) $6a^2b + 4a$

4 Factorise these expressions:

(a) $4x^2y - 2xy$ (b) $10pq - 15p$ (c) $8ab - 12a$

(d) $3a^3b^2 - 12ab$ (e) $8s^2t - 6st^2$ (f) $11p^2q^3 + 33pq^2$

2.4 Fractions in algebra

To add and subtract fractions you have to find equivalent fractions with the same denominator. That denominator is the least common multiple (LCM) of the two denominators.

For example: $\frac{2}{3} + \frac{3}{5} = \frac{10}{15} + \frac{9}{15}$

$$= \frac{19}{15}$$

$$= 1\frac{4}{15}$$

You can use the same method to add and subtract algebraic fractions.

■ **To add and subtract algebraic fractions find equivalent fractions with the same denominator.**

Example 9

Simplify $\dfrac{4x}{3} + \dfrac{8}{y}$

You need to find equivalent fractions with the same denominator:

Equivalent fractions:

$$\frac{2}{3} \overset{\times 5}{\underset{\times 5}{=}} \frac{10}{15}$$

$$\frac{3}{5} \overset{\times 3}{\underset{\times 3}{=}} \frac{9}{15}$$

$$\frac{4x}{3} \overset{\times y}{\underset{\times y}{=}} \frac{4xy}{3y} \qquad \frac{8}{y} \overset{\times 3}{\underset{\times 3}{=}} \frac{24}{3y}$$

The least common multiple of 3 and y is $3y$.

So $\quad \dfrac{4x}{3} + \dfrac{8}{y} = \dfrac{4xy}{3y} + \dfrac{24}{3y}$

$\qquad\qquad = \dfrac{4xy + 24}{3y}$

$\qquad\qquad = \dfrac{4(xy + 6)}{3y}$ ——————— Simplify your answer as much as possible.

Example 10

Simplify $\dfrac{y^2}{4x} - \dfrac{2y}{x^2}$

Find equivalent fractions with the same denominator:

$\overset{\times x}{\curvearrowright}$

$\dfrac{y^2}{4x} = \dfrac{xy^2}{4x^2}$

$\underset{\times x}{\curvearrowright}$

$\overset{\times 4}{\curvearrowright}$

$\dfrac{2y}{x^2} = \dfrac{8y}{4x^2}$

$\underset{\times 4}{\curvearrowright}$

The least common multiple of $4x$ and x^2 is $4x^2$.

So $\quad \dfrac{y^2}{4x} - \dfrac{2y}{x^2} = \dfrac{xy^2}{4x^2} - \dfrac{8y}{4x^2}$

$\qquad\qquad\quad = \dfrac{xy^2 - 8y}{4x^2}$

$\qquad\qquad\quad = \dfrac{y(xy - 8)}{4x^2}$

Exercise 2D

1 Supraj wrote this down in his homework book:

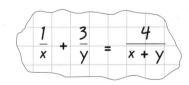

$$\dfrac{1}{x} + \dfrac{3}{y} = \dfrac{4}{x + y}$$

   (a) Substitute values for x and y into the expression to show that Supraj was wrong.

   (b) Simplify $\dfrac{1}{x} + \dfrac{3}{y}$.

2 Simplify these expressions:

(a) $\dfrac{x}{2} + \dfrac{1}{y}$ (b) $\dfrac{m^2}{2n} + \dfrac{1}{n^2}$ (c) $\dfrac{xy}{3} + \dfrac{3x}{2y^2}$

(d) $\dfrac{1}{m^2n} + \dfrac{m}{n^2}$ (e) $\dfrac{4d}{e} + \dfrac{e^2f}{d}$ (f) $\dfrac{3xy}{2z} + \dfrac{z^2}{x^2y}$

3 Simplify these expressions:

(a) $\dfrac{m}{4} - \dfrac{3}{2n}$ (b) $\dfrac{a^2}{3b} - \dfrac{b}{a}$

(c) $\dfrac{2x^2}{y} - \dfrac{y^2x}{3}$ (d) $\dfrac{4}{2n^2} - \dfrac{3m}{4n}$

(e) $\dfrac{4p^2q}{r^2} - \dfrac{p}{q^2r}$ (f) $\dfrac{2x}{y^2z} - \dfrac{xy}{3z^2}$

E 2.5 Multiplying bracketed expressions

Sometimes you will need to multiply two expressions with brackets.

Example 11

Write without brackets:

$$(x+2)(x+5)$$

This means $(x + 2) \times (x + 5)$.

There are two ways of expanding this expression.

Method 1
This rectangle has sides of length $(x + 2)$ and $(x + 5)$.
The total area of the rectangle is $(x + 2)(x + 5)$.
By dividing the rectangle into smaller sections
you can see that:

$$(x+2)(x+5) = x^2 + 2x + 5x + 10$$
$$= x^2 + 7x + 10 \quad\text{——— Collect like terms}$$

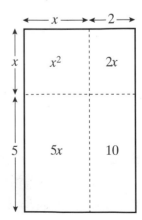

Method 2
You can multiply out the brackets in two stages.

$$(x+2)(x+5) = x(x+5) + 2(x+5)$$
$$= x^2 + 5x + 2x + 10$$
$$= x^2 + 7x + 10$$

Exercise 2E

1 Write these expressions without brackets using **Method 1**.

(a) $(y+1)(y+2)$ (b) $(a+2)(a+4)$

(c) $(x+4)(x+5)$ (d) $(4+t)(3+t)$

(e) $(2n+1)(n+2)$ (f) $(m+6)(3+4m)$

2 Use this diagram to expand $(x-3)(x-2)$.

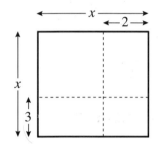

3 Expand these expressions using **Method 2**.

(a) $(p+1)(p+5)$ (b) $(2r+1)(3+r)$

(c) $(y-3)(y+5)$ (d) $(2-x)(3-x)$

(e) $(p+2)^2$ (f) $(w-8)^2$

(g) $(x-3)(1-2x)$ (h) $(2x+1)(3x-6)$

(i) $(4-2q)^2$ (j) $(r-3)(2r-9)$

4 Use this diagram to expand $(a+b)^2$.

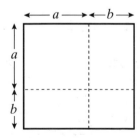

5 Use either of the methods given to write these expressions without brackets.

(a) $(x+y)(x+z)$ (b) $(a+b)(c+d)$

(c) $(m-n)^2$ (d) $(p+q)(p-q)$

(e) $(e+f)(e-g)$ (f) $(w+x)(y-z)$

E 2.6 Fractional and negative powers

So far you have only used whole number positive powers in algebra. You can apply the laws of indices to fractional and negative powers as well.

$$x^{\frac{1}{2}} \times x^{\frac{1}{2}} = x^{\frac{1}{2}+\frac{1}{2}} = x^1 = x$$

So $x^{\frac{1}{2}} = \sqrt{x}$

Remember:
$\sqrt[n]{x}$ means 'the nth root of 'x'.
$\underbrace{\sqrt[n]{x} \times \sqrt[n]{x} \times \ldots \times \sqrt[n]{x}}_{n \text{ times}} = x$

■ $x^{\frac{1}{n}} = \sqrt[n]{x}$

You also need to be able to work with negative powers.

$$\frac{1}{x^2} = \frac{x^0}{x^2} = x^{0-2} = x^{-2}$$

■ $x^{-n} = \dfrac{1}{x^n}$

Example 12

Write $\sqrt[3]{(m^2)}$ as a fractional power.

$$\sqrt[3]{(m^2)} = (m^2)^{\frac{1}{3}} = m^{2 \times \frac{1}{3}} = m^{\frac{2}{3}}$$

Example 13

Write $\dfrac{q}{q^4}$ as a negative power.

$$\frac{q}{q^4} = q^{1-4} = q^{-3}$$

Exercise 2F

1   Write these expressions as fractional powers
(a) $\sqrt[3]{x}$ (b) $\sqrt[3]{(p^4)}$ (c) $\left(\sqrt[3]{p}\right)^4$ (d) $\sqrt[6]{z}$

2   Write these expressions as negative powers
(a) $\dfrac{1}{y^3}$ (b) $q^3 \div q^8$ (c) $\dfrac{4}{r^2}$ (d) $\dfrac{s^3}{s^4}$

3 Write down the number that should be in the box.

$$\frac{x^{-2}}{\sqrt[3]{x}} = x^{\boxed{}}$$

Hint:
Write the denominator
as a fractional power first.

Summary of key points

1 In algebra a collection of letters and numbers is called a *term*.

2 A collection of terms is called an *expression*.

3 Terms that contain exactly the same letters are called *like terms*.

4 To multiply powers of numbers or letters, add the indices together: $x^a \times x^b = x^{a+b}$

5 To divide powers of numbers or letters, subtract the indices: $x^a \div x^b = x^{a-b}$

6 To find a power of a power multiply the indices: $(x^a)^b = x^{ab}$

7 Any letter raised to the power of zero is equal to 1: $x^0 = 1$

8 Factorising is the reverse process to removing brackets.

9 To add and subtract algebraic fractions find equivalent fractions with the same denominator.

E $x^{\frac{1}{n}} = \sqrt[n]{x}$

E $x^{-n} = \dfrac{1}{x^n}$

3 Area, volume and measure

The Greek mathematician Archimedes, born almost 2300 years ago, discovered many beautiful results:

The volume of a cylinder (where height = diameter) is equal to the sum of the volumes of the sphere and cone that fit inside.

3.1 Revision of area

Shape	Name	Area
	Rectangle	$l \times w$
	Parallelogram	$b \times h$
	Triangle	$\frac{1}{2} \times b \times h$
	Trapezium	$\frac{(x+y)}{2} \times h$
	Kite	$\frac{1}{2} \times l \times w$

Remember to express all lengths in the same units before you calculate an area.

Example 1

Work out the area of this trapezium in:

(a) cm^2 **(b)** mm^2

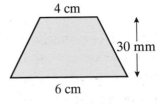

(a) Convert the height in millimetres to centimetres:

$$30\,\text{mm} = 3\,\text{cm}$$

Now work out the area:

$$\text{Area} = \frac{(6+4)}{2} \times 3$$
$$= 5 \times 3$$
$$= 15\,\text{cm}^2$$

(b) Convert the base and top side in centimetres to millimetres:

$$6\,\text{cm} = 60\,\text{mm} \text{ and } 4\,\text{cm} = 40\,\text{mm}$$

Now work out the area:

$$\text{Area} = \frac{(60+40)}{2} \times 30$$
$$= 50 \times 30$$
$$= 1500\,\text{mm}^2$$

Exercise 3A

1 Work out the area of each shape in:

   (i) cm^2 **(ii)** mm^2

(a)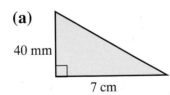

(b)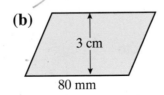

(c)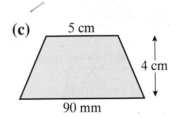

2 Work out the area of each shape in:

   (i) m^2 **(ii)** cm^2

(a)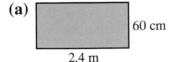

(b)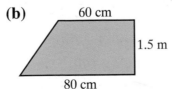

(c)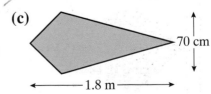

3 Work out the area of this shape in:

(a) cm² (b) mm²

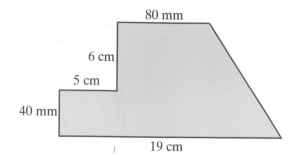

4 This flag is triangular with a white rectangle. Work out the area of the shaded region in:

(a) m² (b) cm²

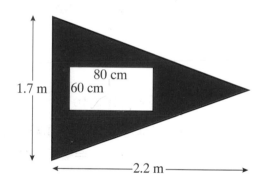

3.2 Conversion between area units

The area of this square is $(1 \times 1)\,\text{cm}^2 = 1\,\text{cm}^2$

$$1\,\text{cm} = 10\,\text{mm}$$

So the area of the square is also
$(10 \times 10)\,\text{mm}^2 = 100\,\text{mm}^2$

$$1\,\text{cm}^2 = 100\,\text{mm}^2$$

■ **To convert cm² to mm², multiply by 100.**
To convert mm² to cm², divide by 100.

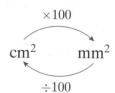

Example 2

Convert **(a)** $3.6\,\text{cm}^2$ to mm^2 **(b)** $23\,\text{mm}^2$ to cm^2

(a) $3.6\,\text{cm}^2 = (3.6 \times 100)\,\text{mm}^2$
$\qquad\qquad = 360\,\text{mm}^2$

(b) $23\,\text{mm}^2 = (23 \div 100)\,\text{cm}^2$
$\qquad\qquad = 0.23\,\text{cm}^2$

You can use a similar approach to convert between m^2 and cm^2.

The area of this square is $(1 \times 1)\,\text{m}^2 = 1\,\text{m}^2$

$\qquad 1\,\text{m} = 100\,\text{cm}$

So the area of the square is also
$(100 \times 100)\,\text{cm}^2 = 10\,000\,\text{cm}^2$

$\qquad 1\,\text{m}^2 = 10\,000\,\text{cm}^2$

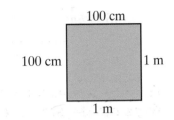

■ **To convert m^2 to cm^2, multiply by 10 000.**
   To convert cm^2 to m^2, divide by 10 000.

Example 3

Convert **(a)** $4.7\,\text{m}^2$ to cm^2 **(b)** $2400\,\text{cm}^2$ to m^2

(a) $\quad 4.7\,\text{m}^2 = (4.7 \times 10\,000)\,\text{cm}^2$
$\qquad\qquad = 47\,000\,\text{cm}^2$

(b) $2400\,\text{cm}^2 = (2400 \div 10\,000)\,\text{m}^2$
$\qquad\qquad = 0.24\,\text{m}^2$

Exercise 3B

1 Convert:
   (a) $7\,\text{cm}^2$ to mm^2 **(b)** $900\,\text{mm}^2$ to cm^2
   (c) $5.92\,\text{cm}^2$ to mm^2 **(d)** $87\,\text{mm}^2$ to cm^2

2 Convert:
   (a) $6\,\text{m}^2$ to cm^2 **(b)** $30\,000\,\text{cm}^2$ to m^2
   (c) $8.24\,\text{m}^2$ to cm^2 **(d)** $200\,\text{cm}^2$ to m^2

3 **(a)** Work out, in mm^2, the area
         of this triangle.
     (b) Express your answer to **(a)** in cm^2.

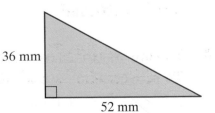

36 mm

52 mm

4 (a) Work out, in m², the area of this rectangle.

(b) Express your answer to (a) in cm².

5 Work out the number of mm² in 1 m².

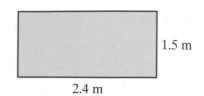

1.5 m

2.4 m

3.3 Circumference and area of a circle

■ **Circumference of a circle, $C = \pi \times$ diameter or πd**

$$= 2 \times \pi \times \textbf{radius or } 2\pi r$$

You already know that

area of a circle, $A = \pi \times \text{radius}^2$ or πr^2

Since

radius $= \frac{1}{2} \times$ diameter or $r = \frac{1}{2}d$

then

area of a circle, $A = \pi \left(\dfrac{d}{2}\right)^2 = \dfrac{\pi d^2}{4}$

■ **area of a circle $= \pi r^2$ or $\dfrac{\pi d^2}{4}$**

You may be asked to use different approximations to π such as 3 or $\frac{22}{7}$. You might also be asked to leave your answer in terms of π. Unless told otherwise you should use 3.14 or the $\boxed{\pi}$ key on your calculator.

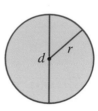

Example 4

Work out the perimeter and area of this shape.

Perimeter of semi-circle $= \frac{1}{2}\pi d$

$\qquad\qquad = \frac{1}{2} \times 3.14 \times 28$

$\qquad\qquad = 44\,\text{cm}$

Perimeter of shape $= 44 + 28 + (2 \times 35)$

$\qquad\qquad = 142\,\text{cm}$

Area of semi-circle $= \frac{1}{2}\pi r^2$

$\qquad\qquad = \frac{1}{2} \times 3.14 \times 14^2$

$\qquad\qquad = 308\,\text{cm}^2$

Area of shape $= 308 + (28 \times 35)$

$\qquad\qquad = 308 + 980$

$\qquad\qquad = 1288\,\text{cm}^2$

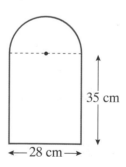

35 cm

←28 cm→

Example 5

The circumference of a circle is 20 cm. Work out the diameter of the circle in units of π.

$$C = \pi d$$

so $$d = \frac{C}{\pi}$$

so diameter $= \dfrac{20}{\pi}$ cm (in units of π)

Exercise 3C

Unless told otherwise, use $\pi = 3.14$ or the $\boxed{\pi}$ key on your calculator in this exercise.

1 The diameter of a circle is 43 cm.
  Work out:
  (a) the circumference
  (b) the area of the circle.

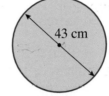

2 The radius of a circle is 35 cm.
  Using $\pi = \frac{22}{7}$, work out:
  (a) the circumference
  (b) the area of the circle.

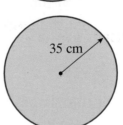

3 The diameter of a circle is 8 cm.
  Work out, in units of π:
  (a) the circumference
  (b) the area.

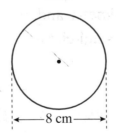

4 Work out the area of the shaded region.

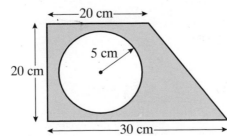

5 Two circles with the same centre have diameters of 8 cm and 10 cm.

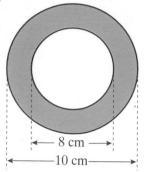

Circles with the same centre are called concentric circles.

Work out the area of the shaded ring between the circles.

6 The diagram shows a rug. Work out:

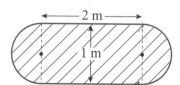

(a) the perimeter of the rug

(b) the area of the rug.

7 A semi-circular shelf has a diameter of 60 cm. Work out:

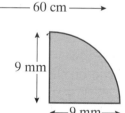

(a) the perimeter of the shelf

(b) the area of the shelf.

8 Work out:

(a) the perimeter

(b) the area of this shape.

9 The circumference of a circle is 35 cm. Work out the diameter of the circle.

10 The area of a circle is 314 cm². Work out the radius of the circle.

11 The London Eye has a diameter of 135 m. Each ride lasts for one revolution of the wheel. How far do you travel during a ride on the London Eye?

12 Jeremy's gerbil is running in a playwheel of radius 5 cm. If each revolution of the wheel takes 0.6 s, how long does it take his gerbil to run 5 m?

13 Katrine is waiting for a train. It's 3 o'clock and her train is due at twenty-five to four. If the train is on time and the minute hand of the station clock is 20 cm long, what area will the minute hand sweep through before Katrine catches her train?

3.4 Surface areas of solids

The cuboid in the diagram has 6 rectangular faces.

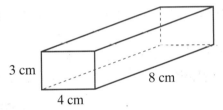

You can see this more clearly if you sketch the net of the cuboid:

The surface area of the cuboid is the total area of the 6 rectangles. You can shorten the working by using the fact that opposite faces of a cuboid are congruent and so have the same area.

$$\text{Surface area} = 2 \times 3 \times 8 + 2 \times 4 \times 8$$
$$+ 2 \times 4 \times 3$$
$$= 48 + 64 + 24$$
$$= 136 \text{ cm}^2$$

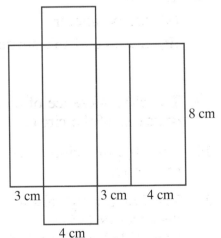

Example 6

Work out the surface area of this cylinder.

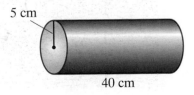

The net of the cylinder is made up of a rectangle and two circles. The length of the rectangle is 40 cm and its width is equal to the circumference of the circles.

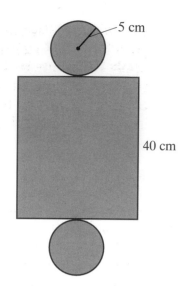

$$\text{Circumference of circle} = \pi \times \text{diameter}$$
$$= 3.14 \times 10$$
$$= 31.4 \text{ cm}$$

$$\text{Surface area} = 40 \times 31.4 + 2 \times \pi \times 5^2$$
$$= 1256 + 157$$
$$= 1413 \text{ cm}^2$$

Exercise 3D

1 Work out the surface area of each of these shapes.

(a)

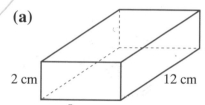

2 cm, 12 cm, 5 cm

(b)

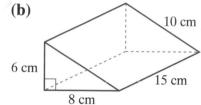

10 cm, 6 cm, 15 cm, 8 cm

(c)

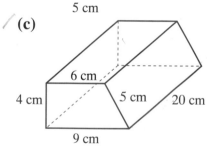

6 cm, 4 cm, 5 cm, 20 cm, 9 cm

(d)

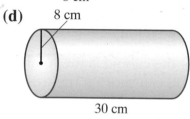

8 cm, 30 cm

(e)

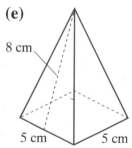

8 cm, 5 cm, 5 cm

(f)

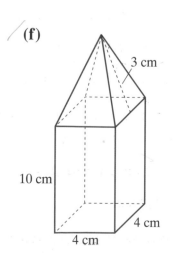

3 cm, 10 cm, 4 cm, 4 cm

2 Daniel has designed a step. Before it goes into production, he decides to apply for a patent. The sketch that he sends to the patent office is shown opposite. Find the total surface area of the step (including the base).

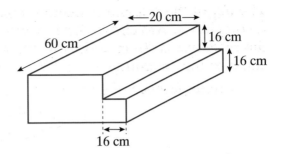

3 Harshini is going to make a mobile to hang from her bedroom ceiling. She makes the mobile from rectangular, triangular and semi-circular pieces of card.

   (a) Find the area of card in cm² that she will need to make the mobile.

   (b) Write this area in mm².

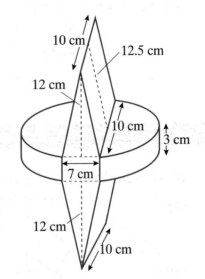

3.5 Volume and capacity

- The volume is the amount of space that a shape takes up in three dimensions.
- The amount of space inside a hollow three-dimensional shape is its capacity.
- Volume of a cuboid = length × width × height.

A cuboid is a prism, because it has a uniform cross-section. This means that you get the same shape, a rectangle, if you cut through the cuboid anywhere parallel to its base.

The volume of this cuboid is $3 \times 2 \times 10 = 60\,\text{cm}^3$.

Its area of cross-section is $3 \times 2 = 6\,\text{cm}^2$.

Volume of a cuboid = area of cross-section × height

This result is true for any prism.

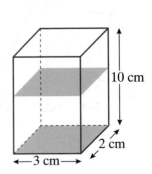

■ **Volume of a prism = area of cross-section × height**

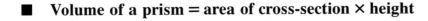

Example 7

Work out the volume of this prism.
Its cross-section is a trapezium.

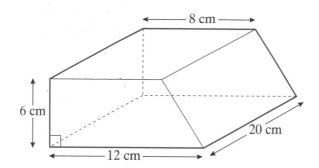

Area of cross-section $= \dfrac{(x+y)}{2} \times h$

$$= \dfrac{(12+8)}{2} \times 6$$

$$= 10 \times 6$$

$$= 60 \, cm^2$$

Volume of prism $=$ area of cross-section $\times$ height

$$= 60 \times 20$$

$$= 1200 \, cm^3$$

Example 8

Work out the volume of this cylinder.

A cylinder is a circular prism.

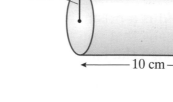

Area of cross-section $= \pi r^2$

$$= 3.14 \times 4^2$$

$$= 50.2 \, cm^2$$

Volume of prism $=$ area of cross-section $\times$ height

$$= 50.2 \times 10$$

$$= 502 \, cm^3$$

Exercise 3E

1 Work out the volume of each of these solids:

(a)

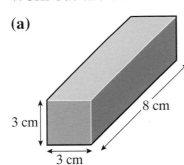

3 cm · 3 cm · 8 cm

(b)

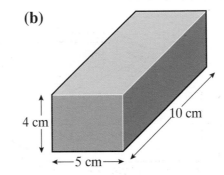

4 cm · 5 cm · 10 cm

(c) 6 cm

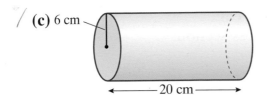

20 cm

(d)

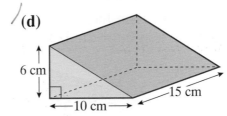

6 cm · 10 cm · 15 cm

(e)

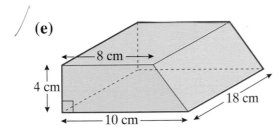

8 cm · 4 cm · 10 cm · 18 cm

(f)

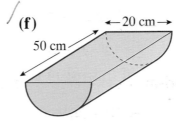

20 cm · 50 cm

2 A cylindrical can has a base radius of 8 cm and a height of 24 cm. Work out the capacity of the can in:

(a) cm^3

(b) litres.

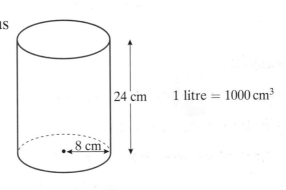

24 cm · 8 cm

1 litre = 1000 cm^3

3 The diagram shows the cross-section of a swimming pool.
The length of the swimming pool is 10 m. Work out the volume of water in the pool.

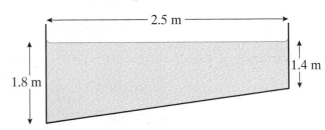

2.5 m · 1.8 m · 1.4 m

4 This cuboid has a volume of 4800 cm³.
Work out its length.

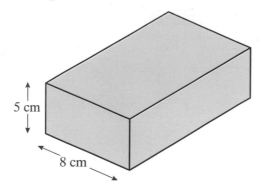

5 This triangular prism has a volume of 120 cm³.
Work out the length of the base of its cross-section.

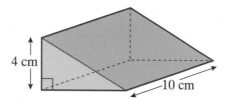

6 The cross-section of this prism is a trapezium.
Its volume is 2240 cm³.
Work out the length of the base of the trapezium.

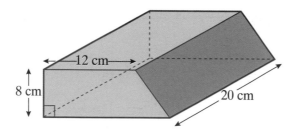

7 The volume of this cylinder is 6160 cm³.

Using $\pi = \frac{22}{7}$, work out the height of the cylinder.

3.6 Conversion between volume units

The volume of this cube is $(1 \times 1 \times 1)\,\text{cm}^3 = 1\,\text{cm}^3$

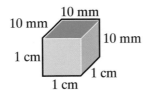

$1\,\text{cm} = 10\,\text{mm}$

So the volume of the cube is also

$(10 \times 10 \times 10)\,\text{mm}^3 = 1000\,\text{mm}^3$

$1\,\text{cm}^3 = 1000\,\text{mm}^3$

■ **To convert cm^3 to mm^3, multiply by 1000.
   To convert mm^3 to cm^3, divide by 1000.**

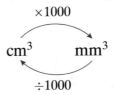

Example 9

Convert (a) $2.4\,\text{cm}^3$ to mm^3
        (b) $32\,000\,\text{mm}^3$ to cm^3

(a) $2.4\,\text{cm}^3 = (2.4 \times 1000)\,\text{mm}^3$
        $= 2400\,\text{mm}^3$

(b) $32\,000\,\text{mm}^3 = (32\,000 \div 1000)\,\text{cm}^3$
        $= 32\,\text{cm}^3$

You can use a similar approach to convert between m^3 and cm^3.

The volume of this cube is

$(1 \times 1 \times 1)\,\text{m}^3 = 1\,\text{m}^3$

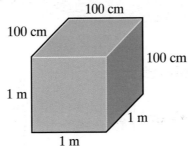

$1\,\text{m} = 100\,\text{cm}$

So the volume of the cube is also
$(100 \times 100 \times 100)\,\text{cm}^3 = 1\,000\,000\,\text{cm}^3$

$$1\,\text{m}^3 = 1\,000\,000\,\text{cm}^3$$

■ **To convert m³ to cm³, multiply by 1000 000.**
To convert cm³ to m³, divide by 1000 000.

$\times 1000\,000$

m³   cm³

$\div 1000\,000$

Example 10

Convert   **(a)** $3.26\,\text{m}^3$ to cm^3
           (b) $7400\,\text{cm}^3$ to m^3

(a) $3.26\,\text{m}^3 = (3.26 \times 1000\,000)\,\text{cm}^3$
                 $= 3260\,000\,\text{cm}^3$

(b) $7400\,\text{cm}^3 = (7400 \div 1000\,000)\,\text{m}^3$
                 $= 0.0074\,\text{m}^3$

Exercise 3F

1 Convert:
   (a) $9\,\text{cm}^3$ to mm^3 **(b)** $80\,000\,\text{mm}^3$ to cm^3
   (c) $7.43\,\text{cm}^3$ to mm^3 **(d)** $4710\,\text{mm}^3$ to cm^3

2 Convert:
   (a) $4\,\text{m}^3$ to cm^3 **(b)** $3000\,\text{cm}^3$ to m^3
   (c) $8.9\,\text{m}^3$ to cm^3 **(d)** $37\,800\,\text{cm}^3$ to m^3

3

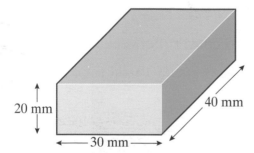

20 mm   40 mm   30 mm

   (a) Work out, in mm^3, the volume of this cuboid.
   (b) Express your answer to **(a)** in cm^3.

4   **(a)** Work out, in m^3, the volume
         of this prism.
   (b) Express your answer to **(a)** in cm^3.

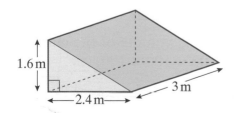

1.6 m   3 m   2.4 m

5   Work out the volume of this prism:
   (a) in mm^3
   (b) in cm^3.

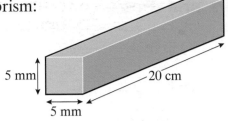

5 mm
5 mm
20 cm

6   Work out the volume of this prism:
   (a) in m^3
   (b) in cm^3.

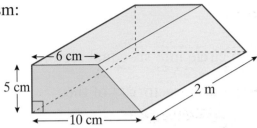

6 cm
5 cm
10 cm
2 m

7   Work out the volume of
   this cylinder:
   (a) in mm^3
   (b) in cm^3.

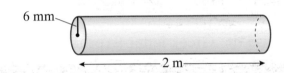

6 mm
2 m

8   Work out the number of mm^3 in 1 m^3.

9   When you buy a soft drink the volume of liquid in the
   bottle is often given in litres where

   1 litre = 1000 cm^3

   (a) Copy and complete:

   To convert litres to cm^3, multiply by _____.

   To convert cm^3 to litres, divide by _____.

   (b) Riccardo buys a 1.5-litre bottle of lemonade.
      What is this in cm^3?

   (c) Work out the volume
      of this prism in litres.

   (d) Work out the volume
      of the prism in millilitres.

Fizz
McFizz
WINNER OF LAST
YEARS FIZZ
COMPETITION
1.5 l

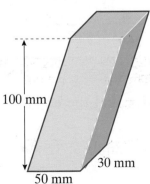

100 mm
30 mm
50 mm

1 litre ≡ 1000 millilitres

E 3.7 Sectors and arcs

In this section you will look at some formulae that arise
from the maths you have been doing on circles.

Consider a circle of radius r.

Its area is πr^2.

Divide the circle into six equal sectors:

The area of each sector is $\frac{1}{6}$ of the
area of the whole circle.

$$\text{Area of a sector} = \frac{\pi r^2}{6}$$

You can use the Greek letter θ (pronounced 'theta')
to represent the angle in degrees between the two
radii of the sector. For this circle $\theta = 360° \div 6 = 60°$.

The fraction of the area of the whole circle

that the sector occupies is $\dfrac{\theta}{360°}$.

So   area of a sector = area of circle × fraction of circle occupied by sector

$$= \pi r^2 \times \frac{\theta}{360°}$$

■ **area of a sector $= \pi r^2 \times \dfrac{\theta}{360°}$**

**where θ is the angle in degrees between the two
bounding radii and r is the radius of the circle.**

You can obtain the following result in a similar way:

■ **arc length $= 2\pi r \times \dfrac{\theta}{360°}$**

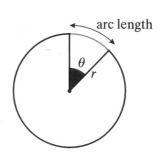

arc length

Example 11

Find the area of the sector and the length of the arc
shown in the diagram.

From the diagram $\theta = 45°$ and $r = 5\,\text{cm}$

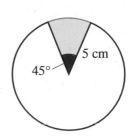

5 cm

45°

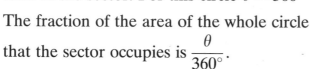

so   area of sector $= \pi \times 5^2 \times \dfrac{45°}{360°}$

$= 3.14 \times 25 \times \dfrac{1}{8}$

$= 9.8 \, \text{cm}^2$

and   arc length $= 2 \times \pi \times 5 \times \dfrac{45°}{360°}$

$= 2 \times 3.14 \times 5 \times \dfrac{1}{8}$

$= 3.9 \, \text{cm}$

Exercise 3G

1   Find the areas of the sectors and the lengths of the arcs:

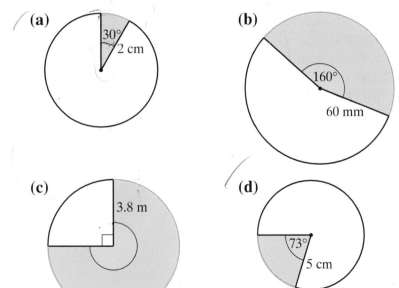

(a)   30°   2 cm

(b)   160°   60 mm

(c)   3.8 m

(d)   73°   5 cm

2   Vacek buys a pizza with a cheese-filled crust and shares it evenly amongst his seven friends. If the pizza has radius 20 cm, what is the area of each slice and what length of crust does each person get?

3 Explain why
$$\text{arc length} = 2\pi r \times \frac{\theta}{360°}$$

4 Given that all the curves are semicircles of radius 0.5 cm, find the area and perimeter of this jigsaw piece.

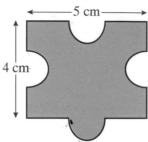

5 The park in the village of Sedgewick is to have a new pond. Below is the final design for the pond, which includes angles and dotted lines showing how it was constructed. Each centimetre on the design represents one metre.
Using an angle measurer and a ruler, find the perimeter and area of the pond.
You can use **Activity Sheet 1** to help you.

You could find the lengths and angles exactly using trigonometry. There is more about this in chapter 17.

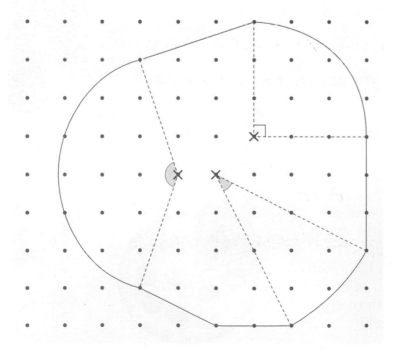

E 3.8 Cylinders

In this section you will look at the formulae for the surface area and volume of a cylinder.

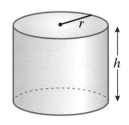

Consider the net of a cylinder of height h, radius r and surface area A.

The length C is the circumference of the cylinder

so $\quad C = 2\pi r$

The surface area of the cylinder is the sum of the area of the circles and the area of the rectangle.

So $\quad A =$ area of circles $+$ area of rectangle

$\qquad = 2 \times \pi r^2 + 2\pi r \times h$

$\quad A = 2\pi r^2 + 2\pi rh$

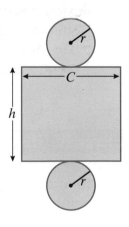

■ **The total surface area A of a cylinder of height h and radius r is given by the formula**

$$A = 2\,\pi r^2 + 2\,\pi rh$$

In section 3.5 you saw the result

$\qquad$ Volume of a prism $=$ area of cross-section $\times$ height

Cylinders are prisms so you can use this formula to find the volume of a cylinder:

area of cross-section $= \pi r^2$

height $= h$

so volume of cylinder, $V = \pi r^2 \times h$

■ **The volume V of a cylinder of height h and radius r is given by the formula**

$$V = \pi r^2 h$$

Example 12

Find the surface area and volume of this cylinder.

The surface area of the cylinder is

$$A = 2\pi r^2 + 2\pi rh$$

where $r = 5\,\text{cm}$ and $h = 12\,\text{cm}$.

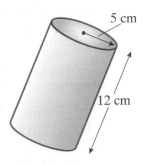

So
$$\begin{aligned} A &= 2 \times \pi \times 5^2 + 2 \times \pi \times 5 \times 12 \\ &= 50\pi + 120\pi \\ &= 170\pi \\ &= 534\,\text{cm}^2 \end{aligned}$$

The volume of the cylinder is

$$\begin{aligned} V &= \pi r^2 h \\ &= \pi \times 5^2 \times 12 \\ &= 300\pi \\ &= 942\,\text{cm}^3 \end{aligned}$$

Always write down the formula first.

The surface area of the cylinder is $534\,\text{cm}^2$ and the volume is $942\,\text{cm}^3$.

Exercise 3H

1 Find the surface areas and volumes of the cylinders below.

(a)

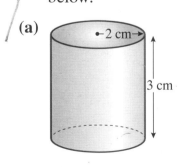

(b)

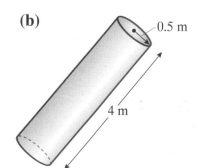

(c) 13 m

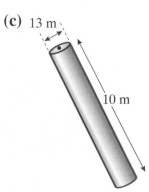

(d)

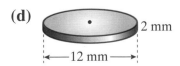

2 Rewrite the formulae for the surface area and volume of a cylinder in terms of d, the diameter of the cylinder.

3 Gwyneth's money box holds 100 two pence pieces. The money box is a cylinder with the same radius as a two pence piece. Find:

(a) the surface area and volume of a two pence piece.

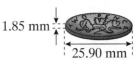

1.85 mm
25.90 mm

(b) the height, surface area and volume of the money box.

The mass of a two pence piece is 7.12 grams.

(c) Find the mass of the money in the box when it is full.

4 Find the volume and surface area (including the inside surface) of these tubes:

(a) 1 m   0.5 m

3 m

(b) 13 mm   9 mm

112 mm

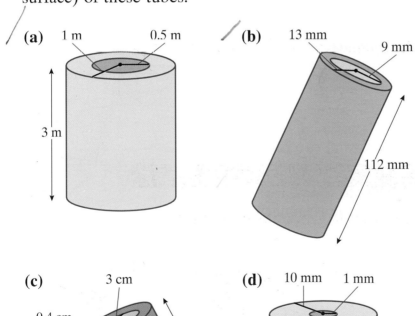

(c)   3 cm

0.4 cm

23 cm

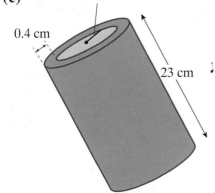

(d) 10 mm   1 mm

2 mm

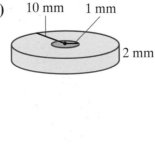

5 The Channel Tunnel runs under the English Channel, connecting Britain and France by rail. The trains travel in concrete tunnels which are 50 km long and have an inside diameter of 7.6 m. The tunnel walls are 1.5 m thick. Calculate the volume of concrete used to build one tunnel.

E 3.9 Accuracy of measurements

How long is this line?
Adam says 'It's 3 cm to the nearest centimetre'.
Bhavana says 'It's 3.2 cm to the nearest millimetre'.

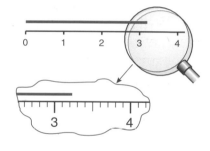

Both answers are correct because both Adam and Bhavana have said how accurate their answers are.

Neither answer is perfectly accurate, however, as *any* answer obtained by measurement is approximate, even if you are very careful and use sophisticated measuring instruments.

'The length of a line is 7 cm, to the nearest centimetre' means that the length of the line is somewhere between 6.5 cm and 7.5 cm.

The line could not be any length greater than 7.5 cm.

This is the least upper bound for the length.

Its least possible length is 6.5 cm.

This is the greatest lower bound for the length.

If *l* is the length of the line in cm, you can write the range of possible values for *l* as

$$6.5 \leqslant l < 7.5$$

7 cm may, therefore, be inaccurate by up to 0.5 cm.

There is more on lower and upper bounds in section 1.2.

Exercise 3I

For each of the following measurements, give the greatest
and least possible values.

1   9 cm to nearest cm   **2**   18 mm to nearest mm

3   20 s to nearest s   **4**   24°C to nearest °C

5   218 g to nearest g   **6**   400 m to nearest m.

Measuring area

Example 13

The measurements of this rectangle are given
to the nearest centimetre.

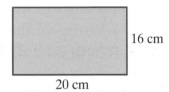

20 cm

16 cm

(a) Work out the greatest possible area.

(b) Work out the least possible area.

(c) Let A be the area of the rectangle in cm^2.
Write down the range of A.

(d) Give the area to a sensible degree of accuracy and
explain your answer.

(a) Greatest possible area $= 20.5 \times 16.5$
$$= 338.25 \, cm^2$$

(b)   Least possible area $= 19.5 \times 15.5$
$$= 302.25 \, cm^2$$

(c) Using the answers to parts **(a)** and **(b)**:
$$302.25 \leqslant A < 338.25$$

(d) Correct to 1 significant figure the answers to **(a)** and
(b) are both $300 \, cm^2$, but to 2 significant figures they
are different ($340 \, cm^2$ and $300 \, cm^2$). $300 \, cm^2$ is,
therefore, the answer to a sensible degree of accuracy.

Exercise 3J

1   The measurements of this rectangle are
given to the nearest centimetre.

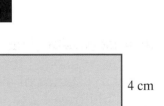

6 cm

4 cm

   (a) Work out the greatest possible perimeter.

   (b) Work out the least possible perimeter.

   (c) Let p be the perimeter of the rectangle in cm.
   Write down the range of p.

   (d) Give the perimeter to a sensible degree of
   accuracy.

2 The diameter of a circle is 6 cm, to the nearest centimetre.

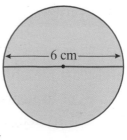

6 cm

   (a) Work out the greatest possible circumference.

   (b) Work out the least possible circumference.

   (c) Representing the circumference by a suitable letter, write down its range.

   (d) Give the circumference to a sensible degree of accuracy. (Use $\pi = 3.14$)

3 The measurements of this rectangle are given to the nearest centimetre.

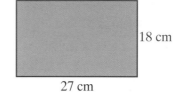

18 cm

27 cm

   (a) Work out the greatest possible area.

   (b) Work out the least possible area.

   (c) Representing the area by a suitable letter, write down its range.

   (d) Give the area to a sensible degree of accuracy.

4 The measurements of this cuboid are given to the nearest millimetre.

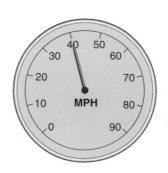

11 mm   19 mm

14 mm

   (a) Work out the greatest possible volume.

   (b) Work out the least possible volume.

   (c) Representing the volume by a suitable letter, write down its range.

   (d) Give the volume to a sensible degree of accuracy.

E ## 3.10 Speed and other compound measures

The diagram shows the speedometer reading of Mr Hill's car as 40 miles per hour.

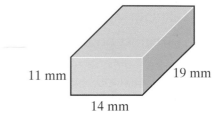

This means that if he drove at the same steady or constant speed for one hour he would travel a distance of 40 miles. In two hours he would travel 2×40 miles $= 80$ miles, and so on.

So for an object moving at a *constant* speed

■ **distance = speed × time**

Rearranging this:

■ $\text{speed} = \dfrac{\text{distance}}{\text{time}}$

■ $\text{time} = \dfrac{\text{distance}}{\text{speed}}$

You can use this triangle to help you remember the formulae.

Example 14

Julie walks for 50 seconds at a constant speed.
She covers a distance of 90 m. Work out her speed.

$\text{speed} = \dfrac{\text{distance}}{\text{time}}$

$\text{speed} = \dfrac{90}{50}$

$\text{speed} = 1.8\text{ metres per second}$

In real life, speeds are usually not constant throughout a journey. You can, however, work out the *average speed* for a journey, where

■ $\text{average speed} = \dfrac{\text{total distance travelled}}{\text{total time taken}}$

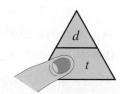

Cover up s and you are left with $\dfrac{d}{t}$ so $s = \dfrac{d}{t}$.

metres per second is usually shortened to m/s:
'per' = '/' = 'for every'

Example 15

Safia drives 220 miles in 4 hours. Work out her average speed.

$\text{average speed} = \dfrac{\text{distance}}{\text{time}} = \dfrac{220}{4}$

$= 55\text{ miles per hour}$

miles per hour is usually shortened to mph

Example 16

David cycles 105 miles at an average speed of 21 mph.
Work out the time for which he cycles.

$\text{time} = \dfrac{\text{distance}}{\text{speed}} = \dfrac{105}{21}$

$= 5\text{ hours}$

Example 17

Lee runs at 8 metres per second for 25 seconds.
Work out the distance he covers.

distance $=$ speed $\times$ time
$$= 8 \times 25$$
$$= 200 \text{ metres}$$

Exercise 3K

1   Tony drove 290 miles in 5 hours. Work out his average speed.

2   Alicia drove 288 miles at an average speed of 48 mph. Work out the time her journey took.

3   Ranjit cycled for 55 seconds at 11 m/s. Work out the distance he cycled.

4   An aeroplane flew 1533 miles in $3\frac{1}{2}$ hours. Work out its average speed.

5   Emma swam for 2 minutes at an average speed of 1.2 m/s. Work out the distance she swam.

6   This question will show you how to convert a speed in metres per second to a speed in miles per hour. If a car is moving at 1 m/s then it travels 1 metre each second.
    (a) Work out the number of seconds in an hour.
    (b) Copy and complete the following sentences, filling in the missing fractions.
        (i)   The car travels _____ metres in an hour.
        (ii) The car travels _____ kilometres in an hour.
        (iii) The car travels _____ miles in an hour.
    (c) Write down the speed of the car in miles per hour.

Use 1 km $= \frac{5}{8}$ miles

7   Idries walks to work at an average speed of 2 m/s.
    (a) Work out his speed in miles per hour.
    (b) If he works $1\frac{1}{2}$ miles from home, how long does it take Idries to get to work?

8 The Blackbird aircraft can travel at 2000 mph.
   (a) Work out this speed in metres per second.
   The distance from London to New York is 5585 km.
   (b) Estimate the time taken for the
      Blackbird aircraft to fly from London
      to New York.

Density

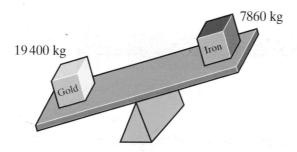

The mass of 1 cubic metre of gold is greater than the mass
of 1 cubic metre of iron. This is because gold has a greater
density than iron.

■ $\textbf{density} = \dfrac{\textbf{mass}}{\textbf{volume}}$

Example 18

The mass of $3\,\text{m}^3$ of aluminium is $8100\,\text{kg}$. Work out the
density of aluminium.

$$\text{density} = \frac{\text{mass}}{\text{volume}}$$

$$= \frac{8100}{3}$$

$$= 2700 \text{ kilograms per cubic metre}$$

usually shortened to kg/m³

The formula for density can be rearranged to give:

■ $\textbf{volume} = \dfrac{\textbf{mass}}{\textbf{density}}$

■ $\textbf{mass} = \textbf{volume} \times \textbf{density}$

You can use this
triangle to help you
remember the
formulae.

Example 19

The density of steel is $7700 \, \text{kg/m}^3$. Work out the mass of $2.5 \, \text{m}^3$ of steel.

$$\text{mass} = \text{volume} \times \text{density}$$
$$= 2.5 \times 7700$$
$$= 19\,250 \, \text{kg}$$

Exercise 3L

Copy this table and work out the missing values.

Substance	Mass in kg	Volume in m^3	Density in kg/m^3
1 Copper	35 840	4	
2 Tin	19 737	2.7	
3 Zinc		4.9	7130
4 Lead	42 408		11 400
5 Balsa wood		5.74	200
6 Concrete	15 686		2300
7 Uranium	20	0.0011	
8 Breeze block	200		1400
9 Magnesium		0.0015	174
10 Platinum	0.08		2145

Pressure

Another compound measure is pressure.

■ $$\textbf{pressure} = \frac{\textbf{force on surface}}{\textbf{surface area}}$$

Force is measured in newtons (N) so pressure is measured in newtons per square metre (N/m^2).

You can use this triangle to help you rearrange the formula.

Example 20

A force of 10 newtons is applied over the
surface of a cube with sides of length 0.5 m.
Find the pressure on the cube.

force on surface area $= 10$ newtons or $10\,$N

surface area of cube $= 6 \times (0.5)^2 = 1.5\,$m^2

so   pressure $= \dfrac{10}{1.5}\,$N/m^2

$= 6.7\,$N/m^2

The unit of pressure
(N/m^2) is sometimes
known as the pascal
(Pa). $1\,$N/m$^2 = 1\,$Pa.

Exercise 3M

1 Find the pressure in each of the following cases:
  (a) force on surface $= 15\,$N
      area $= 2\,$m^2
  (b) force on surface $= 5\,$N
      arca $= 20\,$m^2
  (c) force on surface $= 13\,$N
      area $= 0.5\,$m^2
  (d) force on surface $= 32\,$N
      area $= 8\,$m^2

2 An object has a pressure of $2\,$N/m^2 exerted evenly over
   its surface. If the force applied is $14\,$N, find the surface
   area of the object.

3 A regular polyhedron with faces of area $8\,$m^2 has
   pressure $3\,$N/m^2, due to force $96\,$N, applied evenly over
   its surface. What is the name of the polyhedron?

4 Shula's cat, Rocco, has a weight of $45\,$N. His feet each
   have an area of $15\,$cm^2. Work out the pressure in Pa
   that Rocco exerts on the ground.

5 The swimming pool at Bob's hotel is $5\,$m wide
   and $10\,$m long. On 4 January the air pressure
   at the hotel was 1013.25 millibars where
   $1\,$Pa $= 10$ millibars.
   Work out the force exerted by the air on the
   surface of the swimming pool.

If you listen to the
weather forecast you
will hear air
pressure given in
millibars.

Other compound measures

Many other compound measures are in everyday use. The fuel consumption of a car, for example, can be expressed in miles per gallon (mpg).

Fuel consumption is also expressed in litres/100 km.

Example 21

A car travels 195 miles on 5 gallons of petrol. Work out its fuel consumption in miles per gallon.

$$\text{Fuel consumption} = \frac{\text{distance travelled}}{\text{fuel used}}$$

$$= \frac{195}{5}$$

$$= 39 \, \text{mpg}$$

Exercise 3N

1   A car travels 172 miles on 4 gallons of petrol. Work out its fuel consumption in miles per gallon.

2   The fuel consumption of a car is 32 mpg. How far will it travel on 8 gallons?

3   Jenny types at 93 words per minute. How long will it take her to type 651 words?

4   4500 litres of water flow through a pipe in 5 hours.
    (a) Work out the rate of flow in litres per hour.
    (b) How many litres of water flow through the pipe in 7 hours?

5   5 litres of petrol costs £3.90.
    (a) Work out the cost per litre of petrol.
    (b) Work out the cost of 35 litres of petrol.

Summary of key points

1 To convert cm² to mm², multiply by 100.
To convert mm² to cm², divide by 100.

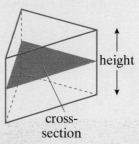

$\times 100$

$\mathrm{cm}^2 \qquad \mathrm{mm}^2$

$\div 100$

2 To convert m² to cm², multiply by 10 000.
To convert cm² to m², divide by 10 000.

$\times 10\,000$

$\mathrm{m}^2 \qquad \mathrm{cm}^2$

$\div 10\,000$

3 Circumference of a circle, $C = \pi \times$ diameter or πd
$\qquad\qquad = 2 \times \pi \times$ radius or $2\pi r$

4 Area of a circle $= \pi r^2$ or $\dfrac{\pi d^2}{4}$

5 Volume of a prism $=$ area of cross-section $\times$ height

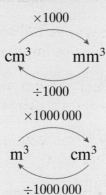

height

cross-
section

6 To convert cm³ to mm³, multiply by 1000.
To convert mm³ to cm³, divide by 1000.

$\times 1000$

$\mathrm{cm}^3 \qquad \mathrm{mm}^3$

$\div 1000$

7 To convert m³ to cm³, multiply by 1000 000.
To convert cm³ to m³, divide by 1000 000.

$\times 1000\,000$

$\mathrm{m}^3 \qquad \mathrm{cm}^3$

$\div 1000\,000$

E Area of a sector $= \pi r^2 \times \dfrac{\theta}{360°}$ where θ is
the angle in degrees between the two bounding
radii and r is the radius of the circle.

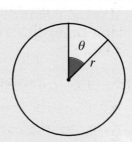

E Arc length $= 2\pi r \times \dfrac{\theta}{360°}$

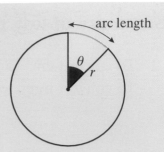

arc length

E The total surface area A of a cylinder of height h and radius r is given by the formula

$$A = 2\pi r^2 + 2\pi rh$$

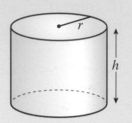

E The volume V of a cylinder of height h and radius r is given by the formula

$$V = \pi r^2 h$$

E Distance $=$ speed $\times$ time

$$\text{speed} = \dfrac{\text{distance}}{\text{time}}$$

$$\text{time} = \dfrac{\text{distance}}{\text{speed}}$$

E Average speed $= \dfrac{\text{total distance travelled}}{\text{total time taken}}$

E Density $= \dfrac{\text{mass}}{\text{volume}}$

$$\text{volume} = \dfrac{\text{mass}}{\text{density}}$$

$$\text{mass} = \text{volume} \times \text{density}$$

E Pressure $= \dfrac{\text{force on surface}}{\text{surface area}}$

4 Averages and spread

This unit reminds you of some facts you have already met and introduces some other ways of describing data.

4.1 Mean, mode, median and range

You already know these facts:

There are three different types of average:
- the mean
- the mode
- the median

The mean of a set of data is the sum of all the values divided by the number of values

$$\text{mean} = \frac{\text{sum of values}}{\text{number of values}}$$

The mode of a set of data is the value which occurs most often.

The median is the middle value when the data is arranged in order of size.
When there is an even number of values the median is the average (mean) of the middle two values.

The range of a set of data is the difference between the highest and lowest values:

$$\text{range} = \text{largest value} - \text{smallest value}$$

When using a frequency table:

$$\text{mean} = \frac{\text{total of (each value} \times \text{frequency)}}{\text{total frequency}}$$

The cumulative frequency is the running total of the frequencies.

The median is the value half-way along the cumulative frequency.

A stem and leaf diagram is a way of simplifying data in a table. It can be used to find the median and the mode.

Example 1

A small business recorded the number of computers that were faulty each day for 100 days.

Find the mode, median and mean for this data.

Number of computers	Frequency
0	24
1	29
2	15
3	10
4	9
5	13

Largest frequency is 29 so the mode is 1 computer.

The mode is the value with the largest frequency.
The mode is 1 computer.

To calculate the median you add an extra column and work out the cumulative frequency.

Number of computers, n	Cumulative frequency
0	24
$n \leqslant 1$	$24 + 29 = 53$
$n \leqslant 2$	$53 + 15 = 68$
$n \leqslant 3$	$68 + 10 = 78$
$n \leqslant 4$	$78 + 9 = 87$
$n \leqslant 5$	$87 + 13 = 100$

The 50th and 51st values are both 1 computer.

The middle values of 100 items are the 50th and 51st values when arranged in order.

So the median is 1 computer.

To calculate the mean you add an extra column to the original table and work out frequency × value.

Number of computers	Frequency	Number of computers × frequency
0	24	$0 \times 24 = 0$
1	29	$1 \times 29 = 29$
2	15	$2 \times 15 = 30$
3	10	$3 \times 10 = 30$
4	9	$4 \times 9 = 36$
5	13	$5 \times 13 = 65$
Total	100	Total $= 190$

This is the total number of faults recorded in 100 days.

Mean $= 190 \div 100 = 1.9$ computers.
Sometimes the data is affected by an extreme value.
During the next night there was a lightning strike and 113 computers did not work.
The mean for 101 days $= (190 + 113) \div 101 = 3$ computers.

You can find the median and mode more easily using a stem and leaf diagram.

In a stem and leaf diagram the stem is often the tens digit and the leaf is often the units digit.

Example 2

This stem and leaf diagram shows the number of minutes a train is late each day for a period of 24 days.
Find the mode, median and range for the data.

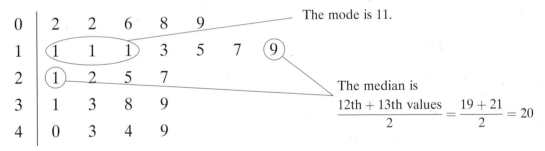

0	2	2	6	8	9
1	1	1	1	3	5	7	9
2	1	2	5	7
3	1	3	8	9
4	0	3	4	9

The mode is 11.

The median is
$$\frac{\text{12th + 13th values}}{2} = \frac{19 + 21}{2} = 20$$

Stem $= 10$ minutes

The mode is 11 minutes.
The median is 20 minutes.

A stem and leaf diagram does not help the calculation of a mean but can be used to calculate the range.
Range $= 49 - 2 = 47$ minutes.

Exercise 4A

1 The frequency table shows the number of days each pupil was absent during the year for a school of 500 pupils.

Number of days absent	Frequency
0	20
1	55
2	60
3	125
4	100
5	73
6	32
7	27
8	8

Work out:

(a) the mode

(b) the mean

(c) the median

(d) the range.

The total frequency equals 500 so you do not need to use a calculator.

2 The number of runs scored by a cricketer for a season are shown in a stem and leaf diagram.

```
0 | 0  0  3  4  5  6  6  6  9
1 | 0  2  4  4  6
2 | 2  2  3  5  6  8  9
3 | 3  3  5  5  7  7  8  8  9
4 | 1  2  2  3  3  4  4
```

Stem = 10 runs

(a) Work out the median.

(b) State the mode and the range.

3 The times taken by 21 runners to complete a half marathon are:

2 h 35 min, 3 h 50 min, 3 h 10 min, 1 h 15 min, 1 h 30 min,
3 h 20 min, 2 h 15 min, 2 h 10 min, 4 h 0 min, 2 h 10 min,
1 h 40 min, 2 h 0 min, 1 h 20 min, 1 h 25 min, 1 h 40 min,
4 h 20 min, 1 h 35 min, 2 h 15 min, 1 h 50 min, 1 h 55 min,
2 h 20 min

   (a) Show this data in a stem and leaf diagram.

   (b) Work out the median and the mode for the data.

4 The table shows the number of accidents per day for the first 355 days the M1 was open.
Calculate:

   (a) the mean

   (b) the median

   (c) the mode

   (d) the range.

Number of accidents	Frequency
0	116
1	113
2	77
3	36
4	8
5	5

4.2 Finding the mean of grouped or continuous data

When data has a wide range of values it makes sense to group sets of values together. This makes it easier to record the data, and to spot any patterns or trends.

It makes life easier if the groups are the same size but they do not have to be.

■ **Groupings of continuous data are called class intervals.**

When continuous data is recorded using class intervals you do not have the exact values of the data. You can calculate an **estimate of the mean** based on the assumption that all values within a class interval are distributed evenly and can be represented by the middle value of the class interval.

The estimate of the mean is an accurate calculation. You do not approximate any values during the calculation!

Example 3

An angler keeps a record of the weight of each fish she lands. Her results are shown in this table.

Find an estimate of the mean for the data.

Weight (kg)	Frequency
$0 < W \leqslant 0.5$	2
$0.5 < W \leqslant 1.0$	10
$1.0 < W \leqslant 1.5$	23
$1.5 < W \leqslant 2.0$	26
$2.0 < W \leqslant 2.5$	27
$2.5 < W \leqslant 3.0$	12

To calculate an estimate of the mean you include a column for the middle values and a column to work out middle value × frequency.

Weight (kg)	Middle value	Frequency	Middle value × frequency
$0 < W \leqslant 0.5$	0.25	2	$0.25 \times 2 = 0.5$
$0.5 < W \leqslant 1.0$	0.75	10	$0.75 \times 10 = 7.5$
$1.0 < W \leqslant 1.5$	1.25	23	$1.25 \times 23 = 28.75$
$1.5 < W \leqslant 2.0$	1.75	26	$1.75 \times 26 = 45.5$
$2.0 < W \leqslant 2.5$	2.25	27	$2.25 \times 27 = 60.75$
$2.5 < W \leqslant 3.0$	2.75	12	$2.75 \times 12 = 33$
	Total	100	Total 176

The estimate for the total weight of fish.

The middle value of each class interval is calculated by

$$\frac{\text{upper limit} + \text{lower limit}}{2}$$

So for the class interval $2.0 < W \leqslant 2.5$,

$$\text{middle value} = \frac{2.0 + 2.5}{2} = 2.25$$

$$\text{estimate of mean} = \frac{\text{total weight of fish}}{\text{total frequency}} = \frac{176}{100} = 1.76$$

Example 4

A village of 120 people takes a census of the ages of the population. Villagers were asked their age last birthday and the results were tabulated.

Age last birthday	Frequency
0–19	23
20–39	19
40–59	38
60–79	34
80–99	6

Find an estimate of the mean age.

Although age is continuous data it is recorded using discrete values. The class interval 20 to 39 is really $20 \leqslant \text{age} < 40$ so care must be taken with class interval middle values.

Age last birthday	Middle value	Frequency	Middle value × frequency
0–19	10	23	$10 \times 23 =$ 230
20–39	30	19	$30 \times 19 =$ 570
40–59	50	38	$50 \times 38 = 1900$
60–79	70	34	$70 \times 34 = 2380$
80–99	90	6	$90 \times 6 =$ 540
	Total	120	Total 5620

$$\text{estimate of mean} = \frac{\text{combined age}}{\text{total frequency}} = \frac{5620}{120} = 46.833\,333\ldots$$

$$= 46.8\dot{3} = 46.83 \text{ to 2 d.p.}$$

46.8$\dot{3}$ years is 46 years 10 months.

Estimate of mean age is 46.83 years.

■ **With grouped data you can calculate an estimate of the mean using the middle value of each class interval.**

Exercise 4B

1 The table shows the length, in centimetres,
   of 120 snakes captured by Steve.

Length of snake (cm)	Frequency
$70 < L \leqslant 80$	8
$80 < L \leqslant 90$	19
$90 < L \leqslant 100$	16
$100 < L \leqslant 110$	32
$110 < L \leqslant 120$	24
$120 < L \leqslant 130$	15
$130 < L \leqslant 140$	6

   Calculate an estimate of the mean length of the snakes
   captured by Steve.

2 The table shows the age, in years, at last birthday of
   240 mothers when their first child was born.

Age	16 to 19	20 to 23	24 to 27	28 to 31	32 to 35	36 to 39
Frequency	45	93	52	23	17	10

   Calculate an estimate of the mean age.

3 The frequency diagram below shows the weekly rainfall
   for a village.

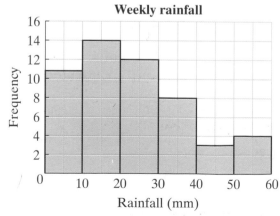

   (a) Make a table for the data.
   (b) Calculate an estimate of the mean weekly rainfall.

4 The table shows the length of stays in a local car park during one day.

Length of stay	Frequency
Under 1 hour	20
1 hour to under 2 hours	14
2 hours to under 4 hours	8
4 hours to under 8 hours	12
8 hours to under 24 hours	16

Be careful – not all the class intervals are of equal width.

(a) Calculate an estimate of the mean length of stay.

The charges for the car park are:

Length of stay	Charge
Under 1 hour	£0.75
1 hour to under 2 hours	£1.50
2 hours to under 4 hours	£2.50
4 hours to under 8 hours	£4.50
8 hours to under 24 hours	£8.00

(b) Calculate an estimate of the mean amount of money charged per car.

The local council wants to change the charges for the car park.

(c) Use your answers to parts (a) and (b) to suggest a fixed hourly rate charge for the car park which will be paid by everyone, no matter how long they stay. Give reasons for your choice and also what you think will be the impact on the use of the car park.

4.3 Finding the median of grouped or continuous data

To find the median for grouped data we first need to draw a cumulative frequency diagram (sometimes called an **ogive**).

■ **The cumulative frequency of grouped data is the running total of the frequency up to the end of each class interval.**

■ **You draw a cumulative frequency diagram by plotting each value of cumulative frequency against the end of the corresponding class interval.**

Example 5

The marks gained for a mathematics test by a Year 9 form
are shown in this table.

Mark	Frequency
0–20	2
21–40	5
41–60	23
61–80	30
81–100	9

Mark, m	Cumulative Frequency
$0 < m \leqslant 20$	2
$0 < m \leqslant 40$	$2 + 5 = 7$
$0 < m \leqslant 60$	$7 + 23 = 30$
$0 < m \leqslant 80$	$30 + 30 = 60$
$0 < m \leqslant 100$	$60 + 9 = 69$

Draw a cumulative frequency diagram and use it to find the
median mark.

The median value is the $\left(\dfrac{69 + 1}{2}\right)$th value, or the 35th value.

To estimate the median from a cumulative frequency diagram:

① Find the halfway value of the
cumulative frequencies (here it is 35)

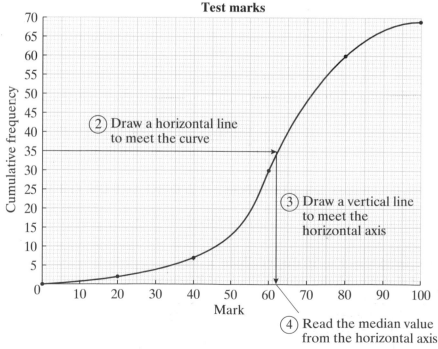

Test marks

② Draw a horizontal line
to meet the curve

③ Draw a vertical line
to meet the
horizontal axis

④ Read the median value
from the horizontal axis

Values are
plotted at the
end of the
class interval.

Estimate of median mark is 62.

Example 6

The table gives the age last birthday, in years, of 100 people attending the out-patients department of a hospital.
Find an estimate of the median for this data.

Age last birthday	Frequency
0 to 19	7
20 to 39	19
40 to 59	36
60 to 79	32
80 to 99	6

The upper class limit of this group is 100 years.

Age last birthday	Cumulative frequency
0 to 19	7
0 to 39	$7 + 19 = 26$
0 to 59	$26 + 36 = 62$
0 to 79	$62 + 32 = 94$
0 to 99	$94 + 6 = 100$

You can estimate the median from the fiftieth value.

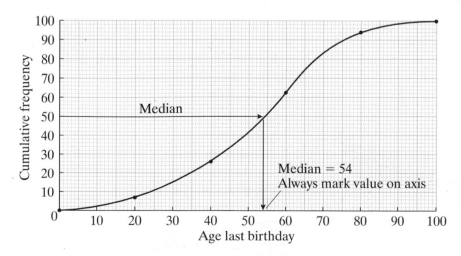

Estimate of median age is 54 years.

Exercise 4C

1 By drawing cumulative frequency diagrams, find an estimate of the median for questions 1, 2 and 3 of Exercise 4B.

2 This table shows the number of fans passing through a turnstile prior to a football match.

Minutes before kick off	Frequency
$60 \geqslant T > 50$	35
$50 \geqslant T > 40$	62
$40 \geqslant T > 30$	95
$30 \geqslant T > 20$	120
$20 \geqslant T > 10$	54
$10 \geqslant T > 0$	34

(a) Draw a cumulative frequency curve to represent the data. (Hint: your x-axis should start at 60 and go down to 0.)

(b) Work out the median.

3 The table of values for an experiment has been spoilt and only certain values can be seen.

Temperature °C	Frequency
$200 < T \leqslant 250$	12
$250 < T \leqslant 300$	23
$300 < T \leqslant 400$	29
$400 < T \leqslant 500$	17
$500 < T \leqslant 700$	9
$700 < T \leqslant$	5

(a) Say why it is not possible to calculate an estimate of the mean.

(b) Draw a cumulative frequency curve with the available data and work out an estimate of the median.

4 An experiment is carried out to see if the yield of tomatoes is different when using a liquid fertilizer.

100 plants are tested, 50 without fertilizer and 50 with fertilizer. The results are shown in the table.

Frequency without fertilizer	Weight of tomatoes (kg)	Frequency with fertilizer
7	$5 < w \leqslant 10$	2
12	$10 < w \leqslant 15$	4
20	$15 < w \leqslant 20$	15
8	$20 < w \leqslant 25$	23
3	$25 < w \leqslant 30$	6

(a) Calculate an estimate of the mean weight of tomatoes for the plants without fertilizer and also for those with fertilizer.

(b) Draw two cumulative frequency curves on the same set of axes and estimate the median weight for both sets of data.

(c) Make a brief statement, backed up with statistics, to describe the effect of the fertilizer.

5 The frequency diagram shows the March rainfall, r, for a district.

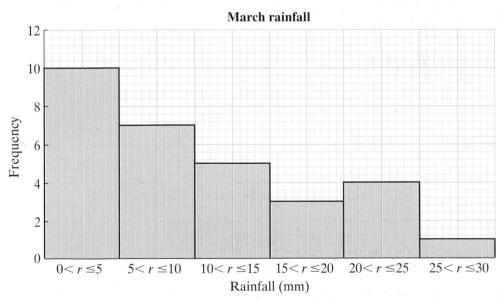

March rainfall

(a) Construct a frequency table for the data.

(b) Calculate an estimate of the mean.

(c) Draw a cumulative frequency curve and estimate the median.

6 During the poor weather in winter, trains were a lot later than usual.

A cumulative frequency graph was drawn to work out the median length of time trains were late.

(a) Copy the tables and use the graph to complete them by entering the cumulative frequencies first and then calculating the frequencies.

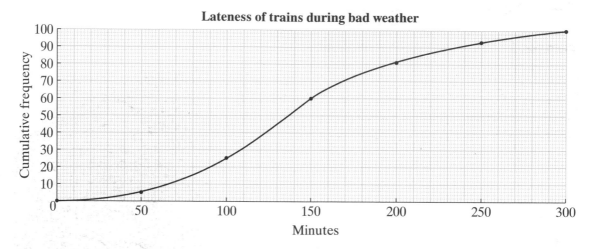

Lateness of trains during bad weather

Time late (minutes)	Frequency
$0 < T \leqslant 50$	
$50 < T \leqslant 100$	
$100 < T \leqslant 150$	
$150 < T \leqslant 200$	
$200 < T \leqslant 250$	
$250 < T \leqslant 300$	

Time late (minutes)	Cumulative frequency
$T \leqslant 50$	
$T \leqslant 100$	
$T \leqslant 150$	
$T \leqslant 200$	
$T \leqslant 250$	
$T \leqslant 300$	

(b) Work out an estimate of the mean from your table.

E 4.4 Upper and lower quartiles

In this chapter you have met the median – the middle value when the data is arranged in order of size. The data can also be split into quartiles.

■ **When the data is arranged in ascending order of size:**

  ● **the lower quartile is the value one quarter of the way into the data**
  ● **the upper quartile is the value three quarters of the way into the data.**

As with the median, for a large set of grouped data you can estimate the upper and lower quartiles from a cumulative frequency graph.

Example 7

An independent music store recorded the number of CDs it sold each day over a period of 100 days. The manager then drew this cumulative frequency graph from the data:

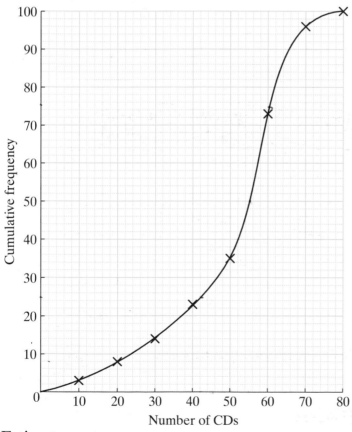

Estimate
(a) the median
(b) the lower quartile
(c) the upper quartile.

An estimate of the median is the

$$\left(\frac{1}{2} \times 100\right) \text{th} = 50\text{th value.}$$

An estimate of the lower quartile is the

$$\left(\frac{1}{4} \times 100\right) \text{th} = 25\text{th value.}$$

An estimate of the upper quartile is the

$$\left(\frac{3}{4} \times 100\right) \text{th} = 75\text{th value.}$$

So

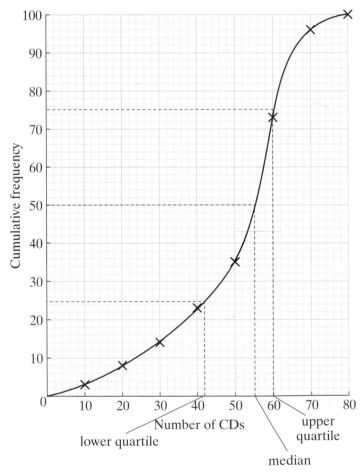

From the graph an estimate of
(a) the median is 55 CDs
(b) the lower quartile is 42 CDs
(c) the upper quartile is 60 CDs.

Exercise 4D

For each set of data below, draw a cumulative frequency graph and use it to estimate:

(a) the median

(b) the lower quartile

(c) the upper quartile.

1 Tracey decided to record to the nearest hour the number of hours of sunshine received by the village of Sedgeford each week. Her tabulated results are shown below.

Hours of sunshine, s	Number of weeks in this class interval
$0 \leqslant s < 15$	2
$15 \leqslant s < 30$	6
$30 \leqslant s < 45$	9
$45 \leqslant s < 60$	21
$60 \leqslant s < 75$	30
$75 \leqslant s < 90$	18
$90 \leqslant s < 105$	6

2 Nihar measures the height to the nearest centimetre of his 31 classmates and records them in a table:

Height, h, in cm	Number of pupils in this class interval
$150 < h \leqslant 155$	4
$155 < h \leqslant 160$	8
$160 < h \leqslant 165$	10
$165 < h \leqslant 170$	7
$170 < h \leqslant 175$	2

3   Katsura travels up Barbury Road to work every
    weekday morning. She recorded to the nearest minute
    the duration of her journey each day for ten weeks.
    Her results are shown below.

Duration of journey, d, in minutes	Number of days in this class interval
$10 < d \leqslant 13$	1
$13 < d \leqslant 16$	2
$16 < d \leqslant 19$	15
$19 < d \leqslant 22$	19
$22 < d \leqslant 25$	12
$25 < d \leqslant 28$	0
$28 < d \leqslant 31$	0
$31 < d \leqslant 34$	1

4   Daniel asks his friends' parents what age
    they were at their last birthdays.
    Daniel recorded his data in a table:

Age at last birthday	Number of parents in this interval
21–25	1
26–30	0
31–35	0
36–40	13
41–45	5
46–50	6
51–55	0
56–60	1
61–65	1

5   David asked 30 people to the nearest 0.1% what interest
     they were receiving on the money in their main bank
     account. His results were recorded in a tally table below:

Interest rate, $r\%$	Number of people in this class interval
$1.0 \leqslant r < 2.0$	‖
$2.0 \leqslant r < 3.0$	ЖТ ЖТ ЖТ ЖТ	
$3.0 \leqslant r < 4.0$	
$4.0 \leqslant r < 5.0$	│
$5.0 \leqslant r < 6.0$	│
$6.0 \leqslant r < 7.0$	ЖТ

E 4.5 Interquartile range

The interquartile range is the difference between the upper
and lower quartiles.

■   **interquartile range = upper quartile − lower quartile**

Example 8

Find the interquartile range of the data in Example 7.

The lower quartile is 42 CDs.
The upper quartile is 60 CDs.

So the interquartile range = upper quartile − lower quartile
$$= \quad 60 \quad - \quad 42$$
$$= \quad 18 \text{ CDs}$$

You already know from section 4.1 that

     range = highest value − lowest value

However, when the data is grouped you do not know the
highest and lowest values. In this case you estimate the range.

■   **For grouped data you can estimate the range using**

$$\textbf{range} = \begin{pmatrix} \textbf{highest possible value} \\ \textbf{in last class interval} \end{pmatrix} - \begin{pmatrix} \textbf{lowest possible value} \\ \textbf{in first class interval} \end{pmatrix}$$

Example 9

Reagan's stopwatch records times to the nearest 0.1 seconds. She records in a table the time taken for each of her friends to run 100 m. The top and bottom of the table are shown here.

Time taken, t, in seconds	Number of friends in this class interval
$12.0 \leqslant t < 13.0$	2
$13.0 \leqslant t < 14.0$	5
$20.0 \leqslant t < 21.0$	4
$21.0 \leqslant t < 22.0$	1

Estimate the range of Reagan's data.

If Reagan records a time of 15.0 seconds for her friend Chris, his actual time t could be any time in the range $14.95 \leqslant t < 15.05$ because Reagan's stopwatch only records times to the nearest 0.1 seconds.

So the first class interval is really $11.95 \leqslant t < 12.95$ and the last class interval is really $20.95 \leqslant t < 21.95$. An estimate of the range is $21.95 - 11.95 = 10$ seconds.

Exercise 4E

1   Find the range and interquartile range of each set of data in Exercise 4D.

2   What do you think the interquartile range tells you about a set of data? Why might it be more useful than the range?

3   Alvaro and Brigitte are flatmates. They both work at the same supermarket and cycle there every weekday morning.

Alvaro always cycles on Route A whilst Brigitte always takes Route B.

They decide to record their journey times each day over the course of six weeks.

Their results are shown in the table on the next page.

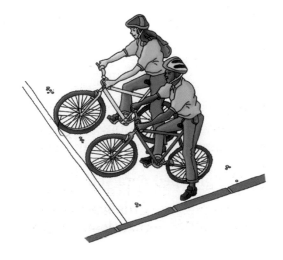

Journey time, t, in minutes	Number of journeys in this class interval	
	Alvaro	Brigitte
$25 < t \leqslant 30$	2	0
$30 < t \leqslant 35$	5	1
$35 < t \leqslant 40$	9	12
$40 < t \leqslant 45$	8	14
$45 < t \leqslant 50$	5	2
$50 < t \leqslant 55$	1	1

On the same axes, draw and label cumulative frequency graphs of Alvaro's and Brigitte's journey times.

For both sets of data estimate

(a) the median **(b)** the interquartile range **(c)** the mean.

In what ways do Alvaro's and Brigitte's journey times differ? Think of reasons to explain your findings.

E 4.6 More questions on averages

Through this unit you have extended your knowledge and use of the mean, mode and median. You can now solve problems involving these averages.

Example 10

Ruud and Marta are contestants in a television game show, playing to win a snowboarding holiday.

Ruud is in an isolation booth and has 5 cards in front of him, each of which has a number greater than 0 written on it.

Marta has to work out the number on each card, but Ruud is only allowed to tell her the range, mode and mean of four or more of the cards.

Ruud explains, "My 5 cards have range 17, mean 13 and mode 18. I take one card away and the four remaining cards have range 7 and mean 16. What are the numbers on my five original cards?"

Ruud has 5 cards with   range $= 17$
       mean $= 13$
       mode $= 18$

one card is taken away and then
there are 4 cards with   range $= 7$
       mean $= 16$

Let the numbers on each of the cards be

     C_1, C_2, C_3, C_4, C_5

then to start with   mean $= 13$

so
$$\frac{C_1 + C_2 + C_3 + C_4 + C_5}{5} = 13$$

therefore $C_1 + C_2 + C_3 + C_4 + C_5 = 65$ **(1)**

Say that C_1 is taken away.
Ruud now claims that   mean $= 16$

so
$$\frac{C_2 + C_3 + C_4 + C_5}{4} = 16$$

therefore $C_2 + C_3 + C_4 + C_5 = 64$ **(2)**

Subtract **(2)** from **(1)**, to get $C_1 = 1$

You now know that the cards are numbered

     $1, C_2, C_3, C_4, C_5$

You are told that all the numbers are greater
than zero. This means that 1 must be the
smallest number on the cards.

Let C_5 be the largest number.

Ruud says that the range of $1, C_2, C_3, C_4, C_5$ is 17.

so $C_5 - 1 = 17$

therefore $C_5 = 17 + 1 = 18$

Ruud also says that the range of C_2, C_3, C_4, C_5 is 7, so

            $C_5 - C_2 = 7$

but $C_5 = 18$, so $18 - C_2 = 7$

therefore $C_2 = 18 - 7 = 11$

You now know that the cards are numbered

     $1, 11, C_3, C_4, 18$

The mode of the five cards is 18, so there are more cards numbered 18 than any other number.

Therefore at least one of the two remaining unknown cards is numbered 18.

Say $C_4 = 18$

The cards are   1, 11, C_3, 18, 18

so from **(1)** $1 + 11 + C_3 + 18 + 18 = 65$

and $C_3 = 65 - 18 - 18 - 1 - 11 = 17$

So for Ruud and Marta to win their holiday, Marta should answer:

   1, 11, 17, 18, 18

You can check your answer by working out whether Ruud's original statement was correct for these numbers.

Exercise 4F

1   Gavin records five tracks for his new solo album.
He claims that the lengths of the tracks in minutes
have a range of 5, a mean of 6 and a mode of 7.
Is this possible?

2   Aseel cycles to her Aunt's house at a
speed of 20 km/h and cycles home at
a speed of 10 km/h. Work out her
average speed for the round trip.
(Hint: the answer is not 15 km/h)

3   Dancho decides to go clubbing in London. He could travel there by bus, by express coach or by train. He discovers that the train ticket would be most expensive and the bus ticket would be cheapest.
The three tickets have a median price of £25 and a mean price of £27. Given that the range of the prices is £12, find the cost of each ticket.

4   Amita, Benny and Caimile are each asked by a street magician to think of one number between 1 and 20. The magician concentrates hard, trying to read their thoughts, but can only gather that the mean of their numbers is 13 and the range is 9. The embarrassed magician correctly works out the smallest possible value of

(a) the smallest of their three numbers

(b) the largest of their three numbers.

What are his answers?

Summary of key points

1   There are three different types of average:
   • the mean
   • the mode
   • the median

2   The mean of a set of data is the sum of all the values divided by the number of values:

$$\text{mean} = \frac{\text{sum of values}}{\text{number of values}}$$

3   The mode of a set of data is the value which occurs most often.

4   The median is the middle value when the data is arranged in order of size. When there is an even number of values the median is the average (mean) of the middle two values.

5   The range of a set of data is the difference between the highest and lowest values:

$$\text{range} = \text{largest value} - \text{smallest value}$$

6 When using a frequency table:

$$\text{mean} = \frac{\text{total of (each value} \times \text{frequency)}}{\text{total frequency}}$$

7 The cumulative frequency is the running total of the frequencies.

8 The median is the value half-way along the cumulative frequency.

9 A stem and leaf diagram is a way of simplifying data in a table. It can be used to find the median and the mode.

10 Groupings of continuous data are called class intervals.

11 With grouped data you can calculate an estimate of the mean using the middle value of each class interval.

12 The cumulative frequency of grouped data is the running total of the frequency up to the end of each class interval.

14 You draw a cumulative frequency diagram by plotting each value of cumulative frequency against the end of the corresponding class interval.

E When the data is arranged in ascending order of size:
the lower quartile is the value one quarter of the way into the data
the upper quartile is the value three quarters of the way into the data.

E interquartile range = upper quartile − lower quartile

E For grouped data you can estimate the range using

$$\text{range} = \begin{pmatrix} \text{highest possible value} \\ \text{in last class interval} \end{pmatrix} - \begin{pmatrix} \text{lowest possible value} \\ \text{in first class interval} \end{pmatrix}$$

5 Formulae, equations and inequalities

Scientists use formulae to calculate the tension on the surface of a bubble.

5.1 Solving linear equations

Linear equations have no powers.

■ **To solve linear equations you always use the inverse operation.**

Remember:
$-$ is the inverse of $+$
$+$ is the inverse of $-$
$\div$ is the inverse of $\times$
$\times$ is the inverse of $\div$

Example 1

Solve the equation
$$p - 5 = -2$$

$+5$ is the inverse of -5

so add 5 to both sides:
$$p = -2 + 5$$
$$p = 3$$

Exercise 5A

Solve these equations:

1 $x + 4 = 7$ **2** $x - 7 = 2$ **3** $x + 5 = 1$

4 $2x = 5$ **5** $3x = 2$ **6** $5x = 3$

7 $\dfrac{x}{2} = 5$ **8** $\dfrac{x}{3} = 5$ **9** $\dfrac{x}{5} = \dfrac{1}{10}$

10 $\dfrac{x}{2} = \dfrac{2}{3}$ **11** $5x = 17$ **12** $x + 3 = -2$

5.2 Equations with two operations

You can use inverse operations to solve equations with two operations.

Example 2

Solve the equation:

$$\frac{x}{5} + 2 = 5$$

Method 1

Subtract 2 from both sides:

$$\frac{x}{5} + 2 - 2 = 5 - 2$$

$$\frac{x}{5} = 3$$

Multiply both sides by 5:

$$\frac{x}{5} \times 5 = 3 \times 5$$

$$x = 15$$

Method 2

Multiply both sides by 5:

$$\left(\frac{x}{5} + 2\right) \times 5 = 5 \times 5$$

$$x + 10 = 25$$

Subtract 10 from both sides:

$$x + 10 - 10 = 25 - 10$$

$$x = 15$$

Exercise 5B

Solve these equations:

1 $2x + 1 = 9$ **2** $\frac{x}{3} - 4 = 5$ **3** $\frac{x}{5} + 3 = 18$

4 $3x - 2 = 0$ **5** $2x + 1 = 1$ **6** $\frac{x}{3} + 7 = 1$

7 $\frac{x}{2} - 5 = 4$ **8** $7x - 1 = -3$ **9** $\frac{x}{6} + 3 = 1$

10 $\frac{x}{3} - 3 = 1$ **11** $5x + 1 = 3$ **12** $4x + 5 = 3$

13 $4 = 3 + \frac{x}{2}$ **14** $5 = \frac{x}{2} - 9$ **15** $2 = \frac{x}{7} + 5$

5.3 Equations with brackets

You can solve equations with brackets in them by
multiplying out the brackets.

- **When solving equations with brackets, always multiply
  out the brackets first.**

Example 3

Solve the equation: $2(3x - 5) = 12$

Multiply out the brackets first:

$$6x - 10 = 12$$
$$(+10) \qquad 6x = 22$$
$$(\div 6) \qquad x = 3\tfrac{4}{6} \text{ or } 3\tfrac{2}{3}$$

Exercise 5C

Solve these equations:

1 $2(x + 1) = 8$	**2** $3(x - 1) = 12$	**3** $4(x + 3) = 20$
4 $2(3x + 1) = 12$	**5** $2(3x + 1) = 13$	**6** $5(2x - 1) = 21$
7 $5(2x - 1) = 10$	**8** $3(2x + 1) = 3$	**9** $3(2x + 1) = 1$
10 $3(x + 5) = 3$	**11** $3(x + 4) = 2$	**12** $5(2x - 3) = 15$
13 $5(2x - 2) = 2$	**14** $2(7x + 1) = 10$	**15** $7(3x - 2) = 21$

5.4 Equations with the variable on both sides

- **When you solve equations with the variable on both
  sides use the inverse method. You need the variable on
  its own on one side.**

Example 4

Solve the equation:

$$4x - 5 = 2(3x + 6)$$

Multiply out the brackets:

$$4x - 5 = 6x + 12$$

$(-6x)$ $\qquad -2x - 5 = 12$

$(+5)$ $\qquad -2x = 17$

$(\div-2)$ $\qquad x = -8\frac{1}{2}$

Exercise 5D

Solve these equations:

1 $3x + 2 = 2x + 5$ **2** $3x + 1 = 5x - 7$ **3** $2(x + 1) = x + 5$

4 $5x - 2 = 2(2x + 3)$ **5** $4(x + 1) = 5(x - 3)$ **6** $3x - 2 = 7x + 6$

7 $2(x + 3) = 3 - x$ **8** $5(x - 1) = 7 - x$ **9** $4(x + 6) = 3(x - 1)$

10 $10(3 - x) = x - 3$ **11** $4x + 1 = 2x - 7$ **12** $3y + 7 = 7y - 1$

13 $5q - 1 = 2 - 4q$ **14** $2 - 5r = 4 - 2r$ **15** $4q + 7 = -(5 - 2q)$

5.5 Writing and solving your own linear equations

Word problems often describe everyday situations. You can simplify them by writing them as equations. You can then solve them much more easily.

Example 5

A rectangle is twice as long as it is wide. Find the length and width of the rectangle when the perimeter is 18 cm.

Write the width as x cm.
The length is then $2x$ cm.

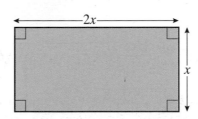

It is a good idea to draw a diagram.

The perimeter is 18 cm so:

$$x + 2x + x + 2x = 18$$
$$6x = 18$$
$$x = 3$$

So the rectangle is 6 cm long and 3 cm wide.

You can check the solution by putting the numbers back into the problem:

$$6\,\text{cm is twice }3\,\text{cm}$$
$$6 + 6 + 3 + 3 = 18 \checkmark$$

Exercise 5E

Write an equation and then solve it to find the answer to these problems.

1 The equal sides of an isosceles triangle are twice as long as the base. The perimeter of the triangle is 20 cm. Work out the lengths of the sides.

Hint:

2 The cost of printing an exam paper is 10p per copy plus the setting up charge of 75p. Mr Keane spends £3.95 printing exam papers. How many does he print?

3 The cost, C, of a mobile phone is made up of a monthly rental of £15 plus a call charge of 10p per minute. One month Pat paid a bill of £25. For how many minutes had she used her phone?

Hint: Work in pence or pounds.

4 The cost C of hiring a car is made up of a daily rate of £50 plus 20p per mile. Alex hires a car for 1 day and it costs him £80. How far did he drive?

5 The base angles of an isoceles triangle are twice as big as the other angle. Work out the sizes of the angles.

6 Jack and Jill have a combined age of 25. Jack is 3 years older than Jill. How old are they?

7 Helen and her dad have a combined age of 51. Helen is half her dad's age. How old is Helen?

8 The length and width of a rectangle are in the ratio 3 : 2. The perimeter of the rectangle is 50 cm. Find the length of the rectangle.

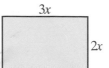

9 The base angles of an isosceles triangle are in the ratio $5:2$ with the other angle. Work out the size of the angles.

10 The cost of printing is made up from a setting up charge of 25p plus a cost of £1 per 100 sheets. Robin paid £5.50 for his printing. How many sheets did he have printed?

Hint:

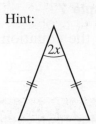

5.6 Fractional equations

Sometimes you will be asked to solve equations that involve fractions.

There is a very simple rule to deal with equations like this:

- **If an equation involves fractions, multiply everything by the lowest common denominator.**

You do this to get rid of the fractions in the equation.

> The lowest common denominator is the lowest number that the numbers on the bottom of a fraction will divide into (i.e. the least common multiple of the denominators).

Example 6

Solve the equation:

$$\frac{x}{2} + \frac{x}{3} = 5$$

Step 1: Multiply both sides by 6, the lowest common denominator

$$\frac{6 \times x}{2} + \frac{6 \times x}{3} = 6 \times 5$$

Step 2: Cancel and solve the equation

$$\frac{{}^{3}\cancel{6} \times x}{\cancel{2}_{1}} + \frac{{}^{2}\cancel{6} \times x}{\cancel{3}_{1}} = 30$$

$$3x + 2x = 30$$

$$5x = 30$$

$$x = 6$$

> The lowest common denominator of $\frac{x}{2}$ and $\frac{x}{3}$ is 6 because 6 is the lowest number that 2 and 3 will divide into.

Example 7

Solve the equation:

$$\frac{x+2}{3} = \frac{x-3}{5}$$

Multiply both sides by 15:

$$\frac{15(x+2)}{3} = \frac{15(x-3)}{5}$$

The lowest common denominator is 15.

Cancel factors:

$$\frac{{}^{5}\cancel{15}(x+2)}{\cancel{3}_{1}} = \frac{{}^{3}\cancel{15}(x-3)}{\cancel{5}_{1}}$$

Now solve the equation in the usual way:

$$5(x+2) = 3(x-3)$$
$$5x + 10 = 3x - 9$$
$$5x - 3x + 10 = -9$$
$$2x + 10 = -9$$
$$2x = -19$$

so

$$x = -9\tfrac{1}{2}$$

Exercise 5F

Solve these equations:

1 $\dfrac{x}{2} + \dfrac{x}{3} = 10$ **2** $\dfrac{x}{3} + \dfrac{x}{4} = 7$ **3** $\dfrac{x}{2} + \dfrac{x}{5} = 7$

4 $\dfrac{x}{4} + \dfrac{x}{5} = 9$ **5** $\dfrac{x+2}{3} = \dfrac{x+3}{2}$ **6** $\dfrac{x-2}{2} = \dfrac{x-3}{3}$

7 $\dfrac{3x}{2} - \dfrac{4x}{3} = 6$ **8** $\dfrac{x-2}{3} = \dfrac{x+3}{2}$ **9** $\dfrac{x}{2} + x = 1$

10 $\dfrac{x}{2} + \dfrac{x}{3} = 1$ **11** $\dfrac{3x}{4} - \dfrac{2x}{3} = 3$ **12** $\dfrac{(x+2)}{3} + \dfrac{(x-3)}{4} = 1$

5.7 Substituting into formulae

The brightness of the sun is given by the formula $B = \dfrac{K}{d^2}$,

where K is a constant and d is the distance from the sun.

In this section you are going to substitute positive and negative numbers and fractions into formulae.

Example 8

The formula for the distance travelled by a stone dropping from a cliff is given by

$$s = ut + \tfrac{1}{2}at^2$$

Find s when $u = 10$, $t = \tfrac{1}{2}$, $a = -10$

$$s = 10 \times \tfrac{1}{2} + \tfrac{1}{2} \times (-10) \times \left(\tfrac{1}{2}\right)^2$$

No brackets so indices first:

$$s = 10 \times \tfrac{1}{2} + \tfrac{1}{2} \times (-10) \times \tfrac{1}{4}$$

Division and multiplication next:

$$s = 5 + (-5) \times \tfrac{1}{4}$$
$$s = 5 + -\tfrac{5}{4}$$

Then addition and subtraction:

$$s = 5 - 1\tfrac{1}{4}$$
$$s = 3\tfrac{3}{4}$$

Don't forget
B rackets
I ndices
D ivision
M ultiplication
A ddition
S ubtraction

$\tfrac{1}{2} \times 10 = 5$
so $\tfrac{1}{2} \times -10 = -5$

Exercise 5G

1   Use the formula

$s = ut + \frac{1}{2}at^2$ to find the value of s when:

(a) $u = 0, t = 2, a = -10$

(b) $u = 10, t = 5, a = -10$

(c) $u = 20, t = \frac{1}{2}, a = 10$

(d) $u = -10, t = \frac{1}{2}, a = 10$

(e) $u = 2, t = \frac{1}{4}, a = -5$

2   The formula $C = \frac{5}{9}(F - 32)$ changes degrees
Fahrenheit into degrees Celsius. Find C when:

(a) $F = 212°$

(b) $F = 32°$

(c) $F = 0°$

(d) $F = 14°$

(e) $F = -13°$

3   Use the formula

$V = \sqrt{u^2 - 2as}$ to find the value of V when:

Remember:
$\sqrt{u^2 - 2as}$ can also
be written as
$\sqrt{(u^2 - 2as)}$

(a) $u = 0, a = -10, s = 5$

(b) $u = 10, a = -10, s = 5$

(c) $u = 5, a = -2, s = 10$

(d) $u = 2, a = \frac{1}{2}, s = 3$

(e) $u = 1, a = -\frac{1}{2}, s = 2$

5.8 Rearranging formulae

When you substitute numbers into a formula you might have
to rearrange the formula to find the variable you need.

Example 9

Kolya throws a ball into the air. The formula for its speed
is given by

$v = u + at$

Find a when $v = -10$, $u = 10$ and $t = 2$

$$v = u + at$$

so $-10 = 10 + a \times 2$

$-20 = a \times 2$

$\dfrac{-20}{2} = a$

so $a = -10$

Exercise 5H

1   The cost in pounds, C, of hiring a car is given by the formula

$$C = 20 + \tfrac{1}{2}m$$

Find the number of miles m travelled if C is:

(a) 44   (b) 82   (c) 220   (d) 32   (e) 100

2   The simple interest I gained by investing P pounds for T years at $R\%$ is given by the formula

$$I = \frac{P \times T \times R}{100}$$

Work out the time T when:

(a) $I = 10$, $P = 100$, $R = 5$

(b) $I = 12$, $P = 200$, $R = 3$

(c) $I = 24$, $P = 60$, $R = 4$

(d) $I = 50$, $P = 250$, $R = 5$

3 The formula for the speed of a rocket is

$$V = u + at$$

Work out the value of t when:

(a) $V = 100$, $u = 0$, $a = 5$
(b) $V = 50$, $u = 10$, $a = 5$
(c) $V = 50$, $u = -10$, $a = 6$
(d) $V = 1000$, $u = 100$, $a = -10$

4 The formula to change °F to °C is

$$C = \tfrac{5}{9}(F - 32)$$

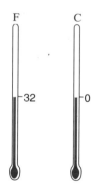

Find F when C is:

(a) 20   (b) 40   (c) -10 (d) -5 (e) 200

5 The formula for the time T taken when the pendulum on a clock travels from one side to another and back is

$$T = 2\pi\sqrt{\dfrac{l}{g}}$$

where l is the length of the pendulum and $g = 9.81$.

Using $\pi = 3.14$ or the π key on your calculator, find l when T is:

(a) 1   (b) 10   (c) 2   (d) 5   (e) 0.5

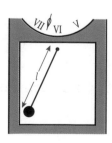

5.9 Changing the subject of a formula

Sometimes you have to change the subject of a formula. This is especially important when you aren't given numbers to put into the formula.

$P = \pi r + 2(a + b)$
Here P is the subject of the formula.

$$r = \frac{P - 2(a + b)}{\pi}$$)

Here r is the subject of the formula.

Example 10

$$P = \pi r + 2(a + b)$$

is the formula for the perimeter of this shape.

Make a the subject of the formula.

$$P = \pi r + 2(a + b)$$

$(-\pi r)$ $\qquad P - \pi r = 2(a + b)$

$(\div 2)$ $\qquad \dfrac{P - \pi r}{2} = a + b$

$(-b)$ $\qquad \dfrac{(P - \pi r)}{2} - b = a$

so $\qquad a = \dfrac{(P - \pi r)}{2} - b$

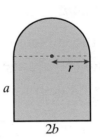

Example 11

Make l the subject of the formula

$$T = 2\pi \sqrt{\frac{l}{g}}$$

$(\div 2\pi)$ $\qquad \dfrac{T}{2\pi} = \sqrt{\dfrac{l}{g}}$

Square each side to get rid of the square root:

$$\frac{T^2}{4\pi^2} = \frac{l}{g}$$

$(\times g)$ $\qquad \dfrac{T^2 g}{4\pi^2} = l$

Exercise 5I

1   The formula for the perimeter of a rectangle is
$P = 2(l + w)$. Make l the subject of the formula.

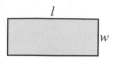

2   The area of a circle is given by the formula $A = \pi r^2$.
Make r the subject of the formula.

3   The cost C of hiring a car and driving m miles is given
by the formula

$$C = 0.4m + 20$$

Make m the subject of the formula.

4   The time T taken for a pendulum to swing is given by

the formula $T = 2\pi \sqrt{\dfrac{l}{g}}$, where l is the length of the

pendulum. Make g the subject of the formula.

5   Make x the subject of the formula

$$F = \frac{g}{x^2}$$

6   These formulae are used in circles and cylinders.
Make r the subject in each case.

   (a) $C = 2\pi r$ **(b)** $V = 2\pi r^2 h$

   (c) $A = \dfrac{\pi r^2 \theta}{360}$ **(d)** $A = Ch + 2\pi r^2$

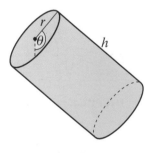

5.10 Non-linear equations

Non-linear equations are equations where the variable is
raised to a power other than 1.
Sometimes you have to simplify the equation to see this.

Example 12

Solve these equations:

(a) $x^2 - 4 = 0$ **(b)** $\dfrac{1}{y} = y$ **(c)** $\dfrac{1}{y-1} = y - 1$

(a) $x^2 - 4 = 0$

so $x^2 = 4$

Take the square root of both sides:

$$x = \pm\sqrt{4}$$

so $x = +\sqrt{4} = 2$ or $x = -\sqrt{4} = -2$

therefore $x = 2$ or $x = -2$

Section 1.6 has more on square roots.

(b) $\dfrac{1}{y} = y$

so $1 = y^2$

and $y^2 = 1$

Take the square root of both sides:

$$y = \pm\sqrt{1}$$

so $y = \sqrt{1} = 1$ or $y = -\sqrt{1} = -1$

therefore $y = 1$ or $y = -1$

(c) $(y - 1) = \dfrac{1}{(y-1)}$

so $(y - 1)^2 = 1$

Take the square root of both sides:

$$y - 1 = \pm\sqrt{1}$$

so $y - 1 = +\sqrt{1}$ or $y - 1 = -\sqrt{1}$

             $y - 1 = 1$ or $y - 1 = -1$

therefore $y = 2$ or $y = 0$

Exercise 5J

1   Solve these equations (to one decimal place where appropriate):

     (a) $x^2 = 9$ **(b)** $y^2 - 36 = 0$ **(c)** $n^2 - 144 = 0$

     (d) $\dfrac{1}{w+2} = w + 2$ **(e)** $2x = \dfrac{72}{x}$ **(f)** $3z^2 - 147 = 0$

(g) $2y^2 = 18$ **(h)** $q^2 - 17 = 271$ **(i)** $\dfrac{3x^2}{2} = 96$

(j) $p + 1 = \dfrac{1}{p + 1}$ **(k)** $\dfrac{16}{q - 5} = 4(q - 5)$ **(l)** $2y + 5 = \dfrac{25}{2y + 5}$

2 Simplify and solve these equations:

(a) $\dfrac{1}{a} + \dfrac{3}{a} = a$ **(b)** $\dfrac{5}{b^3} + \dfrac{4}{b^3} = \dfrac{1}{b^2}$

(c) $\dfrac{17}{(c + 3)^3} + \dfrac{2}{(c + 3)^3} = \dfrac{8}{(c + 3)^2} + \dfrac{11}{(c + 3)^2}$

(d) $\dfrac{18d^4}{d^5} = \dfrac{2d^6}{d^5}$

5.11 Solving equations by trial and improvement

To solve an equation you have to have an exact solution. Sometimes it is not possible to solve an equation using an algebraic method. You then need to try a trial and improvement method.

Example 13

Solve the equation $x^2 + x = 5$

Give your answer to two decimal places.

Start with a guess near the answer.

Try $x = 1$:
$1^2 + 1 = 2$ Too small.

Try $x = 2$:
$2^2 + 2 = 6$ Too big.

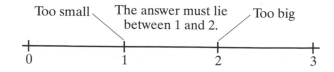

Too small   The answer must lie   Too big
between 1 and 2.

It is a good idea to put your working in a table.

Value of x	Value of $x^2 + x$	Results compared to 5
1	2	Too small
2	6	Too big
1.5	3.75	Too small
1.8	5.04	Too big
1.7	4.59	Too small
1.75	4.8125	Too small
1.78	4.9484	Too small
1.79	4.9941	Too small
1.795	5.017 025	Too big

Remember:
You always try
between values that
are too big and too
small.

This value of x lets
you check whether
1.79 or 1.80 is the
closest answer.

x lies between 1.79 and 1.795.

So the solution correct to two decimal places is $x = 1.79$.

Example 14

The volume of this brick is $50\,\text{cm}^3$.

Work out the lengths of each of the edges
correct to two decimal places.

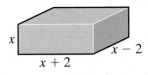

You need to solve the equation $x(x + 2)(x - 2) = 50$

  or $x^3 - 4x = 50$.

Value of x	Value of $x^3 - 4x$	Results compared to 50
4	48	too small
5	105	too big
4.5	73.125	too big
4.2	57.283	too big
4.1	52.521	too big
4.05	50.230 125	too big (just)
4.04	49.779 264	too small
4.045	50.004 391 125	too big

x lies between 4.04 and 4.045.

The value of x correct to two decimal places is 4.04.

So the lengths of the edges are 2.04, 4.04 and 6.04.

Exercise 5K

1 Solve these equations by trial and improvement.
Give your answers correct to one decimal place.
   (a) $x^2 = 20$ (b) $x^2 = 17$
   (c) $x^3 = 40$ (d) $x^2 + x = 10$
   (e) $x^2 + x = 12$ (f) $x^2 - x = 10$

2 Solve these equations by trial and improvement.
Give your answers correct to two decimal places.
   (a) $x^2 = 26$ (b) $x^3 = 26$
   (c) $x^3 + x^2 = 52$ (d) $x^2 - 3x = 10$
   (e) $x^3 - x^2 = 1$ (f) $x^2 + 5x = 120$

3 The area A of this rectangle is given by the formula
   $$A = x^2 - 9$$
   If the area is $40\,\text{cm}^2$ find the value of x correct to
   two decimal places.

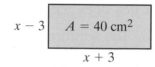

4 The volume of this cuboid is given by the formula
   $$V = x^3 - 25x$$

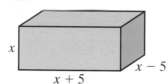

   Find the value of x when $V = 100\,\text{cm}^3$.

E **5.12 Inequalities**

One fish weighs less than 1 kg. You can
show this in an inequality:

   $$f < 1$$

where f is the mass of the fish in kilograms.

■ $>$ means 'greater than'
   $<$ means 'less than'
   $\geqslant$ means 'greater than or equal to'
   $\leqslant$ means 'less than or equal to'

Example 15

Solve the inequality $\quad 2x + 1 \geqslant 4$

Subtract 1 from both sides:

$$2x \geqslant 4 - 1$$
$$2x \geqslant 3$$

Divide both sides by 2:

$$x \geqslant 3 \div 2$$
$$x \geqslant 1\tfrac{1}{2}$$

You solve inequalities in exactly the same way as solving equations.

Sometimes the variable is on the right hand side of the inequality sign. In this case you can swap both sides of the inequality and change the direction of the inequality sign:

$\quad 4 < x$ is the same as $x > 4$

If you multiply or divide by a negative number you must change the direction of the inequality.

$\quad -x < 3$ is the same as $x > -3$

$\quad -4x \geqslant 8$ is the same as $x \leqslant -2$

If 4 is less than x then x is greater than 4.

$$-x < 3$$
Add x to each side:
$$0 < 3 + x$$
so $\quad -3 < x$
Swap sides:
$$x > -3$$

Example 16

Solve the inequality $\quad 4(3 - x) \leqslant 16$

Multiply out the brackets:

$$12 - 4x \leqslant 16$$
(-12) $\qquad -4x \leqslant 4$
$(\div 4)$ $\qquad -x \leqslant 1$
so $\qquad x \geqslant -1$

If you change the signs you have to change the direction of inequality.

Exercise 5L

Solve these inequalities:

1 $2x + 1 < 5$ **2** $x - 3 < 2$ **3** $2x + 5 \leqslant 7$

4 $3(x + 1) > 2$ **5** $2(3x - 2) \geqslant 6$ **6** $5y - 4 \leqslant 6$

7 $3(p - 2) > 9$ **8** $5(q - 4) < 6$ **9** $5 < p - 1$

10 $2 > p - 6$ **11** $8 \leqslant 2(p - 1)$ **12** $10 \geqslant 5(p + 2)$

13 $3 - x < 2$ **14** $4 - 2x > 6$ **15** $3 - x \leqslant 5$

16 $2 \geqslant 3 - x$ **17** $4 < 2 - 3x$ **18** $5 > 10 - 2x$

19 $2(3 - x) > 8$ **20** $15 \geqslant 5(3 - x)$ **21** $8 < 4(2 - x)$

22 $5 - 2x \leqslant 3 - 4x$ **23** $7 + 2x \geqslant 3(4 - x)$ **24** $7(3 - x) < 3(4 - 2x)$

E 5.13 Inequalities on a number line

You can show inequalities by shading a number line.

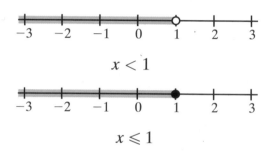

$x < 1$

$x \leqslant 1$

If the inequality sign is $<$ or $>$ then the circle is **not shaded**.

If the inequality sign is $\leqslant$ or $\geqslant$ then the circle is **shaded**.

When there are two inequalities to be satisfied it is sometimes neater to write them as one expression.

e.g. $x > -2$ AND $x \leqslant 1$

can be written as $-2 < x \leqslant 1$

This can be shown on a number line:

However, sometimes two inequalities cannot be written as one expression.

e.g. $x < -2$ AND $x \geqslant 1$

Exercise 5M

1 Write down the inequalities shown on these number lines:

(a)

$$\text{number line from } -3 \text{ to } 3, \text{ open circle at } 2, \text{ shading to the left}$$

(b)

$$\text{number line from } -3 \text{ to } 3, \text{ filled circle at } 2, \text{ shading to the left}$$

(c)

$$\text{number line from } -3 \text{ to } 3, \text{ filled circle at } -2, \text{ shading to the right}$$

(d)

$$\text{number line from } -3 \text{ to } 3, \text{ open circle at } -1, \text{ shading to the right}$$

(e)

$$\text{number line from } -3 \text{ to } 3, \text{ open circle at } 3, \text{ shading to the left}$$

(f)

$$\text{number line from } -3 \text{ to } 3, \text{ open circle at } -1, \text{ shading to the right}$$

(g)

$$\text{number line from } -3 \text{ to } 3, \text{ open circles at } -2 \text{ and } 1, \text{ shading between}$$

(h)

$$\text{number line from } -3 \text{ to } 3, \text{ open circle at } -1, \text{ filled circle at } 2, \text{ shading between}$$

(i)

$$\text{number line from } -3 \text{ to } 3, \text{ filled circle at } -1, \text{ open circle at } 3, \text{ shading between}$$

(j)

$$\text{number line from } -3 \text{ to } 3, \text{ filled circles at } -2 \text{ and } 2, \text{ shading between}$$

2 Draw six number lines from -3 to $+3$. Use them to show these inequalities:

(a) $x < 3$ **(b)** $x > -1$

(c) $x \leqslant 2$ **(d)** $x \geqslant -1$

(e) $x > 0$ **(f)** $x \leqslant 1$

3 Draw six number lines from -3 to $+3$. Use them to show these combined inequalities:

(a) $-1 < x < 1$ **(b)** $-1 < x \leqslant 2$

(c) $-2 \leqslant x < 1$ **(d)** $-1 \leqslant x \leqslant 2$

(e) $-3 \leqslant x < 0$ **(f)** $-1 < x \leqslant 3$

E 5.14 Solving combined inequalities

Sometimes you need to use more than one technique in a single problem.

Example 17

Show this inequality on a number line $-1 \leqslant 2x + 4 < 5$.

Write down the possible values of x if x is an integer.

You need to split this into two inequalities:

$$-1 \leqslant 2x + 4 \quad \text{and} \quad 2x + 4 < 5$$

$(-4) \quad -5 \leqslant 2x \qquad \text{and} \qquad 2x < 1$

$(\div 2) \quad -2\tfrac{1}{2} \leqslant x \qquad \text{and} \qquad x < \tfrac{1}{2}$

So $-2\tfrac{1}{2} \leqslant x < \tfrac{1}{2}$

This can be shown on a number line as

So if x is an integer then x is -2, -1 or 0.

Example 18

The variable x satisfies both

$$5x + 4 > 14 \tag{1}$$

and $2x + 9 \leqslant 3$ **(2)**

Show on a number line the values that x can take.

Using **(1)** $5x + 4 > 14$

so $5x > 14 - 4$

    $5x > 10$

therefore $x > 2$

Using **(2)** $2x + 9 \leqslant 3$

so $2x \leqslant 3 - 9$

    $2x \leqslant -6$

therefore $x \leqslant -3$

So $x \leqslant -3$ and $x > 2$.

This can be shown on a number line as:

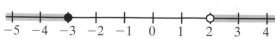

Exercise 5N

1 Show these combined inequalities on number lines from -4 to $+4$.

(a) $-1 \leqslant 2x + 1 < 5$

(b) $-4 \leqslant 3x - 2 \leqslant 7$

(c) $-8 < 3x + 1 \leqslant 10$

(d) $-5 \leqslant 2x - 1 < 3$

(e) $4 < 5 - x < -2$

(f) $7 < 3 - 2x \leqslant -4$

2 x is an integer. List all the values of x that satisfy these combined inequalities.

(a) $-2 \leqslant x + 4 < 7$ (b) $-3 < x - 3 \leqslant 5$

(c) $-6 < 3x \leqslant 9$ (d) $-2 < 3x - 5 \leqslant 7$

(e) $-5 \leqslant 2 + x < -1$ (f) $-4 < 5 + x \leqslant -4$

(g) $-5 \leqslant 2x - 3 \leqslant 7$ (h) $-7 < 5x - 1 \leqslant 8$

(i) $-3 < 3x + 1 \leqslant 10$ (j) $-10 \leqslant 2x + 1 < 9$

3 Show on a number line the values that p can take if it satisfies:

(a) $p + 3 \leqslant 2$ and $p > 0$

(b) $3p + 1 \geqslant 13$ and $4p + 2 < 10$

(c) $p + 2 \geqslant 2$ and $2 > 1 + 2p$

(d) $2p - 7 < 9$ and $5p + 2 > 57$

(e) $4p + 2 \leqslant 30$ and $2p - 10 \geqslant 1$

(f) $p + 3 \geqslant -10$ and $2p + 40 < 9$

4 Daniel designs a flag.

For each of the shaded corners, write down three inequalities that describe them.

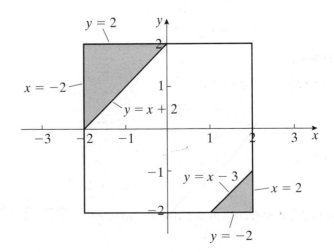

E 5.15 Solving simultaneous equations using graphs

Simultaneous equations are equations that are true at the same time.

Simultaneous means 'at the same time'.

When two straight lines cross, they cross only once.
Each line can have an equation.

e.g. $y = x - 1$
        $y = -x + 3$

The coordinates of each point on a straight line satisfy the equation of the straight line.

■ **When you solve a pair of simultaneous equations you are finding the point where the lines cross.**

Example 19

Solve the simultaneous equations:

$y = x - 1$
$y = -x + 3$

You need to draw the straight lines first:

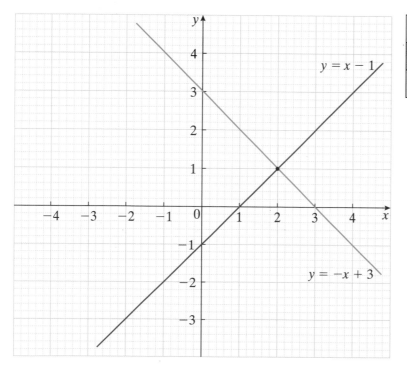

x		-1	0	3
$y = x - 1$		-2	-1	2
$y = -x + 3$		4	3	0

The two lines cross at $(2, 1)$.
At this point both $y = x - 1$
and $y = -x + 3$ are true.

At $(2, 1)$, $x = 2$ and $y = 1$. This is the solution.

> When you solve a pair of simultaneous equations you are finding the coordinates of the point where their lines cross.

Exercise 5O

1   Write down the solution to the simultaneous equations represented by these lines.
    Show that both equations are true at this point.

(a)

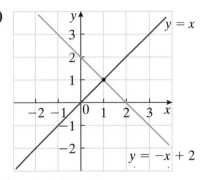

(b)

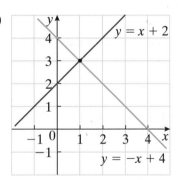

(c)

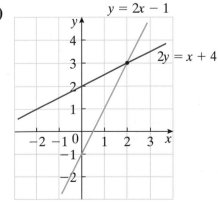

(d)

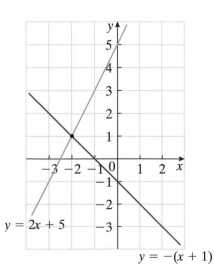

(e)

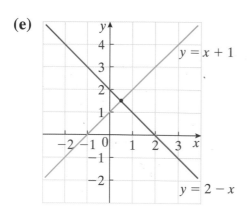

(f)

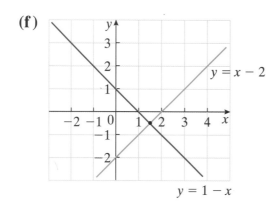

2 By drawing straight line graphs solve these simultaneous equations. (Draw your axes from -4 to $+4$ for both x and y.)

(a) $y = x$ **(b)** $y = x + 1$ **(c)** $y = 2x + 1$

$y = 2 - x$ $y = 1 - x$ $y = -(x + 1)$

(d) $y = 3 - x$ **(e)** $y = 2x + 1$ **(f)** $y = 2x - 1$

$y = x - 1$ $y = -x + 1$ $y = 3 - x$

E 5.16 Solving simultaneous equations by substitution

Solving simultaneous equations by drawing graphs is very time consuming.

One method of solving a pair of simultaneous equations using algebra is to substitute one equation into another.

Example 20

Solve these simultaneous equations by substitution.

$$x + y = 5$$
$$x = 2$$

First label the equations **(1)** and **(2)**:

$$x + y = 5 \hspace{4cm} \textbf{(1)}$$
$$x = 2 \hspace{4.2cm} \textbf{(2)}$$

Substitute equation **(2)** into equation **(1)**:

$$2 + y = 5$$
so $\hspace{1cm} y = 5 - 2 = 3$

So the solution is $x = 2$ and $y = 3$.

> If you label the equations it makes your working much clearer.

Sometimes both equations include x and y.

Example 21

Solve these simultaneous equations by substitution.

$$2x + y = 3 \hspace{3cm} \textbf{(1)}$$
$$x + y = 1 \hspace{3.2cm} \textbf{(2)}$$

From equation **(1)**,

$$y = 3 - 2x$$

Substitute into equation **(2)**:

$$x + (3 - 2x) = 1$$
$$x + 3 - 2x = 1$$
$$-x = 1 - 3 = -2$$
so $\hspace{2cm} x = 2$

Substitute $x = 2$ into equation **(2)**:

$$x + y = 1$$
$$2 + y = 1$$
$$y = 1 - 2 = -1$$

So the solution is $x = 2$ and $y = -1$.

It does not matter which equation or variable you decide to start your working with. In this example, **(1)** was used and y was expressed in terms of x.

> You use the other equation to check your solution at the end.

> Check this solution using equation **(1)**
> $$2x + y = 2 \times 2 - 1$$
> $$= 4 - 1$$
> $$= 3 \checkmark$$

Exercise 5P

1   Solve the simultaneous equations from Example 21 again. This time start with equation **(2)** and write x in terms of y.

2   Solve these simultaneous equations by substitution:

   (a) $x + y = 3$
       $x = 1$

   (b) $3x + 2y = 7$
       $4x = 12$

Remember to always check your solution.

   (c) $y = 2x - 5$
      $6y = 24$

   (d) $y = 2$
      $x = 3y - 9$

   (e) $7x = 10 + 4y$
      $2x = -2$

   (f) $2x - 3y = 10$
      $11y = 44$

3   Solve these simultaneous equations by substitution:

   (a) $x + y = 3$
      $x + 2y = 2$

   (b) $x = -4 + 2y$
      $2x - y = 1$

   (c) $3x - y = -2$
      $x + 3y = 16$

   (d) $x + 2y = 7$
      $3x + y = 11$

   (e) $3x + 2y = 10$
      $2x - 6y = 14$

   (f) $2x + 5y = -2$
      $3x + 9y = -6$

   (g) $10x - 5y = 15$
      $7x - 9y = 5$

   (h) $51x + 17y = 34$
      $13x - 11y = 24$

E 5.17 Solving simultaneous equations by elimination

Often the easiest way to solve simultaneous equations is to add or subtract them. This is called solving **by elimination**.

Example 22

Solve these simultaneous equations by elimination.

$$2x + y = 5$$
$$x - y = 1$$

Add the equations:

$$
\begin{array}{r}
2x + y = 5 \\
+ \quad x - y = 1 \\
\hline
3x = 6
\end{array}
$$

$+y - y = 0$

So $\qquad x = 2$

Substitute this value of x into one of the equations:

$$x - y = 1$$
$$2 - y = 1$$
$$y = 1$$

So the solution is $x = 2$, $y = 1$.

You can check your
answer using the
other equation:
$$2x + y = 5$$
$$4 + 1 = 5 \checkmark$$

If the signs in front of the variable you are eliminating
are the same, you need to subtract one equation from
the other.

Example 23

Solve these simultaneous equations by elimination.

$$4x + y = 18$$
$$x + y = 4$$

Subtract one equation from the other:

$$4x + y = 18$$
$$- \quad x + y = \ \ 4$$
$$\overline{\qquad 3x = 14}$$
$$x = 4\tfrac{2}{3}$$

Substitute this value of x into one of the equations:

$$x + y = 4$$
$$4\tfrac{2}{3} + y = 4$$
$$y = -\tfrac{2}{3}$$

Check:
$$4x + y = 18$$
$$18\tfrac{2}{3} - \tfrac{2}{3} = 18 \checkmark$$

So the solution is $x = 4\tfrac{2}{3}$, $y = -\tfrac{2}{3}$.

■ **You can solve a pair of simultaneous equations by**
  eliminating one variable.

  ● **If the signs in front of the variable are different**
    you add the equations.
  ● **If the signs in front of the variable are the same**
    you subtract one equation from the other.

Exercise 5Q

Solve these simultaneous equations by elimination:

1 $x + y = 3$
   $x - y = 1$

2 $2x + y = 5$
   $x + y = 3$

3 $x + y = 7$
   $x - y = 3$

4 $x + 2y = 5$
   $x - y = -1$

5 $x + 3y = 10$
   $x + y = 4$

6 $2x - y = 5$
   $x + y = 4$

7 $3x + y = 4$
   $x - y = 0$

8 $2p - q = 10$
   $p + q = 2$

9 $3a + 2b = 4$
   $3a - b = 7$

More complicated equations

In all the questions you have tackled so far either one or other of the variables in both equations have had the same number in front. If they are not the same then you have to make them the same.

You do this by multiplying the whole equation by a number.

Example 24

Solve the simultaneous equations:

   $2x + y = 4$ **(1)**

   $3x + 2y = 7$ **(2)**

Look at the numbers in front of x and y. There are two ways of getting x or y to have the same number in front.

Either:
You could multiply equation **(1)** by 2. This would make the y's have the same number in front.

The equations would then be

   $2 \times (2x + y = 4) \Rightarrow 4x + 2y = 8$
   $3x + 2y = 7$

You must multiply all the parts by 2.

or:
You could multiply equation **(1)** by 3 to get $6x$ and equation **(2)** by 2 to get $6x$.

This time the equations would be

   $3 \times (2x + y = 4) \Rightarrow 6x + 3y = 12$
   $2 \times (3x + 2y = 7) \Rightarrow 6x + 4y = 14$

The first method is the easier one so

   $4x + 2y = 8$
   $3x + 2y = 7$

Subtract the second equation from the first:

$$4x + 2y = 8$$
$$-3x + 2y = 7$$
$$\overline{x = 1}$$

Substitute $x = 1$ into equation **(2)**

$$3 + 2y = 7$$
$$2y = 4$$
$$y = 2$$

The solution is $x = 1$, $y = 2$.

Check in the other equation
$4x + 2y = 8$
$4 + 4 = 8\checkmark$

Exercise 5R

Solve these simultaneous equations by elimination:

1 $x + 2y = 5$
$2x + y = 4$

2 $x + 3y = 6$
$3x + y = 10$

3 $2x + y = 3$
$x + 2y = 0$

4 $x - y = 2$
$2x + 3y = -1$

5 $x - y = 7$
$2x + 3y = -1$

6 $3x + y = 5$
$2x - y = 5$

7 $4x + 3y = -2$
$x + 2y = -3$

8 $3x + 3y = 0$
$x + 2y = 2$

9 $x + 2y = 1$
$2x + 3y = -1$

10 $5p + 2q = 9$
$3p + q = 5$

11 $3a + 4b = -5$
$5a - 2b = 9$

12 $4r - 2s = 22$
$6r - 6s = 36$

Summary of key points

1   To solve linear equations you always use the inverse operation.

2   When solving equations with brackets, always multiply out the brackets first.

3   When you solve equations with the variable on both sides use the inverse method. You need the variable on its own on one side.

4   If an equation involves fractions, multiply everything by the lowest common denominator.

E $>$ means greater than
$<$ means less than
$\geqslant$ means greater than or equal to
$\leqslant$ means less than or equal to

E   When you solve a pair of simultaneous equations you are finding the point where the lines cross.

E   You can solve a pair of simultaneous equations by eliminating one variable.
  • If the signs in front of the variable are different you add the equations.
  • If the signs in front of the variable are the same you subtract one equation from the other.

6 Angles

You can use angles to describe the position of stars in the night sky.

6.1 Angle types

- **An angle between 0° and 90° is called acute.**

- **An angle between 90° and 180° is called obtuse.**

- **An angle between 180° and 360° is called reflex.**

Exercise 6A

Without measuring, write down the angle types of the angles below.

1

2 91°

3 203°

4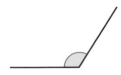

5 17°

6

7

8 162°

6.2 Angles at a point and on a straight line

■ **The sum of the angles at a point is 360°, i.e.**

$$w + x + y + z = 360°$$

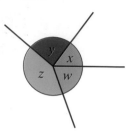

■ **The sum of the angles on a straight line is 180°, i.e.**

$$x + y + z = 180°$$

Example 1

Find the missing angles.

(a)

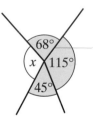

(b)

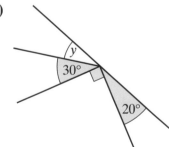

(a) $x + 68° + 115° + 45° = 360°$ (angles at a point)

$$x + 228° = 360°$$

so $\qquad x = 360° - 228° = 132°$

(b) $y + 30° + 90° + 20° = 180°$ (angles on a straight line)

$$y + 140° = 180°$$

so $\qquad y = 180° - 140° = 40°$

Exercise 6B

Work out the unknown angles.

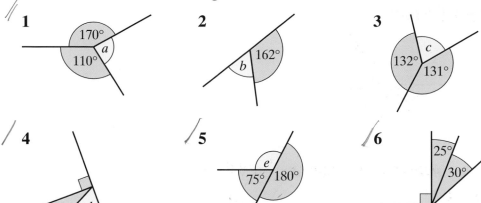

1 170° a 110°

2 162° b

3 c 132° 131°

4 18° d

5 e 75° 180° 180° 75° f

6 25° 30° g

6.3 Intersecting lines

You have seen this result about opposite angles.

■ **When two lines cross they form two pairs of angles opposite each other which are the same size:**

$a = b, c = d$

c a
b d

Proving the result

The two straight lines AB and CD meet at a point.

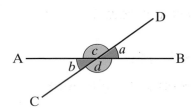

D
A —— c a —— B
b d
C

It 'looks' as if $a = b$ and $c = d$.

You could view the situation as

Start with CD lying along AB

then CD turns:

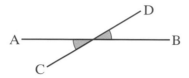

Intuitively the two shaded angles should be equal.

To prove the angles are equal you need to show why it is true:

$$a + c = 180°$$ (angles on a straight line)

In maths, a proof is much more powerful than an intuitive argument.

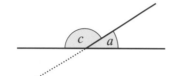

$$b + c = 180°$$ (angles on a straight line)

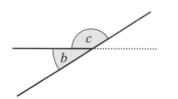

so $a + c = b + c$

therefore $a = b$

You can prove that $c = d$ in the same way.

Exercise 6C

Work out the unknown angles.

1

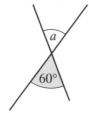

2

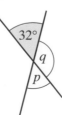

3

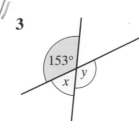

6.4 Angles between parallel lines

You already know these results about parallel lines.

■ **For parallel lines cut by a third line**

● **Alternate angles are equal:**

$$b = e, d = g$$

● **Corresponding angles are equal:**

$$a = e, d = h, b = f, c = g$$

● **The sum of supplementary angles is 180°:**

$$b + g = 180° \quad d + e = 180°$$

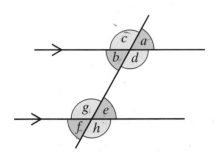

Proving that supplementary angles add to $180°$

These parallel lines are cut by a third line.

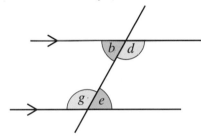

Using the diagram,

$$b + c = 180° \quad \text{(angles on a straight line)}$$

but $\quad c = g \quad$ (corresponding angles)

so $\quad b + g = 180°$

This argument proves that the sum of a pair of supplementary angles is $180°$.

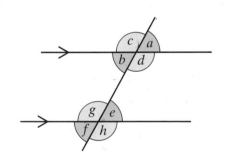

Example 2

Write down, with a reason, the size of the angle

(a) x **(b)** y **(c)** z

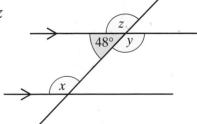

(a) $\qquad x = 180° - 48°$ $\qquad$ (supplementary angles)

$\qquad$ so $\quad x = 132°$

(b) $\qquad y = x$ $\qquad$ (alternate angles)

$\qquad$ so $\quad y = 132°$

(c) $\qquad z = x$ $\qquad$ (corresponding angles)

$\qquad$ so $\quad z = 132°$

Exercise 6D

In each case work out the size of each angle marked with a letter. Give your reasons or show your working.

1

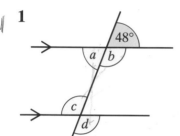

2

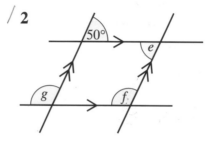

3

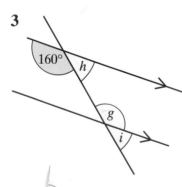

4

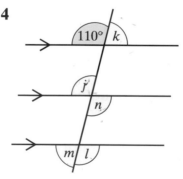

5

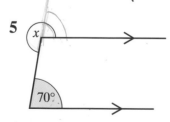

6

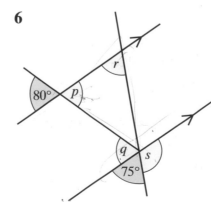

6.5 Angles in a triangle

Draw a triangle, cut it out and tear off each angle.

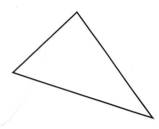 

Arrange each piece so that the angles meet at a point:

You find that they add up to 180°.

You can also prove this result:

ABC is a triangle.
The interior angles of the triangle are
labelled x, y and z.

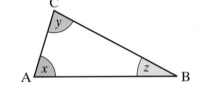

You need to prove that

$$x + y + z = 180°$$

Draw a line, LM, parallel to AC and passing through B:

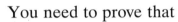

$\angle LBA + y + \angle MBC = 180°$ (angles on a straight line)

but $\angle LBA = x$ (alternate angles)
          $\angle MBC = z$ (alternate angles)

so $x + y + z = 180°$

■   **For any triangle, the sum of the three
interior angles is 180°.**

$$x + y + z = 180°$$

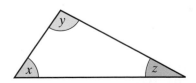

Example 3

Work out the size of the angle marked

(a) x

(b) y

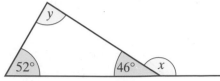

(a) $46° + x = 180°$ (angles on a straight line)

so $x = 180° - 46°$

       $x = 134°$

(b) $52° + 46° + y = 180°$ (angles in a triangle)

so $98° + y = 180°$

              $y = 180° - 98°$

so $y = 82°$

Exercise 6E

1   Work out the size of each angle marked with a letter.
Say which angle facts you use.

(a) 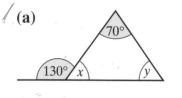   **(b)** 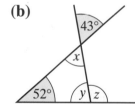   **(c)**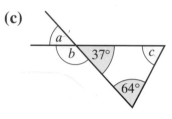

2   ABC is an isosceles triangle

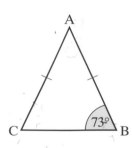

$AB = AC$

$\angle ABC = 73°$

Work out the size of the angle

(a) ACB

(b) BAC

Remember: the base
angles in an
isosceles triangle are
equal.

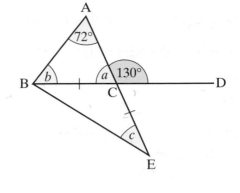

3 BD, AE and BE are straight lines.

$$BC = CE$$
$$\angle ACD = 130°$$
$$\angle BAC = 72°$$

Work out the size of the angles marked *a*, *b* and *c*. Say which angle facts you use.

4 Explain why this triangle is isosceles.

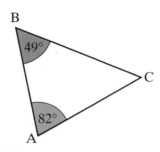

6.6 Angles in a quadrilateral

Draw a quadrilateral, cut it out and tear off each angle.

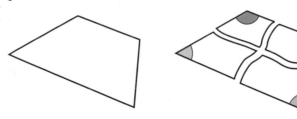

Arrange the pieces so that the angles meet at a point:

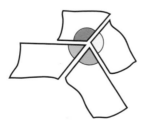

You find that they add up to 360°.

■ **The sum of the interior angles of a quadrilateral is 360°:**

$$a + b + c + d = 360°$$

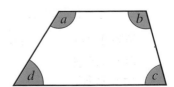

You can also prove this result:

ABCD is any quadrilateral.
The interior angles of the quadrilateral are labelled a, b, c and d.

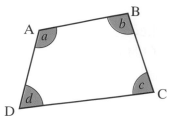

Draw the diagonal from A to C, splitting the quadrilateral into two triangles:

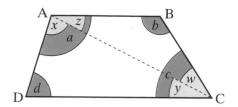

$$x + z = a$$
$$y + w = c$$

Now, $x + y + d = 180°$ (angles in a triangle)
    $z + w + b = 180°$ (angles in a triangle)

Adding these two equations gives:

$$\underbrace{x + z}_{a} + \underbrace{y + w}_{c} + d + b = 360°$$

so $a + b + c + d = 360°$

Example 4

Calculate the angle marked

(a) x (b) y

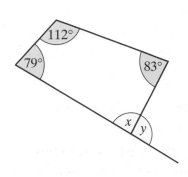

(a) $79° + 112° + 83° + x = 360°$
                $274° + x = 360°$
                        $x = 360° - 274° = 86°$

(b) $x + y = 180°$
      $86° + y = 180°$
           $y = 180° - 86°$
           $y = 94°$

Exercise 6F

1   Calculate each of the unknown angles.

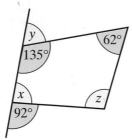

2   Work out each of the unknown angles.

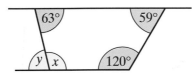

3   Showing all your working and stating all of your reasons, work out the size of the angle CDE.

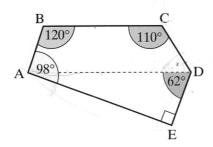

6.7 Angles in any polygon

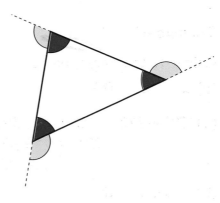

The triangle shown has its interior angles marked in red and its exterior angles marked in blue.

At each vertex the sum of the interior and exterior angles is 180° (angles on a straight line)

The triangle has 3 vertices, so the sum of its interior and exterior angles is

$$3 \times 180° = 540°$$

This result can be extended to polygons with any number of sides:

■   **The sum of the interior and exterior angles of a polygon with *n* sides is *n* × 180°.**

The interior angles of a polygon

So far you know the following results for the sum of the interior angles of a triangle and a quadrilateral:

Polygon	Number of sides	Sum of the interior angles in degrees	Sum of the interior angles in right angles
Triangle	3	180	2
Quadrilateral	4	360	4

Look at this pentagon.

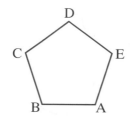

It can be split into three triangles

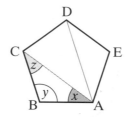

The sum of the angles in each triangle is 180°

i.e. $x + y + z = 180°$

and there are 3 such triangles making up the pentagon.

So the sum of the interior angles of the pentagon ABCDE is

   $3 \times 180° = 540°$

Similarly, this hexagon can be split into 4 triangles.

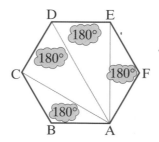

The sum of the interior angles of a hexagon is

   $4 \times 180° = 720°$

You can extend the previous table and make a prediction for a 7-sided figure:

Polygon	Number of sides	Sum of the interior angles in degrees	Sum of the interior angles in right-angles
Triangle	3	$180 = 1 \times 180$	$2 = 2 \times (3 - 2)$
Quadrilateral	4	$360 = 2 \times 180$	$4 = 2 \times (4 - 2)$
Pentagon	5	$540 = 3 \times 180$	$6 = 2 \times (5 - 2)$
Hexagon	6	$720 = 4 \times 180$	$8 = 2 \times (6 - 2)$
Heptagon	7	$900 = 5 \times 180$	$10 = 2 \times (7 - 2)$

and this should be enough to convince you of the **general** result:

n-sided polygon	n	$(n - 2) \times 180$	$2n - 4 = 2(n - 2)$

So for any polygon with n sides, the sum of the interior angles is

$$(n - 2) \times 180°$$

This is because a polygon with n sides can be divided into $n - 2$ triangles.

For example, the 8-sided octagon can be divided into $6 = (8 - 2)$ triangles:

The sum of the angles in each triangle is $180°$

So the sum of the interior angles of the polygon will be $(n - 2) \times 180°$

■   **The sum of the interior angles of a polygon with n sides is**

$$(n - 2) \times 180°$$

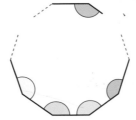

The exterior angles of a polygon

For an *n*-sided polygon:

the sum of the interior and exterior angles $= n \times 180°$

the sum of the interior angles $= (n - 2) \times 180°$

so   the sum of the exterior angles $= n \times 180° - (n - 2) \times 180°$

$$= 2 \times 180°$$
$$= 360°$$

■   **The sum of the exterior angles of any polygon is always 360°.**

Example 5

ABCDE is a regular pentagon.
Calculate the size of

(a) the interior angle *x*
(b) the angle *y*

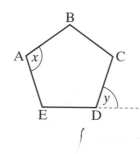

(a) the sum of the interior angles is
$(n - 2) \times 180° = (5 - 2) \times 180°$
$$= 3 \times 180° = 540°$$

There are 5 interior angles. Because the pentagon is regular, these are all equal. So the size of each of the 5 interior angles is *x*.

So $5x = 540°$

$$x = \frac{540°}{5}$$

$$x = 108°$$

(b) $108° + y = 180°$ (angles on a straight line)

so $y = 180° - 108°$

$$y = 72°$$

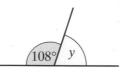

Example 6

The diagram shows part of a regular polygon with *n* sides.

An interior angle of the polygon is 160°.

Work out the number of sides of this polygon.

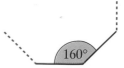

Let the polygon have n sides. So there are n exterior angles.

Because the polygon is regular, each exterior angle is

$$180° - 160° = 20°$$

so $\qquad n \times 20° = 360°$

therefore $\qquad n = \dfrac{360}{20} = 18$

So the polygon has 18 sides.

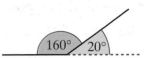

Exercise 6G

1   For a regular octagon, calculate the size of
    (a) each interior angle   **(b)** each exterior angle.

2   Calculate the sum of the interior angles in a polygon
    with
    (a) 10 sides   **(b)** 12 sides   **(c)** 20 sides.

3   ABCDE is a regular pentagon.
    Work out the size of
    (a) the angle x
    (b) the angle y
    (c) the angle z.

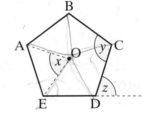

4   Work out the number of sides of a regular polygon that
    has an exterior angle of
    (a) 30°   **(b)** 18°   **(c)** 40°   **(d)** 36°   **(e)** 12°

5   ABCDE is a regular pentagon.
    When BA and DE extended they meet at M.

    Calculate the size of the angle AME.

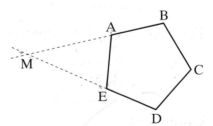

6   ABCDEFGH is a regular octagon.
    (a) Work out the size of the angle HAG.
    (b) Work out the size of the angle BGA.

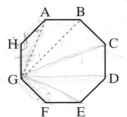

7 The diagram shows part of a regular 10-sided polygon.
AB extended and DC extended meet at P.
Work out the size of the angle BPC.

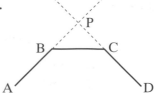

6.8 Three-figure bearings

You have probably used compass bearings to
describe directions. For example this church is
to the North-East.

You can describe directions more accurately
using **three-figure bearings**.

A three-figure bearing describes a direction as
an angle, measured clockwise from North:

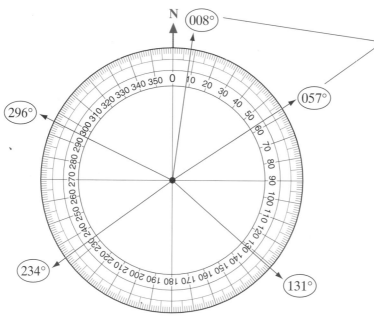

If the angle is less
than 100°, you must
put zeroes in front
of the angle so that
the bearing has
three figures.

You say 'the bearing
of A from O is
140°'.

■ **A three-figure bearing is the angle measured
clockwise from North.**

Example 7

Write these directions as three figure bearings:

(a) North-East
(b) South-West

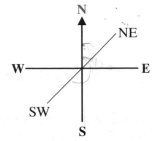

(a) The angle measured clockwise from North to North-East is 45°. The three-figure bearing is 045°.
(b) The angle measured clockwise from North to South-West is 225° (180° + 45°). The bearing is 225°.

Example 8

Draw an accurate diagram to show a bearing of 137°.

Draw the obtuse angle using your protractor as shown here.

You can use a semi-circular protractor to measure bearings up to 180°. For bearings greater than 180° you will either have to add 180° to the angle you measure or subtract it from 360°.

137°

Example 9

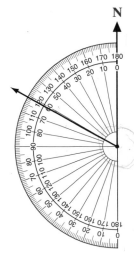

Express the direction shown in the diagram as a three-figure bearing.

Method 1
Measure the angle clockwise from South (119°) and add 180° to it.

$$\text{Bearing} = 119° + 180°$$
$$= 299°$$

Method 2
Measure the angle anticlockwise from North (61°) and subtract it from 360°.

$$\text{Bearing} = 360° - 61°$$
$$= 299°$$

You need to be able to calculate bearings using angle facts.

Example 10

Work out the three-figure bearing of B from A.

Angles on a straight line add to 180°.

    Bearing = 180° − 39°
            = 141°

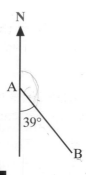

Exercise 6H

1 Write these compass directions as three-figure bearings.
   (a) West   **(b)** South-East   **(c)** North-West

2 Use a protractor to express the directions on the
   diagram as three-figure bearings.

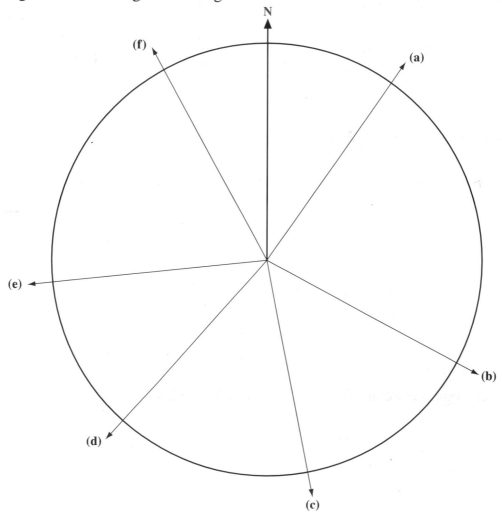

3 Using a protractor, draw a diagram similar to the one above to show these bearings.

(a) 042° **(b)** 163° **(c)** 209° **(d)** 342°

4 Use angle facts to work out the three-figure bearing of B from A for each of the directions below.

(a) 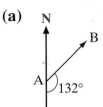 **(b)** 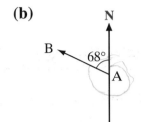 **(c)**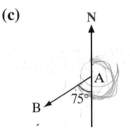

5 An oil tanker is at a bearing of 030° from a yacht. Work out the bearing of the yacht from the tanker.

There is more on bearings in chapter 17.

6 The bearing of point A from point B is 237°. Work out the bearing of point B from point A.

Summary of key points

1 An angle between 0° and 90° is called acute.

2 An angle between 90° and 180° is called obtuse.

3 An angle between 180° and 360° is called reflex.

4 The sum of the angles at a point is 360°

$$w + x + y + z = 360°$$

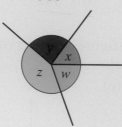

5 The sum of the angles on a straight line is 180°

$$x + y + z = 180°$$

6 When two lines cross they form two pairs of angles opposite each other which are the same size.

$$a = b, c = d$$

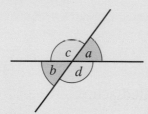

7 Alternate angles are equal: $b = e, d = g$

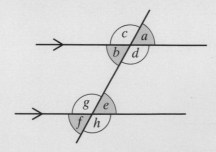

8 Corresponding angles are equal:
$$a = e, d = h, b = f, c = g$$

9 The sum of supplementary angles is 180°:
$$b + g = 180°, d + e = 180°$$

10 For any triangle, the sum of the three interior angles is 180°.

$$x + y + z = 180°$$

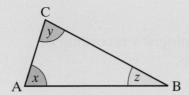

11 The sum of the interior angles of a quadrilateral is 360°:

$$a + b + c + d = 360°$$

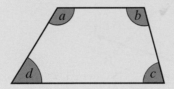

12 The sum of the interior and exterior angles of an n-sided polygon is $n \times 180°$.

13 The sum of the interior angles of an n-sided polygon is $(n - 2) \times 180°$.

14 The sum of the exterior angles of any polygon is always 360°.

15 A three-figure bearing is the angle measured clockwise from North.

7 Graphs

7.1 Straight line graphs

The coordinate grid shows an archaeologist's recording of lines drawn on the entrance to a tomb.

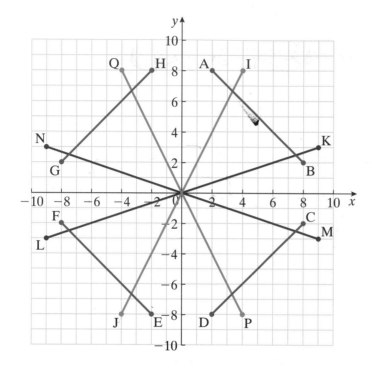

To make the recording easier the archaeologist has labelled the end points of each line.

Example 1

Find the equations of these lines:

(a) AB   **(b)** JI

(a) You need to find a relationship between the x-coordinate and y-coordinate of the points on the line. Choose some points:

$$(2, 8) \qquad (4, 6) \qquad (5, 5) \qquad (8, 2)$$
$$2 + 8 = 10 \qquad 4 + 6 = 10 \qquad 5 + 5 = 10 \qquad 8 + 2 = 10$$

The relationship is *x-coordinate + y-coordinate* = 10
The equation of the line is $x + y = 10$

(b) Choose some points on the line:

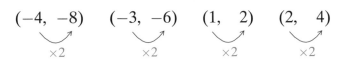

$(-4, -8)$ $\quad$ $(-3, -6)$ $\quad$ $(1, \quad 2)$ $\quad$ $(2, \quad 4)$

$\times 2$ $\qquad\qquad$ $\times 2$ $\qquad\qquad$ $\times 2$ $\qquad\qquad$ $\times 2$

The relationship is *y-coordinate* $= 2 \times$ *x-coordinate*
The equation of the line is $y = 2x$

Exercise 7A

1 Find the equations of the remaining lines on the grid on page 144.

2 Find the equations of the lines on this grid:

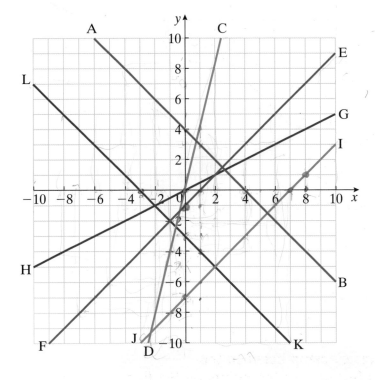

7.2 Drawing straight lines

You can draw straight line graphs by plotting three points on the line.

Example 2

Draw these straight lines:

(a) $y = \frac{1}{2}x$ **(b)** $y = 3x - 2$

(a) Choose three values for x:

x	$y = \frac{1}{2}x$
0	0
−2	−1
6	3

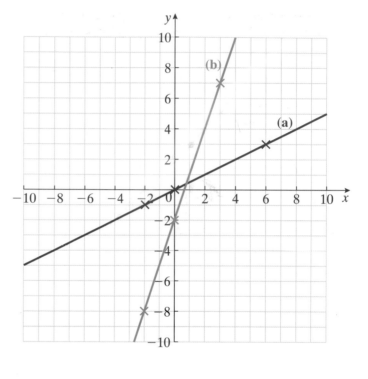

Plot the points and draw a straight line through them.

(b) Choose three values for x:

x	$y = 3x - 2$
0	−2
−2	−8
3	7

Plot the points and draw a straight line through them.

Exercise 7B

1   Draw a coordinate grid from −10 to 10 on each axis. For each equation write down three points on the line and draw the line on your grid.

   (a) $y = x + 2$ **(b)** $y = 3x - 1$ **(c)** $y = -x + 4$
   (d) $y = \frac{1}{3}x$ **(e)** $y = \frac{1}{2}x - 5$ **(f)** $y = 2x - 9$

2 Draw these lines on a coordinate grid.

(a) $y = \frac{1}{2}x + 4$ (b) $y = 3x - 6$ (c) $y = x + 1$

(d) $y = -3x - 2$ (e) $y = -\frac{1}{3}x + 2$ (f) $y = 4x + \frac{1}{2}$

7.3 $y = mx + c$

The equations of the straight lines in section 7.2 all have the same form.

■ **The general form for the equation of a straight line is $y = mx + c$, where m and c are numbers.**

m **is called the gradient.**

The intercept is the point $(0, c)$ where the line crosses the y-axis.

$$y = \frac{1}{2}x + 3 \qquad m = \frac{1}{2}, c = 3$$
$$y = -x - 2 \qquad m = -1, c = -2$$

Example 3

Write down the gradient and intercept of these lines:

(a) $y = 2x + 3$

(b) $y = \frac{x}{4} - 1$

(a) gradient $= 2$
    intercept $= (0, 3)$

(b) Rearrange into the form $y = mx + c$:

$$y = \frac{x}{4} - 1 = \frac{1}{4}x - 1$$

gradient $= \frac{1}{4}$
intercept $= (0, -1)$

Example 4

Find the intercept of these lines.

(a) The line crosses the y-axis at the point $(0, 3)$. The intercept is $(0, 3)$.

(b) The intercept is $(0, -2)$

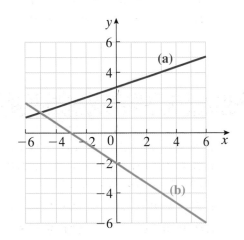

Exercise 7C

1   Write down the gradient and intercept of these lines:

(a) $y = 12x + 9$

(b) $y = -2x - 6$

(c) $y = \dfrac{x}{5} - \dfrac{1}{2}$

(d) $y = \dfrac{2x}{3} + 4$

(e) $y = -5$

(f) $y = -4x$

(g) $y = -\dfrac{x}{4} + 1$

(h) $y = -\dfrac{3x}{2} - 1$

(i) $y = 4 - 2x$

(j) $y = 6 - \dfrac{x}{3}$

(k) $y = -\dfrac{1}{2}x + \dfrac{1}{2}$

(l) $y = -\dfrac{1}{4} - \dfrac{3x}{7}$

2   Find the intercept of these lines:

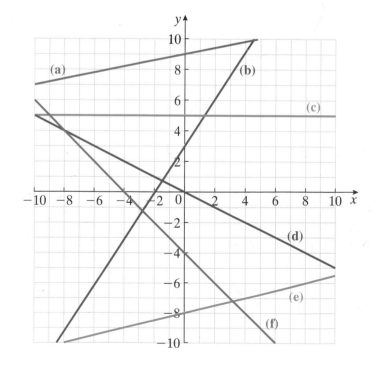

3 These lines are all of the form $y = \frac{1}{2}x + c$ where c is some number.
Write down the equation of each line.

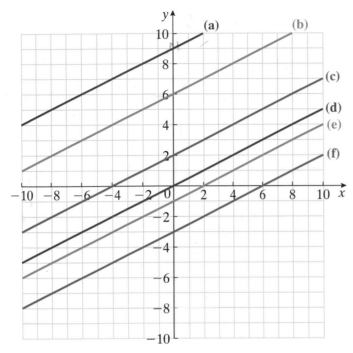

4 Without writing a table of values, draw these lines on a coordinate grid.

(a) $y = x$ **(b)** $y = x - 6$

(c) $y = x + \frac{1}{2}$ **(d)** $y = x + 4$

7.4 Calculating the gradient

Gradient measures the steepness of a line.
The steeper the line, the greater the gradient.

■ **The gradient of a line, m, is a measure of steepness. If a point on the line moves a distance 1 in the x-direction it will move a distance m in the y-direction.**

Positive gradient

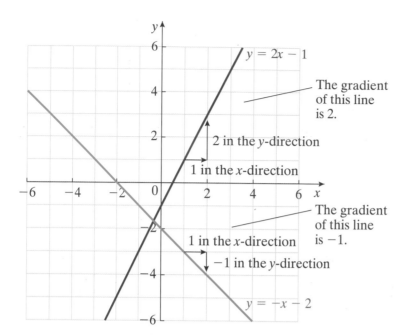

Negative gradient

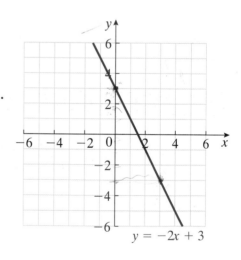

Example 5

Without writing a table of values draw the graph of $y = -2x + 3$.

The intercept is (0, 3). The gradient is -2.

The graph is a straight line through the point (0, 3). If a point on the line moves a distance of 1 in the x-direction, it will move a distance of -2 in the y-direction.

$y = -2x + 3$

You need to be able to calculate the gradient from the graph.

■ **To find the gradient of a straight line, choose any two points on the line:**

$$\text{gradient} = \frac{\text{change in } y\text{-direction}}{\text{change in } x\text{-direction}}$$

Example 6

For each line:

- find the gradient
- write down the equation of the line.

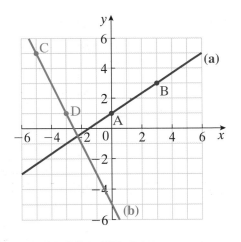

(a) Take two points, A and B, on the line.

$$\text{gradient} = \frac{\text{change in } y\text{-direction}}{\text{change in } x\text{-direction}} = \frac{2}{3}$$

The intercept is $(0, 1)$.

The equation of the line is $y = \frac{2}{3}x + 1$

(b) Take two points, C and D, on the line.

$$\text{gradient} = \frac{\text{change in } y\text{-direction}}{\text{change in } x\text{-direction}}$$

$$= \frac{2}{-4} = -\frac{1}{2}$$

The intercept is $(0, -5)$.

The equation of the line is $y = -\frac{1}{2}x - 5$

Point D is below point C so the change in the y-direction is negative.

positive y-direction

positive x-direction

Exercise 7D

1 Without writing a table of values, draw and label these lines on a coordinate grid.

(a) $y = 2x + 2$ (b) $y = -x + 3$

(c) $y = 4x - 6$ (d) $y = -3x + 1$

(e) $y = 2x - 5$ (f) $y = 8x - 1$

2 For the points A and B on this line write down:

(a) The change in the y-direction.
(b) The change in the x-direction.

Write down:

(c) The gradient of the line.
(d) The intercept.
(e) The equation of the line.

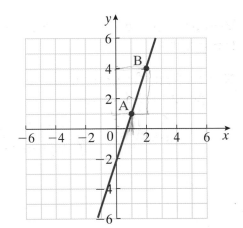

3 For each line on this grid:
  (i) Find the gradient.
  (ii) Write down the equation of the line.

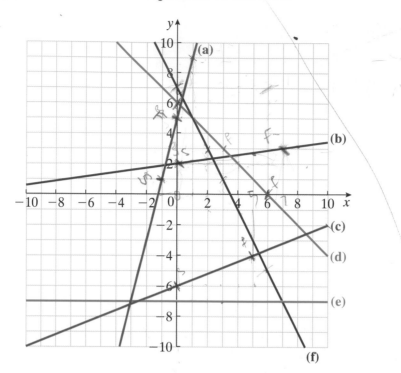

4 This graph shows a section of a straight line.

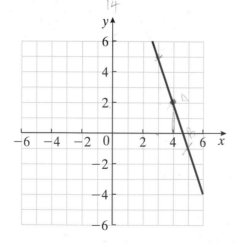

(a) Find the gradient of the line.
(b) Write down a point on the line.
(c) Substitute the values of x and y at that point into the equation $y = mx + c$ to find the value of c.
(d) Write down the intercept and the equation of the line.

5 Find the equations of these lines.

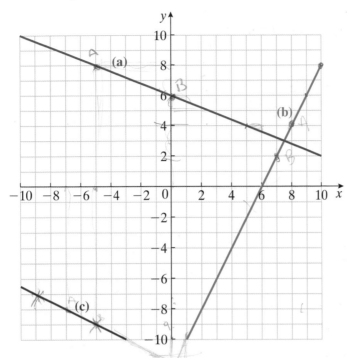

6 William is a car salesman. Each month he earns £400 plus a percentage of the total sales. His income for January–April is shown in the table:

Month	January	February	March	April
Total sales (*S*)	£10 000	£20 000	£1000	£8000
Income (*T*)	£600	£800	£420	£560

Aisha is William's manager. She wants to use a formula to calculate his salary each month.

(a) Draw a graph of income (*y*-axis) against total sales (*x*-axis).

Aisha thinks that the graph can be described by the equation $T = mS + c$.

(b) Find the equation of the graph.

(c) What percentage of total sales does William earn each month?

(d) Use your answer to **(b)** to work out how much William could earn in May if he sells £150 000 worth of cars.

(e) How many cars worth £21 000 each would William have to sell to earn £2500?

Hint:
Choose your scales carefully.

Hint:
Remember the scales on each axis.

7.5 Information graphs

The graph shows a car journey.

The graph is made up of six straight lines.

Each line describes part of the journey.

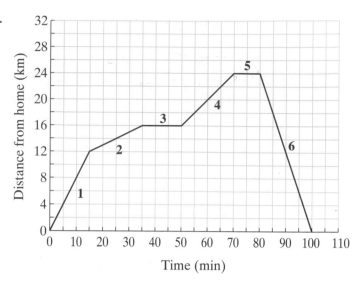

The vertical ↑ axis gives information on distance from home.
Each square represents 2 km.

The horizontal → axis gives information on time.
Each square represents 5 minutes.

Section **1** 12 km travelled in 15 minutes.
The line is straight so the speed is constant.

Section **2** 4 km travelled in 20 minutes.

Section **3** The line is horizontal. 0 km travelled in 15 minutes.
The car has stopped.

Section **4** 8 km travelled in 20 minutes.

Section **5** The car is stationary – destination reached.

Section **6** The car returns home and travels 24 km in 20 minutes.
The line slopes downwards (negative gradient) as the distance from home decreases.

You need to be able to interpret graphs.

Example 7

Look at the graph of the car journey above.
Use it to answer these questions:

(a) How long did the total journey take?

(b) When was the car travelling fastest on the outward journey?
What was this speed?

(c) What was the average speed for:
- the outward journey
- the homeward journey?

(a) The journey took 100 minutes in total.

(b) Steepest gradient gives greatest speed.
For the outward journey this is in Section **1**.
12 km in 15 minutes

$$= \tfrac{12}{15} \text{ km per minute} \quad \text{or} \quad \tfrac{12}{15} \times 60 \text{ km/h}$$

$$= 48 \text{ km/h}$$

(c) average speed = total distance ÷ total time

- Outward journey
$$24 \div 70 = \tfrac{24}{70} \text{ km per minute} \quad \text{or} \quad \tfrac{24}{70} \times 60 \text{ km/h} = 20.57 \text{ km/h}$$

- Homeward journey
$$24 \div 20 = \tfrac{24}{20} \text{ km/min} \quad \text{or} \quad \tfrac{24}{20} \times 60 \text{ km/h} = 72 \text{ km/h}$$

Exercise 7E

1 The graph shows an aeroplane's flight.

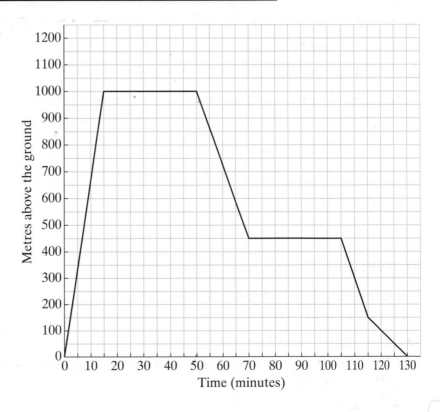

Use the graph on page 155 to answer these questions.

(a) What does 1 small square represent:
  - horizontally
  - vertically?

(b) For how long was the aeroplane climbing?

(c) What was the aeroplane's speed whilst climbing?

(d) How long was the plane in level flight?

Remember to give appropriate units in your answers.

(e) How long did the whole flight take?

(f) What was the aeroplane's average speed on its descent to the ground?

2 The graph shows Bert's bath time.

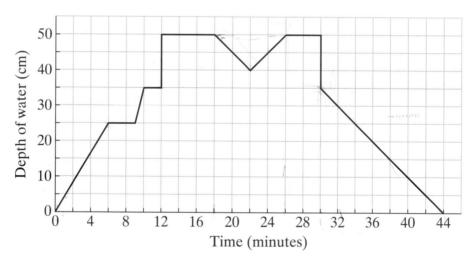

Use the graph to answer these questions.

(a) How deep was the bath when Bert got in?
    How can you tell when this was?

(b) How long did Bert stay in the bath?

(c) How long did the bath take to empty?

(d) What was the speed of emptying?

(e) Describe what might have happened between the 18th and 26th minutes.

3 The graph shows Sally's journey to the local shops.

Use the graph to answer these questions.

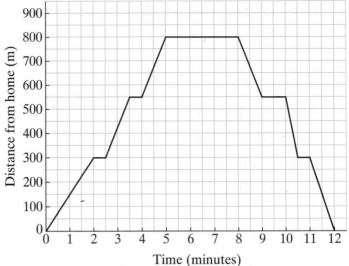

(a) How many roads do you think Sally crossed on the way to the shops? Explain your answer.

(b) How far are the shops from Sally's home?

(c) What was her average speed on the way to the shops?

(d) Between which times was she travelling most quickly?

(e) How long did she spend in the shops?

(f) Did she travel more quickly on her outward or homeward journey? Justify your answer.

4 The graph shows the flight of a space shuttle.

Use it to answer these questions.

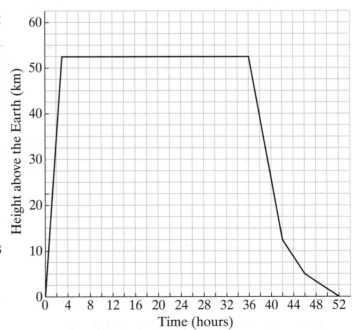

(a) How high above the Earth was the orbit height?

(b) For how long was the space shuttle in orbit?

(c) What was its speed of ascent?

(d) The return journey was in 3 stages.
What was the average speed for the whole descent?

(e) How fast did the shuttle travel, in km/h, on each part of the descent?

(f) Give these speeds in metres per second.

5   The graph shows Sam the Slug's journey from the garden shed to the rockery.

    Use the graph to answer these questions.

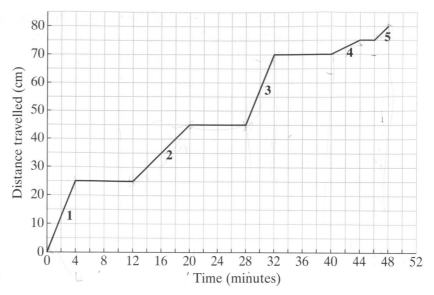

(a) How far is it from the shed to the rockery?

(b) How long did Sam rest for, in total?

(c) Work out Sam's speed for each stage of the journey.

(d) What was Sam's average speed for the whole journey in km/h?

7.6 Sketching and interpreting information graphs

In section 7.5 you saw how to interpret distance–time graphs. You need to be able to draw graphs to represent real-life situations.

Example 8

A square-based pyramid is steadily filled with sand.

Sketch a graph of the height of the sand above the base of the pyramid (y) against time (t).

For questions like this, where you are not given any numerical data, you need to *sketch* the shape of the graph.

It will take much longer for the level of the sand to rise at the beginning than towards the end. This is because the cross-sectional area of the pyramid decreases as the height increases.

So the graph of height against time will look like this:

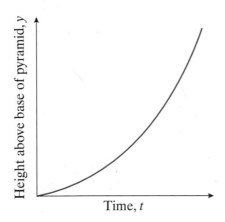

Exercise 7F

1   A cylindrical measuring beaker is steadily filled with water.

Sketch a graph of the height of the water against time.

2   These graphs show different relationships but descriptions of the variables x and y have been left off.

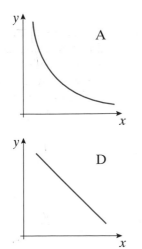

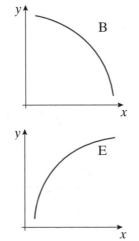

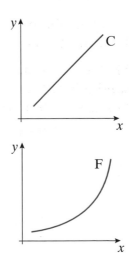

Which of the graphs on page 159 could represent the relationship between:

(a) the speed of an apple falling from a tree (y) and the time it has been falling (x),

(b) the height above water of a diver (y) and the time since she jumped off the diving board (x),

(c) the hotel bill (y) and the number of nights stayed (x),

(d) the number of builders (x) and the time they take to build a house (y),

(e) the number of kilometres walked at 50 pence per km (x) and the sponsor money earned (y),

(f) the circumference (y) and radius (x) of a circle,

(g) the volume (y) and radius (x) of a sphere,

(h) the heat of water in a pan (y) and the time it has been on a fire (x),

(i) the speed of a diver descending in water (y) and the time since he hit the surface (x).

3 A racing driver tests a new car.

A computer draws a graph of the results from sensors on the car.

(a) Describe the journey of the racing driver.

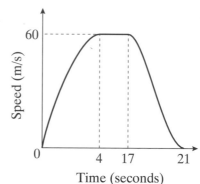

(b) The previous year the same racing driver tested an older model of the car.

The car accelerated from 0 to 60 m/s in 6 seconds, he drove the car for 12 seconds at 60 m/s and then braked. The car came to a stop after a further 8 seconds.

Draw a graph of the racing driver's journey.

E **7.7   Inverses of linear functions**

An expression like $y = 3x + 6$ is sometimes called a **function**. It takes a certain value of x and maps it onto a value of y.

There is more about functions and mappings in chapter 16.

You know how to find the inverse of a function using number machines.

Build up the function starting with x:

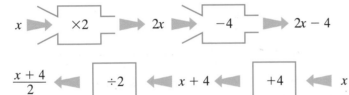

$$x \implies \boxed{\times 3} \implies 3x \implies \boxed{+6} \implies 3x + 6$$

The reverse number machines give the inverse function.

$$\frac{x-6}{3} \impliedby \boxed{\div 3} \impliedby x - 6 \impliedby \boxed{-6} \impliedby x$$

The inverse of $y = 3x + 6$ is $y = \dfrac{(x-6)}{3}$ or $y = \frac{1}{3}x - 2$

Example 9

(a) Find the inverse of the function $y = 2x - 4$

(b) Plot the graphs of the function and its inverse and find the point of intersection.

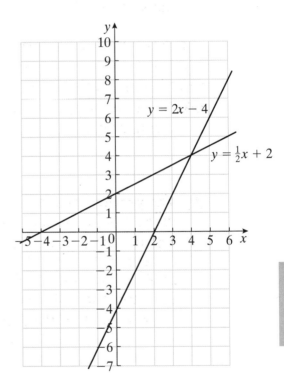

(a)

$$x \implies \boxed{\times 2} \implies 2x \implies \boxed{-4} \implies 2x - 4$$

$$\frac{x+4}{2} \impliedby \boxed{\div 2} \impliedby x + 4 \impliedby \boxed{+4} \impliedby x$$

The inverse is:

$$y = \left(\frac{x+4}{2}\right) \quad \text{or} \quad y = \frac{1}{2}x + 2$$

(b) The point of intersection is $(4, 4)$.

Exercise 7G

1   Find the inverse of each function:
   (a) $y = x - 6$ (b) $y = 4x + 2$ (c) $y = \frac{1}{2}x - 3$
   (d) $y = 6x + 20$ (e) $y = -x + 4$ (f) $y = 2x - 9$
   (g) $y = -3x + 6$ (h) $y = 4 + 6x$

2 Copy these functions and match each to its inverse.
One has been done for you.

$$y = \tfrac{1}{2}x - \tfrac{1}{2} \qquad\qquad y = \tfrac{1}{3}x - 3$$

$$y = 3x + 9 \qquad\qquad y = 5x + 10$$

$$y = \tfrac{1}{2}x + 3$$

$$y = 1 + 2x$$

$$y = 2x - 6 \qquad\qquad y = \tfrac{1}{5}x - 2$$

$$y = 3x - 8 \qquad\qquad y = \tfrac{1}{3}x + \tfrac{8}{3}$$

3 For each function:
- Find the inverse.
- Plot the graph of the function and its inverse.
- Find the coordinates of the point of intersection.

(a) $y = 2x + 3$ (b) $y = x + 4$

(c) $y = 3x - 2$ (d) $y = \tfrac{1}{2}x + 4$

(e) $y = \tfrac{1}{4}x - 8$ (f) $y = -x + 7$

(g) $y = -2x + 5$ (h) $y = -3x - 6$

4 Look at your answers to question **3**. What do you
notice about the points of intersection of a function
and its inverse?

Why do you think this is?

5 Describe the transformation that takes the graph of a
function onto the graph of its inverse.

E 7.8 Parallel and perpendicular lines

You can identify parallel and perpendicular lines
from their gradients.

- **Parallel lines have the same gradient.**

  The lines $y = m_1 x + c_1$

  and $\qquad\quad y = m_2 x + c_2$

  are parallel if $m_1 = m_2$

Remember:

Parallel lines
go in the same
direction.

Perpendicular
lines meet
at right-angles.

Example 10

This graph shows the line

$$y = \tfrac{1}{2}x + 1$$

Write down the equations of two lines parallel to this line, and draw them on a copy of the graph.

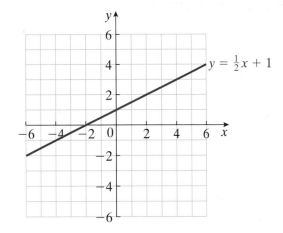

Parallel lines have the same gradient.

These lines will be parallel to the line $y = \tfrac{1}{2}x + 1$:

$$y = \tfrac{1}{2}x - 4$$

$$y = \tfrac{1}{2}x$$

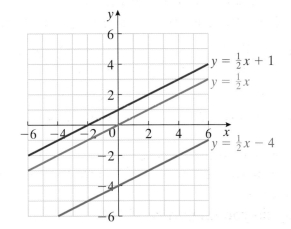

■ **If two lines are perpendicular the product of their gradients is -1.**

The lines $y = m_1 x + c_1$
and $y = m_2 x + c_2$
are perpendicular if $m_1 m_2 = -1$.

Example 11

Which pairs of lines are perpendicular?
Draw graphs to check your answers.

(a) $y = 3x - 2$
     $3y = 4 - x$

(b) $2y = 4x - 2$
     $y = \tfrac{1}{2}x + 3$

(a) Write the equations in the form $y = mx + c$.

$y = 3x - 2$

$y = -\frac{1}{3}x + 4$

$m_1 = 3, m_2 = -\frac{1}{3}$

so $m_1 m_2 = -1$

Lines are perpendicular.

(b) Write the equations in the form $y = mx + c$.

$y = 2x - 1$

$y = \frac{1}{2}x + 3$

$m_1 = 2, m_2 = \frac{1}{2}$

so $m_1 m_2 \neq -1$.

Lines are not perpendicular.

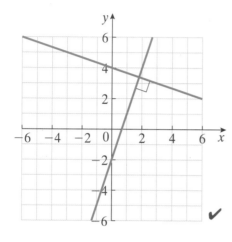

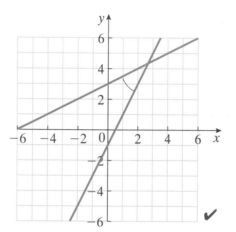

Exercise 7H

1 In each case say if the pairs of lines are parallel, perpendicular or neither.

(a) $y = 4x + 2$
$y = 7x - 4$

(b) $y = -x + 5$
$y = x + 6$

(c) $y = 7 - x$
$y = -x + 9$

(d) $y = 3x - 5$
$3y = 18 - 9x$

(e) $y = 4x - 9$
$4y = 16x + 8$

(f) $y = 8 - 6x$
$6y = x - 12$

(g) $y = 4x$
$4y = 8 - x$

(h) $y = 9x + 27$
$9y = 81x - 18$

(i) $y = 13x - 5$
$13y = x + 26$

2 For each equation write down the equations of two lines perpendicular to the one given.

(a) $y = 2x + 4$

(b) $y = 9x - 8$

(c) $y = x - 4$

(d) $6y = 12x + 24$

(e) $8y = 64x - 24$

(f) $y = 9x + 27$

(g) $y = \frac{1}{4}x - 5$

(h) $y = 8 - \frac{1}{3}x$

(i) $y = 7x + 14$

3 For each equation in question **2** write down the equations of two lines parallel to the one given.

4 Copy these lists and match each equation in the central column to one perpendicular and one parallel to it in the outer columns. One has been done for you.

$2y = x + 6$ $y = 3x + 4$ $y = 4x - 9$

$3y = 9 - x$ $y = 9 - x$ $y = 2 + 8x$

$y = 6 - \frac{1}{4}x$ $y = 4x + 7$ $3y = 9x + 12$

$y = -x + 27$ $y = \frac{1}{2}x - 3$ $2y = -6x - 1$

$8y = 72 - x$ $y = \frac{1}{3}x + 9$ $y = 18 - 2x$

$y = 36 + \frac{1}{3}x$ $y = 9 - \frac{1}{8}x$ $y = x + 4$

Hint: You can mark parallel with // and perpendicular with ⊥

5 Suko sketches a line with gradient m.

(a) Copy the diagram. Rotate triangle ABC 90° about A. Draw this new triangle on the same diagram.

(b) Extend the hypotenuse of the new triangle to form a line.

(c) Use your completed diagram to explain why the product of the gradients of perpendicular lines is −1.

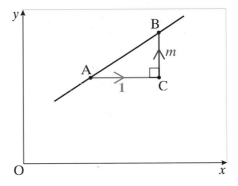

E 7.9 Quadratic graphs

Any equation that can be written in the form $y = mx + c$, where m is the gradient and c is the intercept, will give a straight line.

Equations that contain x^2 or $-x^2$ or $2x^2$ or $-5x^2$ will not give a straight line.

■ **An equation of the form:**
$$y = ax^2 + bx + c$$
where a is any number other than 0 and b and c are any numbers is called a quadratic equation.
The graph of a quadratic equation is a curve.

To draw the graph accurately you need to make a table of values.

Example 12

Draw the graph of $y = \frac{1}{2}x^2 + 3$

Choose values and draw a table:

x	-4	-3	-2	-1	0	1	2	3	4
y	11	$7\frac{1}{2}$	5	$3\frac{1}{2}$	3	$3\frac{1}{2}$	5	$7\frac{1}{2}$	11

Plot the points and join with a smooth curve.

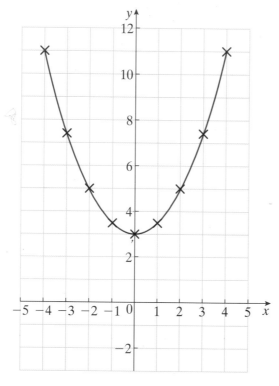

Exercise 7I

For each equation:

● Copy and complete the table of values.

● Plot the points on a coordinate grid.

● Draw and label the curve.

1 $y = x^2 - 3$

x	-4	-3	-2	-1	0	1	2	3	4
y	13								

Hint:
When drawing
curves you might
find it easier to turn
the paper and draw
a curve like this:

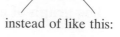

instead of like this:

2 $y = x^2 + 2$

x	−4	−3	−2	−1	0	1	2	3	4
y			6						18

3 $y = 3x^2 - 5$

x	−4	−3	−2	−1	0	1	2	3	4
y	43						7		

4 $y = x^2 + x + 4$

x	−4	−3	−2	−1	0	1	2	3	4
y		10						16	

5 $y = 4 - x^2$

x	−4	−3	−2	−1	0	1	2	3	4
y			0						−12

6 $y = 3x^2 - 2x + 1$

x	−4	−3	−2	−1	0	1	2	3	4
y		34						22	

7 $y = -x^2$

x	−4	−3	−2	−1	0	1	2	3	4
y									

8 $y = -x^2 - x - 1$

x	−4	−3	−2	−1	0	1	2	3	4
y									

E 7.10 Cubics

Equations like

$y = x^3$ $y = 3x^3$ $y = x^3 + x$ $y = x^3 - 4$

are called cubic equations.

This is because they contain a term in x^3.

This table shows some values for the equation $y = x^3$.

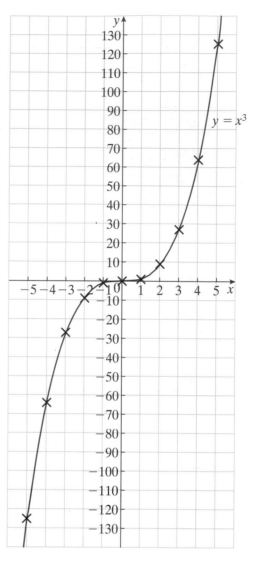

x	−5	−4	−3	−2	−1	0	1	2	3	4	5
y	−125	−64	−27	−8	−1	0	1	8	27	64	125

Remember x^3 means $x \times x \times x$
So $(-5)^3$ means $-5 \times -5 \times -5 = -125$

Notice how the value of y increases rapidly.

This means you need to scale the y-axis sensibly.

Exercise 7J

For each equation:

- Complete the table of values.
- Draw the graph.
  (Be careful to choose a suitable scale for the y-axis.)

1 $y = x^3 + 5$

x	−5	−4	−3	−2	−1	0	1	2	3	4	5
y	−120								32		130

2 $y = x^3 - 10$

x	-5	-4	-3	-2	-1	0	1	2	3	4	5
y		-74			-11					54	

3 $y = 2x^3$

x	-5	-4	-3	-2	-1	0	1	2	3	4	5
y		-128									250

4 $y = 2x^3 + 20$

x	-5	-4	-3	-2	-1	0	1	2	3	4	5
y		-108									270

5 $y = x^3 + x$

x	-5	-4	-3	-2	-1	0	1	2	3	4	5
y		-68						10			

6 $y = x^3 - 2x$

x	-5	-4	-3	-2	-1	0	1	2	3	4	5
y	-115								21		

Summary of key points

1 The general form for the equation of a straight line is $y = mx + c$, where m and c are numbers.

m is called the gradient.

The intercept is the point $(0, c)$ where the line crosses the y-axis.

2 The gradient of a line, m, is a measure of steepness. If a point on the line moves a distance 1 in the x-direction it will move a distance m in the y-direction.

3 To find the gradient of a straight line, choose any two points on the line:

$$\text{gradient of line} = \frac{\text{change in } y\text{-direction}}{\text{change in } x\text{-direction}}$$

E Parallel lines have the same gradient.

The lines $y = m_1x + c_1$

and $y = m_2x + c_2$

are parallel if $m_1 = m_2$.

E If two lines are perpendicular the product of their gradients is -1.

The lines $y = m_1x + c_1$

and $y = m_2x + c_2$

are perpendicular if $m_1m_2 = -1$.

E An equation of the form.

$$y = ax^2 + bx + c$$

where a is any number other than 0 and b and c are any numbers is called a quadratic equation.

The graph of a quadratic equation is a curve.

8 Fractions, ratio and proportion

From about 500 BC, Greek mathematicians tried to explore music using mathematics.

Musical scales are based on the ratios of lengths of strings or columns of air in instruments.

8.1 Revising fractions

In this section you will revise adding, subtracting, dividing and multiplying fractions.

Exercise 8A

1   Work out
   (a) $2\frac{1}{2} - 1\frac{1}{8}$ (b) $3\frac{2}{3} + 2\frac{5}{8}$ (c) $5\frac{1}{4} - 2\frac{2}{3}$

   (d) $4\frac{3}{11} + 9\frac{7}{12}$ (e) $10\frac{5}{7} - 3\frac{4}{5}$ (f) $3\frac{4}{19} - 1\frac{3}{4}$

   Note:
   In part (c) $\frac{1}{4} - \frac{2}{3}$ is negative.

2   Dave, Astrid and Nasrin cycled to meet each other after school. Dave cycled $\frac{5}{8}$ km, Astrid cycled $2\frac{1}{2}$ km and Nasrin cycled $1\frac{3}{4}$ km.

   What is the total distance cycled by the three friends?

3   In 1971 a survey of 54 pupils at a primary school in Sedgeburn revealed that $\frac{2}{3}$ of the pupils owned space hoppers. Of those pupils $\frac{1}{4}$ only ever used them to bounce to the shops, $\frac{1}{3}$ only ever used them to bounce to see their friends and $\frac{2}{9}$ only ever bounced them when their relatives visited. The rest had used them only once. How many pupils had used them only once?

4   Work out:
   (a) $\frac{1}{2} \times \frac{1}{3}$ **(b)** $1\frac{5}{6} \times \frac{2}{5}$ **(c)** $2\frac{3}{8} \times 1\frac{4}{21}$

   (d) $\frac{2}{5} \div \frac{3}{7}$ **(e)** $\frac{1}{2} \div 2\frac{1}{3}$ **(f)** $\frac{9}{5} \div 4\frac{16}{25}$

Remember:
To divide fractions, turn the dividing fraction into its reciprocal and multiply.

5   Selina delivers newspapers and notices that $\frac{3}{5}$ of the houses in her street have satellite dishes. Of these houses, $\frac{3}{4}$ receive newspapers. What fraction of houses in Selina's street have satellite dishes and receive newspapers?

6   Seventh Heaven chocolate bars are divided into seven chunks. One chunk in each bar is $\frac{2}{9}$ nut and $\frac{1}{12}$ raisin. The other chunks do not contain fruit.

Find the fraction of the chocolate bar that is fruit.

7   Bill goes fishing in the North Sea. He needs to catch cod for his fish restaurant, 'The Greasy Behemoth'. The fraction of fish he catches that are cod is $\frac{3}{17}$. Of these he throws $\frac{7}{11}$ back into the sea because they are too small. $\frac{3}{4}$ of the cod he keeps are medium-sized, the rest are large.

How many times does the fraction of large cod Bill lands divide into the total fraction of fish he catches which are cod?

8.2 Fractions and ratio puzzles

You can use fractions to answer questions involving number and shapes, where one quantity is expressed as a proportion of another.

1 Work out the fraction of the shape that is shaded.

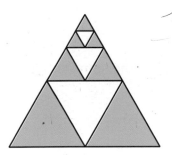

Remember:
To compare fractions you must first write them as equivalent fractions with the same denominator.

2 Calculate:

(a) $\frac{3}{8}\left(1 - \frac{7}{21}\right)$

(b) $\left(2 - \frac{1}{3}\right)\left(3 - \frac{1}{4}\right)$

3 Write $\frac{2}{9}$, 0.24 and $\frac{7}{45}$ in ascending order of size.

4 Jo writes down five numbers:

$$\frac{1}{5}, a, \frac{2}{9}, b, \frac{5}{13}$$

She is told that a is the mean of $\frac{1}{5}$ and $\frac{2}{9}$ and that $b = 2a$. Find a and b.
Has she written the numbers in ascending order of size?
If not, rearrange the numbers from smallest to largest.

5 Write these ratios in their simplest form:

(a) $5:15$ (b) $30:18$ (c) $14:49$

(d) $3:6:12$ (e) $56:24:16$ (f) $18:12:30$

6 Write these ratios in their simplest form.

(a) 350 grams to 7 kg

(b) 2 hours to 180 minutes

(c) £4.50 to 75p

(d) 1 litre of milk to $\frac{1}{2}$ litre of milk

(e) 8 years to 4 years 8 months

Make the units the same before you write each ratio.

7 Paul and Ivalor are making chocolate mousse.
Paul uses 4 ounces of cream to 6 ounces of chocolate.
Ivalor uses 6 ounces of cream to 9 ounces of chocolate.

Which of the following statements are true?

(a) The ratio of cream to chocolate is the same in both Paul and Ivalor's recipes.

(b) The ratio of cream to chocolate in Paul's mousse is $3:2$

(c) $\frac{6}{15}$ of Ivalor's mixture is cream.

(d) $\frac{2}{3}$ of Paul's mixture is cream.

(e) $\frac{3}{5}$ of Ivalor's mixture is chocolate.

(f) The ratio of chocolate to cream is the same in both recipes.

8.3 Proportion

In a football team there are eleven players including one goalkeeper. The ratio of goalkeeper to the other players is $1:10$.

In two football teams there are 22 players including two goalkeepers. The ratio of goalkeepers to the other players is $2:20$.

$1:10$ and $2:20$ are equivalent ratios.

The ratio of goalkeepers to the other players will be the same for any number of football teams.

You say that the number of goalkeepers and the number of players are in **direct proportion**.

■ **Two or more quantities are in direct proportion if their ratio stays the same as the quantities increase or decrease.**

You sometimes say the quantities are **directly proportional** to each other.

Example 1

Petrol consumption and distance travelled are in direct proportion. Karla can drive 40 miles on 3 litres of petrol. How many litres of petrol will she need to drive 120 miles?

The ratio of miles to petrol is 40 : 3. The quantities are in direct proportion so the ratio for the longer journey will be equivalent:

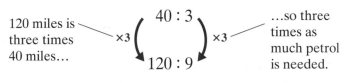

120 miles is three times 40 miles... ×3 $\left(\begin{array}{c} 40 : 3 \\ 120 : 9 \end{array} \right)$ ×3 ...so three times as much petrol is needed.

Karla needs 9 litres of petrol.

Exercise 8C

1 Say whether you think each of these quantities will be in direct proportion or not.
   (a) Number of identical chocolate bars bought and cost.
   (b) Number of pupils in a class and their average height.
   (c) Area of a single tile and area of this whole patio.
   (d) Perimeter of a square and length of one side.

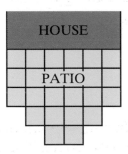

2 Derek's aquarium contains 3 frogs, 2 eels, 4 goldfish and 5 snails.
   (a) Write down the ratio of snails to goldfish to frogs to eels.

   He decides to increase the number of snails to 10. He wants to keep the numbers in the aquarium in direct proportion.
   (b) How many more frogs does he need?
   (c) How many more goldfish does he need?
   (d) How many more eels does he need?

3 Colette makes a fruit punch. The ratio of orange juice to lemonade to grapefruit juice is $4:7:3$.
She keeps the quantities in direct proportion. How much lemonade does she need if she uses:

(a) 400 ml of orange juice

(b) 6 litres of grapefruit juice

(c) 120 ml of grapefruit juice?

4 A carpenter makes cabinets. The ratio of height to width to depth is $5:4:3$.

The carpenter keeps height, width and depth in direct proportion.

(a) How wide should a 105 cm tall cabinet be?

(b) Find the depth of a cabinet that is 88 cm wide.

(c) Find the width and depth of a cabinet that is 3 m tall.

5 Katherine and Ruth have rocking horses. The saddle height and the girls' heights are in direct proportion. Katherine is 60 cm tall and her horse's saddle is 48 cm high.

(a) Write down the ratio of Katherine's height to the height of her saddle.

(b) If Ruth is 75 cm tall, how high is her saddle?

8.4 Calculating with ratios

You will need to be able to solve more difficult ratio problems.

■ **You can solve ratio and proportion problems by reducing one side of the ratio to one.**

Example 2

Faith paints 48 m of fencing in 6 days. How much fencing did she paint in 4 days?

The ratio of number of days to length of fencing painted is:

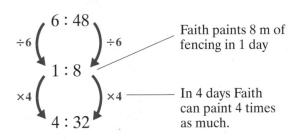

Faith paints 8 m of fencing in 1 day

In 4 days Faith can paint 4 times as much.

Faith painted 32 m of fencing in 4 days.

Example 3

A pancake recipe uses 120 grams of flour and 300 ml of milk for every 2 eggs. How much flour and milk are needed if you make pancakes with 7 eggs?

The ratio of the quantities is

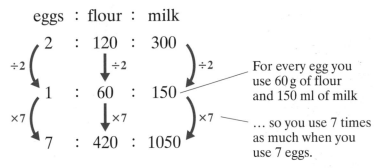

For every egg you use 60 g of flour and 150 ml of milk

… so you use 7 times as much when you use 7 eggs.

You need 420 g of flour and 1050 ml, or 1.05 l of milk.

Exercise 8D

1   Peter walks 10 miles in 3 hours. How long would it take him to walk
    (a) 1 mile   (b) 12 miles?

Hint: Write the time in minutes.

2   Aiden buys 3 CDs for £36. How much would it cost to buy
    (a) 1 CD   (b) 5 CDs?

3 A grasshopper can leap 169 times in 13 minutes.
How many times can it leap in 11 minutes?

4 Pen wants her garden to contain flowers, vegetables and grass in the ratio:

flowers : vegetables : grass
7 : 14 : 28

Her first plan for the garden includes 5 square metres of flowers. What area does she need for:

(a) vegetables   **(b)** grass?

She designs a new plan that uses 12 square metres of flowers. What area does she now need for:

(c) vegetables   **(d)** grass?

5 Three elephants, Rica, Amal and Sanjit get fed peanuts at a wildlife park. The number of peanuts they each get is directly proportional to their weight.

Rica weighs 400 kg, Amal weighs 1600 kg and Sanjit weighs 800 kg.

(a) Write down the ratio of the elephants' weights.

Rica gets 70 peanuts.

(b) How many peanuts does Amal get?

(c) How many peanuts do they get in total?

8.5 Using ratios as scales

Architects often use scale drawings when they are designing houses.

■ **A scale is a ratio used to show the relationship between the length on a diagram or model and the actual length it represents.**

For example, 1 : 100 means 1 cm on the diagram represents 100 cm or 1 m in real life.

Example 4

Jamal makes a model of a battleship with scale
$1:75$.

What do these lengths on the model represent
in real life:

(a) 5 cm   (b) 1.2 m?

(a) 1 cm represents 75 cm in real life.
5 cm represents $5 \times 75 = 375$ cm or 3.75 m.

(b) 1 m represents 75 m in real life.
1.2 m represents $1.2 \times 75 = 90$ m.

Exercise 8E

1   A mobile phone company uses a scale of $1:3$ for a
drawing of a phone used in an advert. The height of
the actual phone is 12 cm.
   (a) What height is the phone shown in the advert?
   (b) On the drawing, the phone is $\frac{2}{3}$ cm wide. How wide
is the actual phone?
   (c) On the drawing the phone has a $\frac{1}{2}$ cm aerial. How
big is the aerial on the actual phone?

2   This Ordnance Survey map uses a scale of
$1:50\,000$. The distance between the Youth
Hostel and the church is $4\frac{1}{2}$ km.
   (a) How many metres are there in a
kilometre?
   (b) How many centimetres are there in a
kilometre?
   (c) How many centimetres are there in
$4\frac{1}{2}$ kilometres?
   (d) What length on the map represents the
distance between the Youth Hostel and
the church?
   (e) David walks from the church to the
campsite, a distance of 14 cm on the map.
What is the actual distance?

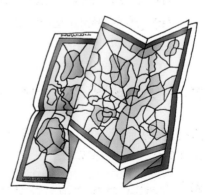

3 An architectural model of a palace uses a scale of 1:50.

   (a) How tall is the actual clock tower if the clock tower on the model is 70 cm tall?

   (b) How wide is the main gate on the model if the actual main gate is 10 m wide?

   (c) If the base of the palace measures 120 m by 70 m, what are the dimensions of the base on the model?

4 An aeroplane has a wingspan of 36 m. What scale would a model be if the wingspan on the model was:

   (a) 1 m   **(b)** 36 cm

   (c) 12 cm   **(d)** 8 m?

E 8.6 Direct proportionality

In section **8.5** you saw some examples of quantities that are in direct proportion.

Example 5

Kisha helps at home to earn his pocket money. His mother pays him £2 per hour.

(a) Draw a table of the number of hours Kisha works, x, and the amount of money he earns, y.

(b) Show that y and x are in direct proportion.

(c) Write down the value of y when $x = 0$.

(d) Write down what happens to y as x doubles. What happens to y as x trebles?

(a)

Number of hours, x	1	2	3	4	9
Amount earned in £s, y	2	4	6	8	18

(b) The ratio between y and x is constant:

   1:2 is the same as 2:4 is the same as 5:10

   so y and x are in direct proportion.

(c) If Kisha does no housework, he does not get paid anything, so when $x = 0$, $y = 0$.

(d)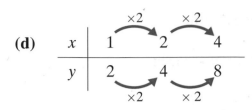

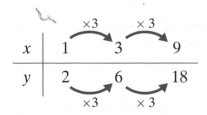

As *x* doubles, *y* doubles. As *x* trebles, *y* trebles.

■ **If two quantities, *y* and *x*, are in direct proportion then:**
  - **when $x = 0$, $y = 0$**
  - **as one quantity doubles, trebles … so does the other.**

■ **These statements have the same meaning:**
  - ***y* and *x* are in direct proportion,**
  - ***y* is directly proportional to *x*,**
  - **$y \propto x$,**
  - **$y = kx$ where k is a constant – k is called the constant of proportionality.**

> You can also say '*y* is directly proportional to *x*'. This is written as $y \propto x$.

Exercise 8F

1 Decide which of the following are examples of direct proportion. Explain your answers.

(a) The number of oranges bought and the cost of each orange.

(b) The number of kilometres walked at 90 pence per kilometre and the sponsor money gained.

(c) The length of a spring and the number of weights attached.

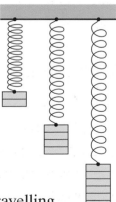

(d) The distance covered by a car travelling at a constant speed and the time it takes.

2 Lizzie is in the park at 12 noon. She notices that the length of the shadow cast by a tree is directly proportional to its height. A tree which is 4 metres high casts a shadow 5 metres long.

(a) What happens to the shadow if the tree is doubled in height?

(b) What happens to the shadow if the tree's height is halved?

(c) How high must the tree be if the shadow is 1.25 metres?

3 Use the table in **Example 5** to explain why writing $y \propto x$ is the same as writing $x \propto y$.

4 Jack's little brother, George, runs around the garden once every 120 seconds until he has completed four laps. He maintains a steady speed, despite his dizziness.

(a) Copy and complete Jack's table:

No. of times around garden, N	0	1	2	3	$3\frac{1}{2}$	4
Time taken, t	0	120				

(b) Show that N is directly proportional to t.

After completing four laps of the garden, George gets distracted by a cat.
He runs after it, barking like a dog.

(c) Jack uses his table to work out how long it would take his brother to run 150 times around the garden. What is his answer? Is this reasonable?

E 8.7 Graphs and direct proportion

The easiest way to visualise direct proportionality is to draw a graph.

Example 6

Kisha from **Example 5** draws a graph of the money he earns, y, against the number of hours he works, x.

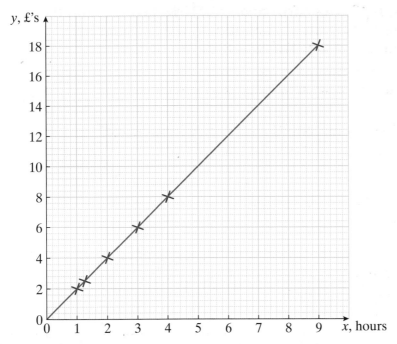

(a) Write down how much money Kisha would earn if he worked for $7\frac{1}{2}$ hours.

(b) Find the equation of the line.

(a) When $x = 7\frac{1}{2}$ hours, $y = £15$

(b) The graph is a straight line with a gradient of 2 and an intercept on the x-axis of 0.
The equation of the line is:

$$y = 2x$$

■ **If two quantities, y and x, are in direct proportion, then the graph of one against the other is a straight line through the origin.**

So $y = kx$

where k is equal to the gradient of the line.

k is called the constant of proportionality.

Exercise 8G

1   Draw a set of axes with the x-axis labelled 'height of tree, x' and y-axis labelled 'length of shadow, y'. By drawing a graph, find the constant of proportionality in question 2 of **Exercise 8F**.

2   Draw a set of axes. Label the horizontal axis 'Time taken, t' and the vertical axis 'Number of laps, N'. Draw a graph to find the constant of proportionality in question 4 of **Exercise 8F**.

3   A deep-sea diver records the pressure of the water at different depths in a swimming pool (disregarding atmospheric pressure).
He thinks the pressure is directly proportional to the depth.
The pool is 7 metres deep.

Depth (m)	1	1.5	3	4	4.5
Pressure (Pa)	10 000	15 000	30 000	40 000	45 000

He draws a graph of the depth (D) against the pressure (P) to see if pressure is directly proportional to depth.

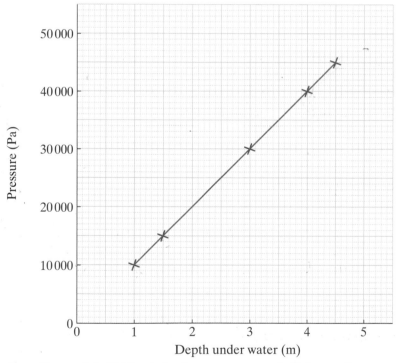

(a) Was the diver right? Explain how you can tell from the graph.

(b) Measure the gradient of the graph.

(c) Use your answer to (b) to write down a formula connecting depth and pressure.
(Hint: the gradient is also the value of the constant of proportionality.)

(d) Use your answer to (c) to predict the water pressure at the bottom of the pool.

4 In an experiment, Rashid measures the diameter and circumference of different circles. He writes his results in a table:

Diameter of circle (cm)	2	6	10	13	18
Circumference (cm)	6.3	18.9	33.4	40.8	56.6

His teacher tells him that the circumference of a circle is directly proportional to its diameter. When he draws a graph of his results, he suspects that one of his measurements is wrong.

(a) By plotting the results on a graph, with diameter on the horizontal axis and circumference on the vertical axis, suggest which of Rashid's measurements is wrong.

(b) Draw a straight line through the points that Rashid measured correctly. Use your graph to find the constant of proportionality.

(c) Use your answer to **(b)** to write down a formula connecting the diameter and circumference of a circle and use it to predict the correct measurement Rashid will get if he repeats his experiment.

5 Sound travels through air at a certain speed. This means that the time it takes for an owl to hear the hoot of another owl depends on how far apart they are. Some values collected by an ornithologist are given in a book for bird watchers:

Distance between owls (m)	10	50	230	400	1000
Time for sound to travel (s)	0.03	0.15	0.69	1.21	3.02

(a) Draw a graph of distance (horizontal axis) against time (vertical axis) and find the constant of proportionality by measuring the gradient.

(b) Use your answer to write down a formula connecting distance between owls and time for sound to travel between them.

(c) Calculate the speed of sound in metres per second.

6 P is directly proportional to Q and when $Q = 12$, $P = 240$.

   (a) Write down a formula connecting P and Q.

   (b) Insert the known values of P and Q into your formula and rearrange it to find the constant of proportionality.

   (c) Use your answer to **(b)** to work out the value of P when:
     (i) $Q = 13$ **(ii)** $Q = 6$ **(iii)** $Q = 1$

7 The speed of sound changes with the temperature of the air it is travelling through. Some examples of this are given in the table.

Air temperature, $T(^\circ C)$	0	10	20	30	40
Speed of sound, v (m/s)	331.0	336.9	342.8	348.7	354.6

   (a) Draw a graph of T against v. Number the horizontal axis from $-40^\circ C$ to $+40^\circ C$ and the vertical axis from 0 to 360 m/s.

   (b) Work out the gradient of your graph and write down the value of v where the line intercepts the vertical axis.

   (c) Does your graph show that speed of sound is proportional to air temperature? What is different about this graph and the graph for direct proportionality in question **3**?

A formula connecting v to T can be written down by adding a constant, f, to the formula for direct proportionality: $v = kT + f$.
The constant of proportionality, k, is still the gradient. The value of f is the point where the graph crosses the vertical axis.

   (d) Use your answer to **(b)** to fill in the values of k and f in the formula.

   (e) Use this formula to work out the speed of sound when the air temperature is:
     (i) $33^\circ C$ **(ii)** $-30^\circ C$.

Eleanor is an ornithologist and wants to find out how quickly sound travels between owls in different climates.

(f) Using your answers to (d) and (e), work out how many seconds it would take for a pair of owls to hear each other if they are

    (i) 900 m apart in Mexico (33°C)

    (ii) 450 m part in Alaska (−30°C)

E 8.8 Further proportionality

Sometimes you can perform a number operation on one quantity to make it directly proportional to another.

Example 7

Lyndsey decides to ride her moped for 100 m and time how long it takes her. She repeats the experiment, travelling at different constant speeds.

Lyndsey then draws a table of her results:

Speed, u (m/s)	5	6	7	8	9
Time, t (s)	20	16.7	14.3	12.5	11.1

(a) Draw a graph of t against u.

Lyndsey's physics teacher suggests that she draws a graph of t against $\dfrac{1}{u}$.

(b) Draw a table with the first row labelled $\dfrac{1}{u}$ and the second row labelled t. Complete the table using the data Lyndsey has gathered.

(c) Draw a graph of t against $\dfrac{1}{u}$.

(d) What can you say about t and $\dfrac{1}{u}$?

(a)

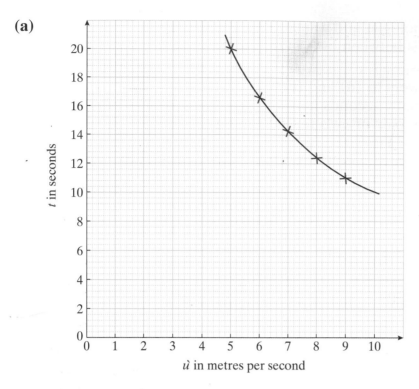

(b)

$\dfrac{1}{u}$	0.2	0.167	0.143	0.125	0.11
t	20	16.7	14.3	12.5	11.1

(c)

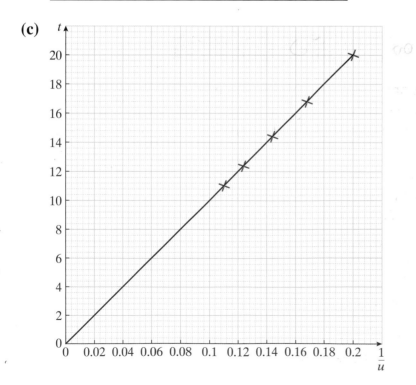

(d) The graph of t against $\dfrac{1}{u}$ is a straight line through $(0, 0)$,

so t is directly proportional to $\dfrac{1}{u}$ or $t \propto \dfrac{1}{u}$.

■ **If $y \propto \dfrac{1}{x}$ then you say 'y is inversely proportional to x'.**

You can write $y = \dfrac{k}{x}$ where k is the constant of proportionality.

Similarly, if $y \propto x^2$ then you can write $y = kx^2$.
You say 'y is proportional to x squared'.

In this example, the graph of t against $\dfrac{1}{u}$ has a gradient of:

$$k = \frac{10 - 0}{0.1 - 0} = \frac{10}{0.1} = 100$$

so $\quad t = 100 \times \dfrac{1}{u}$

or $\quad t = \dfrac{100}{u}$

Here the points $(0.1, 10)$ and $(0, 0)$ are used to find the gradient. Remember you can use any two points on the line.

Exercise 8H

1 A is inversely proportional to B and $A = 12$ when $B = 5$.

(a) Draw a pair of axes with A on the vertical axis and $1/B$ on the horizontal axis. Draw a straight line through the points $(0, 0)$ and $(\frac{1}{5}, 12)$.

(b) Measure the gradient of your graph to find the constant of proportionality, k. Put this value in to the formula $A = k/B$.

(c) Use your answer to **(b)** to find:
   (i) B when $A = 6$
   (ii) A when $B = 10$

(d) Use your graph to check your answer to **(c)**.

(e) If A doubles, what happens to B?

(f) If B is halved, what happens to A?

Remember:
$A \propto 1/B$ means that the graph of A against k/B goes through the origin $(0, 0)$.

2 All of these
rectangles have
an area of 5 cm².

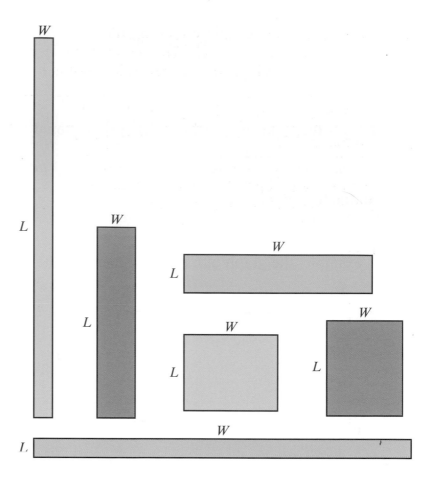

(a) Measure the length and width of each rectangle and record your
results in the table.

Length, L (cm)						
Width, W (cm)						

(b) Work out the value of $1/W$ for each value of W and write them into a
new row in your table.

(c) Plot a graph of L (vertical axis) against $1/W$ (horizontal axis) using the
values in your table. Measure the gradient of your graph.

(d) What do you notice about the value of the gradient?

(e) Write a formula to show the relationship between the length and width
of a rectangle with an area of 5 cm².

(f) Use your formula to predict the width of a rectangle with a length of
6 cm and an area of 5 cm². Use the graph you drew in **(c)** to test your
answer.

3   Ali wants to work out the relationship between the radius and area of a circle. He measures the area and radius of several circles and writes his results in a table.

Radius, R (cm)	1	2	3	4	5	6
Area, A (cm^2)	3.1	12.4	27.9	49.6	77.8	111.6

He draws a graph of area against radius to see if he can find a constant of proportionality.

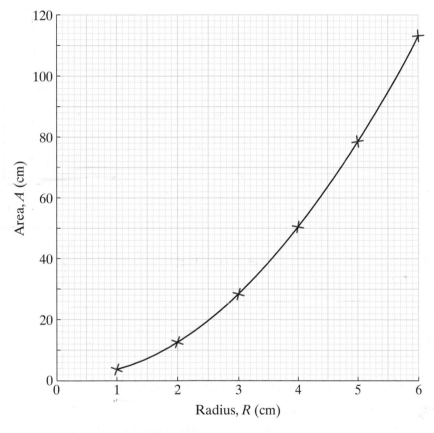

His teacher suggests that he draws a graph of area against radius^2 instead.

(a) Draw a graph with R^2 on the horizontal axis and A on the vertical axis.

(b) Using your graph, find a formula to describe the relationship between R and A.

(c) Ali wants to draw a circle with an area of $60\,\text{cm}^2$. Use your formula to calculate the radius he must set his compasses to.

4 As part of a physics experiment, Zoe drops a ball from different heights. She times how long it takes for the ball to reach the ground from each height. She puts her results into a table:

Distance fallen, d (m)	5	20	45	80	125
Time to reach ground, t (s)	1	2	3	4	5

Zoe draws a graph of her results.

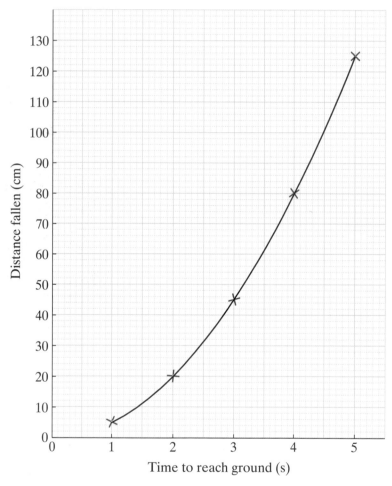

(a) Explain why Zoe's graph shows that distance fallen is not directly proportional to time of fall.

Zoe's teacher tells her that the distance (d) fallen by a free falling object is directly proportional to the square of the time (t) that the object has been falling for. Zoe writes this as an equation:

$$d = kt^2$$

(b) Draw a graph of d (vertical axis) against t^2 (horizontal axis).

(c) Use your graph to find the value of k, the constant of proportionality.

(d) Zoe reads that $k = 0.5g$, where g is the acceleration of a falling object due to gravity.
Use your answer to **(c)** to find an approximate value for g.

(e) The Eiffel Tower in Paris is 300 m tall.
Use Zoe's equation to calculate the time taken for a ball to reach the ground if it is dropped from the top of the Eiffel Tower.

5 Y is directly proportional to the square of x.
This means that the proportionality equation takes the form:

$$y = kx^2$$

When $x = 2, y = 32$. By inserting these numbers into the equation, find the constant of proportionality, k, and use the formula to find the value of y when:

(a) $x = 5$,
(b) $x = 7$,
(c) $x = 21$.

Summary of key points

1   Two or more quantities are in direct proportion
    if their ratio stays the same as the quantities
    increase or decrease.

2   You can solve ratio and proportion problems
    by reducing one side of the ratio to one.

3   A scale is a ratio used to show the relationship
    between the length on a diagram or model and
    the actual length it represents.

E   If two quantities, y and x, are in direct proportion then:
- when $x = 0, y = 0$
- as one quantity doubles, trebles ... so does the other.

E   These statements have the same meaning:
- y and x are in direct proportion,
- y is directly proportional to x,
- $y \propto x$
- $y = kx$ where k is a constant – k is called the constant of
proportionality.

E   If two quantities, y and x, are in direct proportion, then the graph of
one against the other is a straight line through the origin.

so $y = kx$

where k is equal to the gradient of the line.

k is called the constant of proportionality.

E   If $y \propto \dfrac{1}{x}$ then you say 'y is inversely proportional to x'.

You can write $y = \dfrac{k}{x}$ where k is the constant of proportionality.

Similarly, if $y \propto x^2$ then you can write $y = kx^2$. You say 'y is proportional
to x squared'.

9 Handling data

Meteorologists launch over 2000 weather balloons every day to gather data about weather conditions.

9.1 Collecting data

Bibek is gathering data about the heights of pupils in his school.

There are 1400 pupils in Bibek's school. To gather data from the entire population (all the pupils in the school) would take a long time, and it would be difficult to put the data into an easily readable form. To save time, Bibek takes a **sample** of the pupils in his school.

■ **When gathering data from a large population you can look at data from a small group, called a sample.**

Sampling helps you to make conclusions about a large population without having to collect huge amounts of data.

Example 1

Bibek uses his own Year 7 tutor group as a sample for the whole school. He records their heights using a tally chart:

Height, h (cm)	Tally	Frequency
$120 < h \leqslant 130$	|	1
$130 < h \leqslant 140$	ЖН	5
$140 < h \leqslant 150$	ЖН ЖН ЖН	15
$150 < h \leqslant 160$	ЖН ЖН |	11
$160 < h \leqslant 170$	||||	4
$170 < h \leqslant 180$	||	2

(a) Estimate the mean for Bibek's sample.

(b) How do you think the mean height for the whole school will be different from the mean height for this sample?

(c) Suggest a sample with a mean closer to that of the whole population.

(a) Using the middle value from each class interval:

Estimate for mean

$$= \frac{(125 \times 1) + (135 \times 5) + (145 \times 15) + (155 \times 11) + (165 \times 4) + (175 \times 2)}{1 + 5 + 15 + 11 + 4 + 2}$$

$$= \frac{5690}{38} = 149.7 \text{ (1 d.p.)}$$

There is more about estimating the mean of grouped data in section **4.2**.

(b) All the pupils in the sample were from Year 7. It is likely that the mean for the whole school will be greater than the mean for a Year 7 group.

(c) A sample containing one pupil from each tutor group in the school is likely to have a mean much closer to the whole school mean because it is more representative of the school population.

Biased or unbiased?

The sample in **Example 1** was not representative of the whole school. All the pupils were chosen from one year – this made the sample **biased**. It is important to use unbiased samples so that your samples are representative of the whole population.

■   **A sample that is not representative of the whole population is called a biased sample. A representative sample is called an unbiased sample.**

Random sampling
Choosing at random from the population is the easiest way of making sure that a sample is unbiased.

Example 2

The United Nations is trying to gather information about the number of people in Burundi who can read and write. It sends out 100 000 questionnaires at random and receives 4000 responses. Explain why these 4000 responses do not form an unbiased sample of the whole population of the country.

Someone who couldn't read or write may not be able to fill in the survey. The respondents are more likely to be able to read and write so the sample is unrepresentative.

> There may be more than one reason for a sample being unbiased. You can list as many sensible reasons as you can think of.

Exercise 9A

1   Alan and Faith want to gather data about how everyone in their year travels to school. For each sample, say whether it is biased or unbiased. Give reasons for your answers.

   (a) Selecting 15 names from a hat.

   (b) Asking 8 people at a bus stop.

   (c) Asking the first 20 people to arrive at school one morning.

2   The Sun Luck Chinese Takeaway is conducting some market research. It wants to know how often people eat out each month. Say whether each of these samples is biased or unbiased. Give reasons for your answers.

   (a) Asking everyone who visits the restaurant one weekend.

   (b) Polling every 5th person from the local area phone book.

   (c) Conducting a phone survey on a Friday evening.

3 Dominic is surveying the lateness of trains leaving Birmingham New Street station. He chooses a snowy January afternoon and records times for 50 trains. He records his results in a table:

Lateness, l (min)	Frequency
$0 < l \leqslant 30$	9
$30 < l \leqslant 60$	14
$60 < l \leqslant 90$	19
$90 < l \leqslant 120$	6
$120 < l \leqslant 150$	1
$150 < l \leqslant 180$	1

(a) Draw a cumulative frequency diagram for this data.

(b) Estimate the median for the data.

The median lateness for the whole year is 26 minutes.

(c) Give a reason for the difference between the sample median and the median for the whole year. Is this an unbiased sample?

4 Activity – sample sizes

How big a sample should you take? You could take an unbiased sample of just one piece of data, but your results won't tell you very much about the population. In general, the bigger the sample you take, the more you can say about a population. You need to balance the size of the sample with the practicality of gathering the data.

In this activity you will investigate the shoe sizes of people in your class. Read the instructions, then design an appropriate table to record your data.

Find the mean and median shoe sizes for:
- a random sample of 5 people from your class
- a random sample of 10 people from your class
- a random sample of 15 people from your class
- a random sample of 20 people from your class
- the whole class.

How valuable was the data you recorded from your sample of 5 people? How big did your sample need to be for your results to be meaningful?

Estimate the size of sample you would need to take from your whole school to get meaningful data about shoe size.

> **Hint:** You could number everyone in your class and use the random number button on your calculator to take a random sample.
> e.g. If there are 32 people in your class, press RAN# × 32 and round to the nearest whole number.

9.2 Representing data

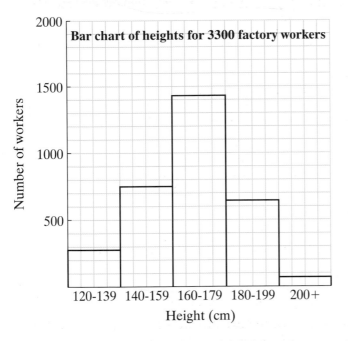

Bar chart of heights for 3300 factory workers

Number of workers

120-139 140-159 160-179 180-199 200+

Height (cm)

This bar chart shows the heights of
workers in a large factory.

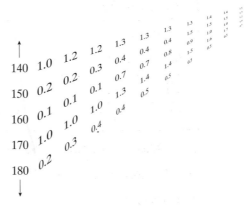

**Stem and leaf diagram for
3300 factory workers**

There are too many pieces of data
to represent these heights on a
stem and leaf diagram.

Not every method of representing data is suitable for every
data set. You need to be able to choose appropriate ways
of representing data.

Example 3

Here are the results of the 2001 general election:

Party	Votes (%)
Labour	40.7
Conservative	31.7
Liberal Democrat	18.3
Others	9.3

(a) Draw a pie chart to represent this data.

(b) Draw a bar-line graph to represent this data.

(c) Which of these provides a clearer representation of the
data?
Give a reason for your answer.

(a) **Pie chart of 2001 general election results by party**

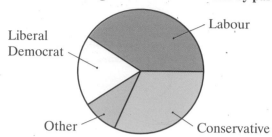

(b) **Bar-line of graph of 2001 general election results by party**

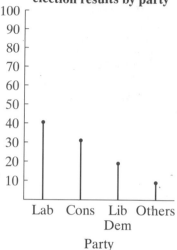

(c) The pie chart provides a much clearer indication of the results. It is a more appropriate form of representation because it shows how the votes were divided up as a proportion of the whole.

Exercise 9B

1 A German oral exam was marked out of 60. The marks for class 9H were:

23	41	52	33	19	37	28	55
46	52	47	56	39	27	32	48
38	16	56	36	51	34	8	44
57	24	53	41	48	20	25	43
51	45	35	12	36	26	45	31

(a) Record this data on a tally chart.

(b) Draw a stem and leaf diagram for this data.

(c) Which of these is a better representation of the data? Give a reason for your answer.

2 The tables on page 201 show the value of prizes given away on a television game show each week for a year.

Value of prize, v (£)	$0 < v \leqslant 50$	$50 < v \leqslant 100$	$100 < v \leqslant 150$	$150 < v \leqslant 200$
Frequency	2	9	17	6

Value of prize, v (£)	$200 < v \leqslant 250$	$250 < v \leqslant 300$	$300 < v \leqslant 350$	$350 < v \leqslant 400$
Frequency	2	4	11	1

(a) Record this data on a pie chart.

(b) Record this data on a histogram.

(c) Which of these is a better representation of the data? Give a reason for your answer.

3 The number of people travelling on the Padstow ferry each day for a month were:

31 24 26 27 24 24 28 21

22 29 27 33 25 23 27 33

30 24 26 25 31 22 20 29

23 27 21 26 29 25

(a) Explain why a stem and leaf diagram is not a suitable way of representing this data.

(b) Choose appropriate class intervals and represent this data using a bar chart.

4 This table shows the frequency distribution of the ages of workers in two companies:

Age	10–19	20–29	30–39	40–49	50–59	60–69
zapp.com	28	41	33	19	5	1
bankcorp	2	18	37	35	28	7

A job applicant wants to compare the distribution of ages for each company. Represent the data in a form that would allow her to do this easily.

5 This table shows the daily temperature and the number of ice creams sold at a wildlife park for two weeks:

Temperature (°C)	25	29	18	31	27	33	22	12	17	26	27	24	30	24
No. of ice creams sold	63	71	26	94	60	89	35	14	21	55	67	40	72	48

Declan wants to know whether there is any link between the daily temperature and the number of ice creams sold.

Represent this data in a way that will help him to do this.

9.3 Interpreting data

You need to be able to interpret and analyse data given in different forms.

■ **When interpreting data you should:**
- **Describe the information you have been given**
- **Say what that information tells you about the situation or data and what predictions you can make based on it.**

Example 4

These scatter graphs show comparisons between French and German test results and between French and Maths test results.

Comment on the correlation between the results.

There is a positive correlation between French and German results. This suggests that a student who is good at French will also be good at German. There appears to be no correlation between French and maths results. It would be impossible to predict someone's maths result from his or her French result.

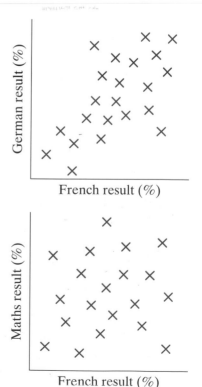

Exercise 9C

1 These frequency polygons show the lengths of
time patients had to wait for an X-ray at two
different hospitals over the course of one week:

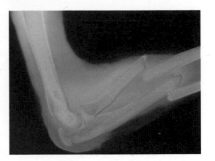

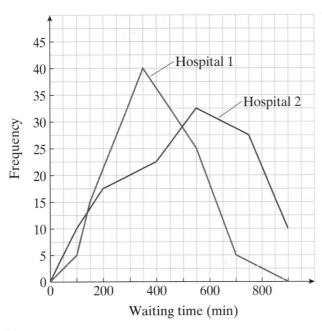

Waiting time (min)

(a) Describe the frequency distribution for each hospital.

(b) Which hospital is performing better? Give a reason for your answer.

2 These two stem and leaf diagrams show the
time taken for the 30 members of a research
group to complete two different exercises:

Exercise Bike
Time taken in minutes

1.0	1	2	4				
2.0	2	3	4	7	8	9	9
3.0	1	1	3	4	5	6	6	7
4.0	0	1	4	8	8	9	
5.0	0	2	5	6			
6.0	2	9					

Rowing machine
Time taken in minutes

1.0							
2.0	0	0	1	2	4	5	5
3.0	1	2	2	3	6	7	7	8	8	8	9
4.0	0	1	3	3	4	5	7	8
5.0	2	5	5	6			
6.0							

(a) Find the mean, median and range for each set of data.

(b) Do you have enough evidence to say that one exercise is more difficult
than the other? Give a reason for your answer.

(c) What additional information could you gather to draw an accurate
conclusion?

3 These two pie charts show the age structure of the UK population in 1880 and 1980:

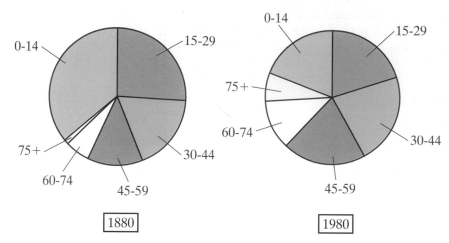

(a) Use the pie charts to describe the main changes in age structure of the UK population between 1880 and 1980.

(b) What percentage of the population were aged 15–44 in:
  (i) 1880
  (ii) 1980?

(c) The **dependent** population of a country is made up of the age groups 0–14, 60–74 and 75+. How many people would you expect to be dependent:
  (i) in a random sample of 500 members of the UK population in 1880?
  (ii) in a random sample of the same size one hundred years later?

9.4 Lines of best fit

When analysing data on a scatter diagram with good correlation you can describe the **trend** in the data by drawing a straight line along the slope of the plotted points.

■ **A straight line that passes as closely as possible to all the plotted points on a scatter graph is called the line of best fit.**

You can use a line of best fit to predict unknown values.

Example 5

Here are ten students' marks for two tests:

Paper 1	44	30	10	22	5	18	40	15	25	34
Paper 2	32	25	16	23	12	18	32	16	20	26

(a) Draw a scatter diagram to represent this data.

(b) Draw a line of best fit and use it to predict the Paper 1 mark of a student who scored 30 on Paper 2.

(c) Predict the Paper 2 mark of a student who scored 8 on Paper 1.

(a)

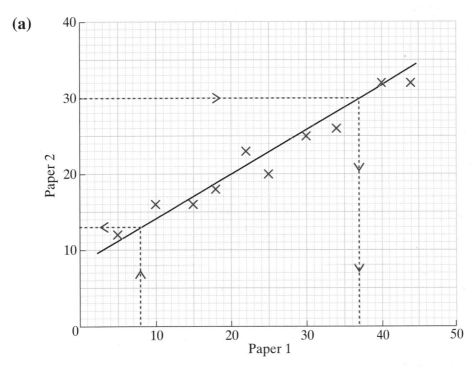

(b) A student who scored 30 on Paper 2 would be expected to score about 37 on paper 1.

(c) A student who scored 8 on Paper 1 would be expected to score about 13 on Paper 2.

Including the mean

You can make more accurate predictions by calculating the mean of each data set and making sure that your line of best fit passes through the point (mean A, mean B).

Example 6

This table shows the heights and
trunk-diameters of the trees
in a park:

Height (m)	33	30	26	35	26	42	47	28	22	38
Diameter (cm)	141	128	125	136	110	148	153	125	110	144

(a) Draw a scatter diagram to illustrate this data.
(b) Calculate the mean height and the mean diameter.
(c) Plot and label the point (mean height, mean diameter).
(d) Draw a line of best fit through this point and use it to predict the diameter
of a tree that is 40 m tall.

(a), (c)

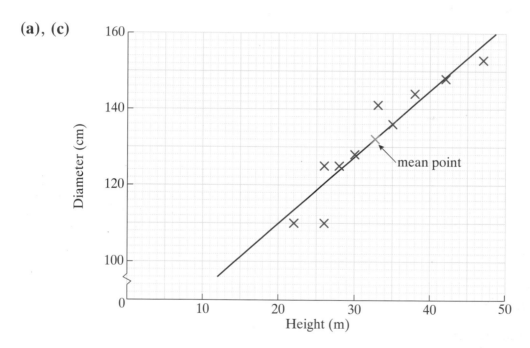

(b) Mean height $= \dfrac{33 + 30 + 26 + 35 + 26 + 42 + 47 + 28 + 22 + 38}{10} = 32.7\,\text{m}$

Mean diameter

$= \dfrac{141 + 128 + 125 + 136 + 110 + 148 + 153 + 125 + 110 + 144}{10} = 132\,\text{cm}$

(d) A tree that is 40 m tall would be expected to have a diameter of about 145 cm.

Exercise 9D

1 This table shows the heights and shoe sizes of ten
   Year 9 pupils:

Height (cm)	160	147	148	157	154	171	132	175	180	156
Shoe size	8	6	5	8	6	10	3	9	9	8

   (a) Draw a scatter diagram to represent this data.

   (b) Describe the relationship between height and shoe
   size.

   (c) Draw a straight line of best fit and use it to predict
   the height of a Year 9 pupil with size 7 shoes.

   (d) Jade is 152 cm tall. What size shoes would you
   expect her to wear?

2 This table shows the number of mobile phones sold by
   two high street shops each month for ten months:

Shop A	160	128	97	92	102	148	116	125	146	188
Shop B	115	130	179	170	152	116	141	128	122	92

   (a) Draw a scatter diagram to represent this data.

   (b) Describe the type of correlation shown and give a
   possible explanation for it.

   (c) Calculate the mean monthly sales for each shop.
   Plot and label the point
   (mean shop A, mean shop B).

   (d) Draw a straight line of best fit through this point.
   The following March, shop A sells 131 phones.
   Predict the number of phones sold by shop B.

   (e) How accurate is your prediction? Suggest a way of
   making your prediction more accurate.

3 Investigation – Football results

FA CARLING PREMIERSHIP 2000/2001 League Table		Home						Away						Total						Pts	GD
		P	W	D	L	F	A	P	W	D	L	F	A	P	W	D	L	F	A		
1	Manchester United	19	15	2	2	49	12	19	9	6	4	29	19	38	24	8	6	78	31	80	47
2	Arsenal	19	15	3	1	45	13	19	5	7	7	18	25	38	20	10	8	63	38	70	25
3	Liverpool	19	13	4	2	40	14	19	7	5	7	31	25	38	20	9	9	71	39	69	32
4	Leeds United	19	11	3	5	36	21	19	9	5	5	28	22	38	20	8	10	64	43	68	21
5	Ipswich Town	19	11	5	3	31	15	19	9	1	9	26	27	38	20	6	12	57	42	66	15
6	Chelsea	19	13	3	3	44	20	19	4	7	8	24	25	38	17	10	11	68	45	61	23
7	Sunderland	19	9	7	3	24	16	19	6	5	8	22	25	38	15	12	11	46	41	57	5
8	Aston Villa	19	8	8	3	27	20	19	5	7	7	19	23	38	13	15	10	46	43	54	3
9	Charlton Athletic	19	11	5	3	31	19	19	3	5	11	19	38	38	14	10	14	50	57	52	−7
10	Southampton	19	11	2	6	27	22	19	3	8	8	13	26	38	14	10	14	40	48	52	−8
11	Newcastle United	19	10	4	5	26	17	19	4	5	10	18	33	38	14	9	15	44	50	51	−6
12	Tottenham Hotspur	19	11	6	2	31	16	19	2	4	13	16	38	38	13	10	15	47	54	49	−7
13	Leicester City	19	10	4	5	28	23	19	4	2	13	11	28	38	14	6	18	39	51	48	−12
14	Middlesbrough	19	4	7	8	18	22	19	5	8	6	26	21	38	9	15	14	44	43	42	1
15	West Ham United	19	6	6	7	24	20	19	4	6	9	21	30	38	10	12	16	45	50	42	−5
16	Everton	19	6	8	5	29	27	19	5	1	13	16	32	38	11	9	18	45	59	42	−14
17	Derby County	19	8	7	4	23	24	19	2	5	12	14	35	38	10	12	16	37	59	42	−22
18	Manchester City	19	4	3	12	20	31	19	4	7	8	21	34	38	8	10	20	41	65	34	−24
19	Coventry City	19	4	7	8	14	23	19	4	3	12	22	40	38	8	10	20	36	63	34	−27
20	Bradford City	19	4	7	8	20	29	19	1	4	14	10	41	38	5	11	22	30	70	26	−40

Using the table above, answer the following questions. You should draw scatter diagrams to provide evidence for your conclusions. When drawing straight lines of best fit, make sure they pass through the point (mean A, mean B).

(a) Investigate the relationship between goals scored (**Total, F**) and points (**pts**).

(b) What type of correlation would you expect to find between goals scored (**Total, F**) and goals conceded (**Total, A**)?
Draw a scatter diagram to test your prediction.

(c) What type of correlation would you expect to find between:
(i) *Away* goals scored and goal difference?
(ii) Points and matches lost?
(iii) *Home* wins and the number of letters in a team's name?

(d) Investigate the relationship between *home* and *away* results for each team.

9.5 Curves of best fit

The relationship between two sets of data can't always be described using a straight line.

■ **You can use a smooth curve to describe the relationship between two sets of data on a scatter diagram. This is called a curve of best fit.**

Example 7

Year 9 are planting trees for charity. They divide into groups and record the time it takes each group to plant five trees. This table shows the number in each group and the length of time taken to plant five trees:

No. in group	2	6	15	1	12	5	1	6	4	2	10	9
Time taken (min)	39	15	8	68	8	18	65	16	26	35	11	10

(a) Draw a scatter diagram to represent this data.

(b) Draw a smooth curve of best fit.

(c) Use your curve of best fit to estimate the length of time taken by a group containing:
    (i) 3 people   **(ii)** 7 people   **(iii)** 13 people.

(a), (b)

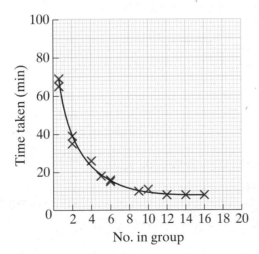

(c) (i) 30 minutes   **(ii)** 13 minutes   **(iii)** 7 minutes

Exercise 9E

1   As part of a physics experiment, Anna drops a stone out of her classroom window and records the distance it falls after certain times. She writes her results in a table:

Time (seconds)	0	0.1	0.2	0.3	0.4	0.5
Distance fallen (m)	0	0.5	2.0	4.5	8.0	12.5

(a) Draw a scatter graph to represent this data.

(b) Draw a smooth curve of best fit.

(c) Use your curve of best fit to estimate:
   (i) the distance that a stone will fall in 0.45 seconds
   (ii) the time that it would take for a stone to fall 6 m.

2   The cost of printing a textbook decreases as you increase the number of books in a print-run.
    Some data provided by a printer is given below:

Number of books printed	Cost per book (£)	Number of books printed	Cost per book (£)
1000	7.16	7000	2.42
1500	5.31	8000	2.32
2000	4.39	9000	2.24
3000	3.47	10 000	2.18
4000	3.01	20 000	1.90
5000	2.73	25 000	1.85
6000	2.55	40 000	1.76

(a) Draw a scatter diagram to represent this data.

(b) Draw a smooth curve of best fit through the points.

(c) A publisher wants to sell textbooks for £10 each. It costs £1.30 to deliver each book to a school and the overhead costs are £5.10 per book. Use your graph to calculate the minimum number of textbooks that must be printed together to make a profit of £1.60 on every book.

3 When a pendulum is at rest, it hangs vertically. Shaziya releases a pendulum 5 cm away from the vertical line of rest and watches it swing. She records the distance of the pendulum from the line at different times after release:

Time (seconds)	0	1	2	3	4	5
Distance from centre (cm)	5	4.5	3.5	0	−3.5	−4.5

Time (seconds)	6	7	8	9	10
Distance from centre (cm)	−5	−4.5	−3.5	0	3.5

Notice that Shaziya has labelled distances to one side of the pendulum as positive and distances to the other side as negative.

(a) Draw a scatter diagram of these measurements, with time on the *x*-axis and distance on the *y*-axis.

(b) Draw a smooth curve of best fit through the points and describe the shape of the curve.

(c) Predict what Shaziya's next five measurements would be if she took them at 5 second intervals, starting with 15 s. Sketch the shape of your graph when these points are added.

The pattern of a pendulum is called **simple harmonic motion**.

4 Henry and Oliver are having a stairs-climbing competition. They see how long it takes each of them to walk up the stairs to different floors in their school. Oliver records his results in a table:

Floor	1	2	3	4	5
Time (*s*)	10	20	35	55	90

Henry's results are:

Floor	1	2	3	4	5
Time (*s*)	10	26	50	80	120

(a) Draw a scatter diagram for each boy and join the points with smooth curves of best fit.

(b) Compare the curves drawn for Henry and Oliver. How can you tell which boy is the fittest?

E 9.6 Reaction times

In this section you will investigate reaction times.

Example 8

Owen holds a 30 cm ruler at the 30 cm mark. Esme's hands are poised 10 cm apart at the 0 cm mark. Owen drops the ruler and Esme closes her hands to catch it. Owen reads the distance that the ruler has fallen and marks the result in a tally chart. They repeat the experiment 15 times.

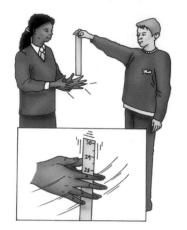

Distance, d (cm)	Tally	Frequency
$0 \leqslant d < 10$		0
$10 \leqslant d < 15$		0
$15 \leqslant d < 20$	||	2
$20 \leqslant d < 22$		0
$22 \leqslant d < 24$	|||	3
$24 \leqslant d < 26$	|||	3
$26 \leqslant d < 28$	⩕	5
$28 \leqslant d < 30$	||	2

Distance, d (cm)	Cumulative frequency
$d < 10$	0
$d < 15$	0
$d < 20$	2
$d < 22$	2
$d < 24$	5
$d < 26$	8
$d < 28$	13
$d < 30$	15

(a) Explain how d is related to Esme's reaction time.

(b) Draw a cumulative frequency diagram for the data.

(c) Estimate the mean and median distances.

(a) The larger d is, the further the ruler has fallen and so it has taken longer for Esme to catch it.
So the larger d is, the longer Esme's reaction time.

(b)

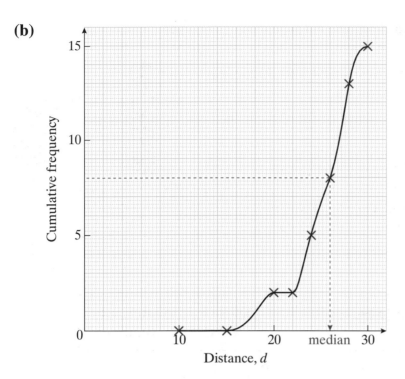

A cumulative frequency curve must pass through all of the plotted points.

(c) Using the middle value for each class interval:

Estimate of mean

$$= \frac{\begin{array}{c}(5 \times 0) + (12.5 \times 0) + (17.5 \times 2) + (21 \times 0) + \\ (23 \times 3) + (25 \times 3) + (27 \times 5) + (29 \times 2)\end{array}}{15}$$

$$= 24.8\,\text{cm}$$

From the cumulative frequency graph:

Estimate of median $= 26$ seconds

Exercise 9F

In this exercise you will repeat Owen and Esme's experiment. You will need a partner.

1 Write down two things that you and your partner should keep the same for each trial.

2 Repeat the reaction time experiment at least 20 times each. Record your results in seperate tables.

3 Draw cumulative frequency curves to represent your results on the same axes.

4 Estimate the mean, median and interquartile range for each set of results. Write down the modal class interval.

5 Using your answers to questions **4** and **5**, compare your reaction time to your partner's.

6 Write down two possible ways of increasing the accuracy of your result.

7 **Investigation**
Investigate reaction times for your whole class. Use the data you collected in this exercise and compare the means of different class members. What is the mean distance for the whole class?

Summary of key points

1 When gathering data from a large population you can look at data from a small group, called a sample.

2 A sample that is not representative of the whole population is called a biased sample. A representative sample is called an unbiased sample.

3 When interpreting data your should:
   - Describe the information you have been given
   - Say what that information tells you about the situation or data and what predictions you can make based on it.

4 A straight line that passes as closely as possible to all the plotted points on a scatter graph is called the line of best fit.

E You can use a smooth curve to describe the relationship between two sets of data on a scatter diagram. This is called a curve of best fit.

10 Geometrical reasoning and construction

10.1 Classifying quadrilaterals

You need to be able to recognise different quadrilaterals and know their properties.

Lines marked ─┼─ or ─╫─ are equal.
Lines marked ─→ or ─⇉ are parallel.

Shape	Name	Properties
	Trapezium	1 One pair of opposite sides parallel
	Parallelogram	1 Opposite sides equal and parallel 2 Opposite angles equal 3 Diagonals bisect each other 4 Rotational symmetry of order 2
	Rhombus	1 All sides equal 2 Opposite sides parallel 3 Opposite angles equal 4 Diagonals bisect each other at right angles 5 Both diagonals are lines of symmetry 6 Rotational symmetry of order 2
	Kite	1 Two pairs of adjacent sides equal 2 One pair of opposite angles equal 3 One line of symmetry 4 Diagonals cross at right angles
	Arrowhead or delta	1 Two pairs of adjacent sides of equal length 2 One interior angle greater than 180° 3 One line of symmetry 4 Diagonals cross at right angles but outside shape

Example 1

Draw a square and write down some of its properties,
as for the shapes in the table.

All sides equal
All angles equal
Four lines of symmetry
Rotational symmetry of order 4
Diagonals cross at right-angles

Example 2

The diagram represents a 3 by 3 pinboard,
which you can use to construct shapes by
using the pins as vertices.

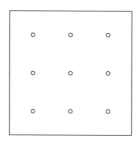

(a) Construct an arrowhead on the pinboard.

(b) Explain why it is not possible to construct an equilateral triangle.

(c) Decide whether or not it is possible to construct a rhombus
that is not a square.

(a)

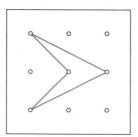

(b) On the 3 by 3 pinboard the triangle must have a base of length

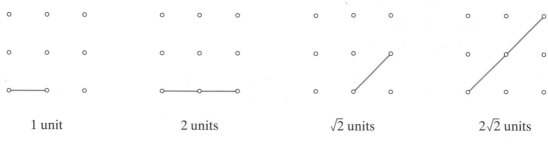

1 unit   2 units $\sqrt{2}$ units $2\sqrt{2}$ units

But in each case you cannot construct two other sides with the same length
as the base. So it is impossible to construct an equilateral triangle.

(c) The sides of a rhombus are all of equal length. One pair of parallel sides of the rhombus would have to be:

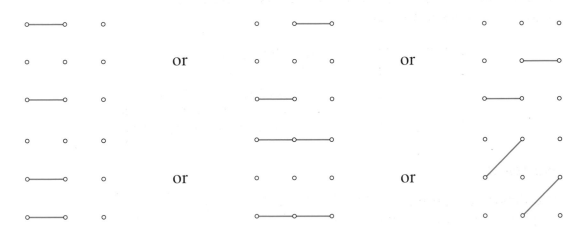

In the first three cases you cannot complete the quadrilateral with two sides of the same length as the two existing sides. In the last three cases you construct a square. So it is impossible to construct a rhombus that is not a square on the pinboard.

Exercise 10A

1 There are many properties of a rhombus that are not listed in the table.
   (a) Draw a diagram to show that
      'Adjacent angles are supplementary'
      is a property of a rhombus.
   (b) By drawing any two pairs of intersecting parallel lines show that:
      'Opposite sides parallel' leads to the property 'Adjacent angles are supplementary'.

2 An isosceles trapezium is a trapezium where the two non-parallel sides are of equal length. Write an entry for the table, describing the properties of an isosceles trapezium.

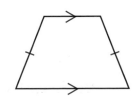

3 Repeat question **2** for a rectangle.

4 Using your answers to questions **3** and **4**, explain whether or not:

(a) a rectangle is a special type of square,

(b) a square is a special type of rectangle.

5 Explain whether or not:

(a) a square is a special type of rhombus,

(b) a rhombus is a special type of square.

6 Explain why a rectangle is a special type of parallelogram but a parallelogram is not a rectangle.

7 The diagram represents a 5 by 5 pinboard. Using the pins as vertices, construct (or explain why it is not possible to construct) on the pinboard:

(a) a kite,

(b) a rhombus,

(c) an equilateral triangle.

8 Find and classify all the different quadrilaterals that can be constructed on a

(a) 3 by 3 pinboard,

(b) 4 by 4 pinboard,

(c) 5 by 5 pinboard.

9 A rectangle has **2** lines of symmetry and rotational symmetry of order **2**. Altogether it has

2 reflective + 2 rotational = 4 symmetries

so there are **4 elements in the symmetry group of a rectangle**.

Work out the number of elements in the symmetry group of

(a) a square,

(b) an equilateral triangle,

(c) a kite,

(d) a regular polygon with n sides.

10.2 Visualization

You can solve many problems more easily
if you visualize what is happening.

Example 3

Find two cross-sections of a cube.

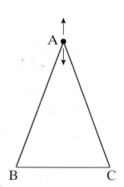

The cube can be sliced by a vertical plane
to create a square cross-section.

The cube can be sliced by a sloping
plane to create a triangular cross-section.

Other cross-sections of a cube can be
created by slicing it with a plane.

Exercise 10B

1   **ABC** is an isosceles triangle.
    The base **BC** is fixed.
    The point **A** can move along the line perpendicular to **BC**.
    Sketch pictures of the various triangles that can be
    constructed.
    What can you say about each of the triangles?

2   In Example **1** you saw two cross-sections of a cube:
    a square and an equilateral triangle.
    Find two other shapes which are
    cross-sections of a cube.

3   The diagram shows a line **L**, a fixed point **A** and
    point **P** which can move. The distance from **P** to **A**
    must always be equal to the perpendicular distance
    from **P** to the line **L**.

    Copy the diagram and then sketch lots of different
    positions for the point **P**.

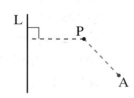

4 Nelly overlaps two equal sized squares and forms a rectangle.

Find as many different shapes as possible that can be created by overlapping:

(a) two equal sized squares,

(b) two equal sized equilateral triangles.

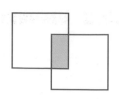

5 A cone can be sliced by planes of varying angles.

Sketch as many different cross-sections of a cone as you can. Describe the plane used to create each cross-section.

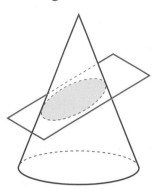

6 The diagram represents a cube. Points have been drawn at the centre of the top face and at three of the vertices on the base.

These points are to be joined by straight lines to form a 3D shape.

Sketch and name the shape formed.

7 Two identical pyramids are joined by their square bases to form another shape.

Sketch and name this shape.

8 Jack wraps a sheet of thin paper several times around the curved surface of a cylinder.

He then slices the cylinder with an oblique plane and unwraps the lower part of the sheet of paper.

Sketch the profile of the top edge of the unwrapped sheet of paper.

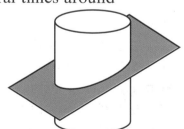

9 A dot is drawn at the centre of each face on a cube. Dots at the centre of adjacent faces of the cube are joined by straight lines to create the outline of another 3D shape.

Sketch and name this shape.

10 A light shines on a solid. The shadow cast by the solid is always a circle. Explain what the solid must be.

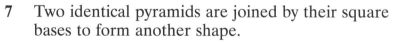

10.3 Tessellations

A honeycomb is an example of a tessellation. Hexagons fit perfectly together to cover a broad frame in the beehive.

■ **A pattern of shapes which fit perfectly together without leaving gaps or overlapping is called a tessellation.**

Example 4

(a) Sketch six hexagons which fit together as part of a honeycomb.

(b) Look at a point where three hexagons meet. By considering the interior angle of a hexagon, decide how you can tell whether a regular polygon will tessellate.

(c) Will a regular pentagon tessellate?

(a)

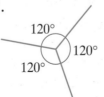

(b) The interior angle of a hexagon is $120°$.

Because 120 is a factor of 360 the hexagons fit together without gaps.

So a regular polygon will tessellate if its interior angle is a factor of $360°$.

> Remember from Chapter 6: sum of interior angles of polygon with n sides $= 180° \times (n - 2)$

(c) The interior angle of a pentagon is

$$\frac{540}{5} = 108°$$

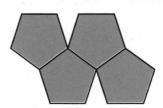

108 is not a factor of 360 so regular pentagons do not tessellate.

■ **A regular polygon will tessellate if its interior angle is a factor of $360°$.**

Most regular polygons do not tessellate on their own. Sometimes you can include another polygon in the pattern to form a tessellation.

A regular octagon has an interior angle of $\dfrac{1080°}{8} = 135°$.

$\dfrac{360}{135} = 2.\dot{6}$ so   135 is not a factor of 360.

So a regular octagon will not tessellate.

However, a regular octagon and a square with sides of the same length as the octagon do tessellate.

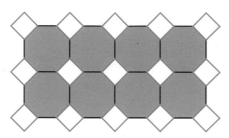

In this case, the sum of the angles at a point is $135° + 135° + 90° = 360°$.

135°

135°

■ **A pattern tessellates if at each point where the shapes meet the sum of the angles is 360°.**

Exercise 10C

1   Copy the grid and show how the shaded shape will tessellate.

You should draw the shape at least 6 times.

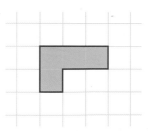

2   Explain whether or not each of these shapes will tessellate:

(a) rectangle,

(b) parallelogram,

(c) regular heptagon,

(d) equilateral triangle,

(e) circle.

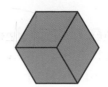

3 A set of tiles are in the form of identical rhombuses.
Three of the tiles can be placed together to form the
regular hexagon shown here.

 (a) Explain why the tiles will tessellate the plane.

 (b) Write down the interior angles of each tile (or
 rhombus).

4 (a) Explain why a regular pentagon will not tessellate.

 (b) Jo places tiles on a flat surface.

 The tiles are regular pentagons.

 She uses quadrilateral tiles to form a tessellation
 with the regular pentagons.

 By drawing or otherwise, find the name of the
 quadrilateral and work out its interior angles.

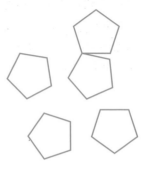

5 Write down all the regular polygons that tessellate.
 (Hint: sum of interior angles of polygon with n sides $= (n - 2) \times 180°$.)

6 (a) Mark a point on a piece of
 paper and draw four straight
 lines radiating from the
 point at any angles you choose.

 (b) Construct a quadrilateral with
 these interior angles.

 (c) Explain why all quadrilaterals tessellate.
 (Hint: In a tessellation, the sum of the
 angles at a point is 360°.)

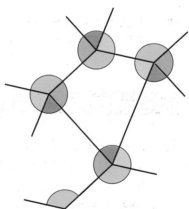

7 Without doing more than one drawing,
 explain why every triangle will
 tessellate.

10.4 Circles

You know that different parts of a circle have special names such as centre, radius, diameter and circumference.

Here is a reminder of some of those words and some new words to do with circles.

	A straight line crossing a circle is called a **chord**.		A section of the circumference is called an **arc**.
	The region of a circle contained by two radius lines and an arc is a **sector**. The circle is divided into a **minor** (smaller) **sector** and a **major sector**.		The region of a circle contained by a chord and an arc is called a **segment**. The circle is divided into a **minor segment** and a **major segment**.
	A straight line that touches a circle at a point is called a **tangent**. The angle between the tangent and the radius is a right angle.		The circle that passes through all the vertices of a given polygon is called a **circumcircle**. It is not possible to **circumscribe** some polygons.
	The centre of a circumcircle is called the **circumcentre**.		A shape that is drawn inside another so that the two shapes touch but do not intersect is **inscribed**.
			The circle inscribed inside a triangle is called an **incircle**. The centre of the incircle is called the **incentre** and the radius is called the **inradius**.

Example 5

Saranga draws a circle and marks six equally spaced points around the circumference. He joins adjacent points with straight lines.

(a) Sketch and describe the inscribed shape.

(b) What shape does Saranga inscribe if he marks n equally spaced points around the circumference?

(a) A regular hexagon.

(b) If he marks eight points he inscribes an octagon. If he marks n points he inscribes a regular polygon with n sides.

Example 6

George draws two circles that intersect at two points, A and B. The radius of one circle is different to the radius of the other. George labels the centre of one circle X and the centre of the other Y.

(a) Draw a diagram to show that the common chord AB is perpendicular to the line joining the two centres XY.

(b) Write down the name of the shape AXBY.

(a)

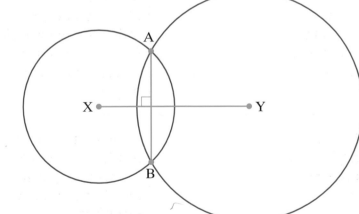

(b) AXB and AYB are both isosceles triangles so AXBY is a kite.

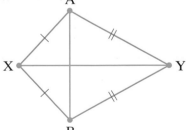

Exercise 10D

1   Rashida draws a chord that divides a circle into two segments.

The segments are the same size.

What can you say about the chord?

2   Two circles can intersect at a maximum of two points.

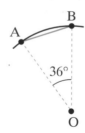

Find the maximum number of points of intersection for three circles.

3   The diagram shows a side AB of a regular polygon inscribed in a circle with centre O.

Work out the number of sides of the regular polygon.

4

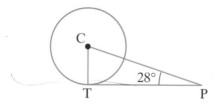

PT is a tangent to the circle centre C.

Work out the angle PCT and explain your working.

5   **(a)** Draw a square with sides of length 6 cm.

(b) Inscribe a circle within your square.

6   Explain fully whether or not it is possible for a kite to have a circumcircle.

10.5 Constructions

Mathematicians in ancient Greece were particularly interested in geometrical constructions and they created many of the mathematical constructions we use today.

Example 7

Construct the perpendicular from the point P to the line AB.

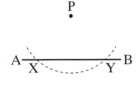

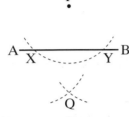

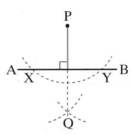

With P as centre draw an arc. Choose a radius so that the arc crosses AB twice, at X and Y.

Choose a radius more than half the length of XY. With X as centre, draw an arc below AB. Keep the radius the same and, with Y as centre, draw a second arc below AB. The two arcs cross at Q.

Join P and Q with a straight line. PQ is the perpendicular from P to the line AB.

Example 8

Construct the perpendicular from the point P on the line AB.

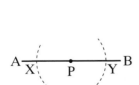

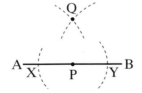

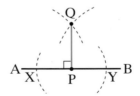

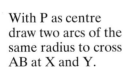

With P as centre draw two arcs of the same radius to cross AB at X and Y.

Choose a radius more than half the length of XY. With X as centre, draw an arc above AB. Keep the radius the same and, with Y as centre, draw a second arc above AB. The two arcs cross at Q.

Join P and Q with a straight line. PQ is perpendicular to the line AB.

Example 9

Construct the perpendicular bisector of the line AB.

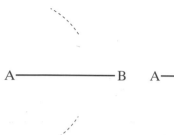
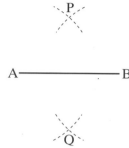
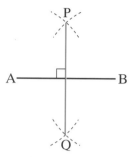

Set your compasses to over half the length of AB. With A as the centre, draw two arcs of the same radius.

Leave your compasses set at the same width. With B as the centre, draw two more arcs. The arcs intersect at P and Q respectively.

Join P and Q. PQ is the perpendicular bisector of the line AB.

Example 10

Construct the bisector of angle BAC.

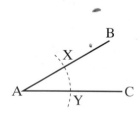
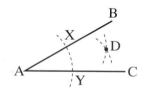
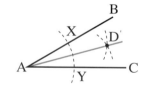

With centre A, draw an arc to cross AB and AC at X and Y respectively.

With centre X, draw an arc. Keep the radius the same and, with Y as centre, draw a second arc. The two arcs cross at D.

Join A and D with a straight line. AD bisects angle BAC.

Example 11

(a) Construct a triangle measuring 4 cm, 5 cm and 7 cm.

(b) Draw the circumcircle for this triangle.

(a)

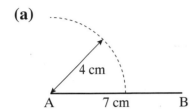

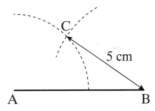

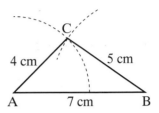

Draw AB 7 cm long.
Set the compasses to
4 cm. With A as the
centre, draw this arc.

Set your compasses
to 5 cm. With B as
the centre, draw
another arc. The
arcs cross at C.

Triangle ABC has
sides of length 4 cm,
5 cm and 7 cm.

(b) The circumcentre of triangle ABC is the point where
the perpendicular bisectors of each of the sides
intersect.

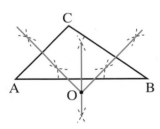

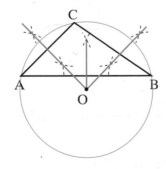

It is only necessary
to draw two
perpendicular
bisectors, but it is a
good check to draw
all three.

Draw the perpendicular
bisector of each side as in
Example 9. The perpendicular
bisectors cross at the
circumcentre.

With O as the centre,
draw a circle that passes
through A, B and C.
This is the circumcircle
of the triangle.

Exercise 10E

1   The incentre of a triangle is the point where the bisectors of each of the angles intersect. Construct the triangle in Example **11(a)** and draw its inscribed circle.

2   Draw a line AB of any length. Without measuring any lengths, construct an equilateral triangle with AB as its base.

3   Thom constructs a triangle. It must have a base of length 5 cm and an angle of 40° adjacent to the base:
    (a) Using a ruler and protractor draw two different triangle with these properties.
    (b) Write down one extra piece of information Thom would need to give to uniquely define his triangle.

4   Construct a triangle ABC with AB = 8 cm, angle BAC = 30° and angle CBA = 70°.
    Explain whether this triangle is unique or not.

5   Using ruler, compasses and pencil only (no protractor) construct a triangle PQR with PQ = 7 cm, PR = 8 cm and angle QPR = 45°.

6   Using a ruler, compasses and a pencil only:
    (a) construct a triangle ABC with BC = 5 cm, AB = 3 cm and AC = 4 cm,
    (b) draw the circumcircle for this triangle,
    (c) draw the inscribed circle for the triangle.

7   (a) Using ruler and compasses only, draw a triangle with sides of length 8 cm, 5 cm and 7 cm.
    (b) Draw the circumcircle and inscribed circle for this triangle.

8   Using ruler, compasses and pencil only:
    (a) draw a regular hexagon with sides of length 5 cm,
    (b) draw the circumcircle and inscribed circle for this hexagon,
    (c) draw an equilateral triangle so that the inscribed circle of the hexagon is the circumcircle for the equilateral triangle.

9   **You will need a circular template or plastic disc.**

    (a) Use a template or disc (not compasses) to draw a circle.

    (b) Use a method of construction to find the exact position of the centre of the circle.

10   Using ruler, compasses and pencil only:

    (a) draw a line segment of length 8 cm,

    (b) draw a circle so that the line segment is a tangent to the circle.

11   Using a ruler, compasses and pencil:

    (a) Construct a triangle ABC with AB = 10 cm, AC = 7 cm and angle ABC = 30°.

    (b) Is this triangle unique?

12   **You may use a protractor.**

    (a) Construct a triangle XYZ where XY = 8 cm, angle ZXY = 50°, and angle ZYX = 70°.

    (b) Explain whether or not this triangle is unique.

    (c) Draw the incircle for this triangle.

    (d) Draw the circumcircle for this triangle.

13   Using ruler and compasses only, construct a regular dodecagon.

A dodecagon has 12 sides.

10.6 Locus

When a point moves according to a given rule, its path is called a **locus**. All the points on the locus obey the rule.

The plural of locus is **loci**.

The jetstream of an aeroplane is an example of a locus

■   **A locus is the path of a point which moves according to a given rule.**

Example 12

A point moves so that it is always 2 cm from a fixed point A.

Draw the locus.

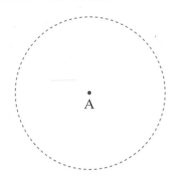

The locus is a circle, centre A, with a radius of 2 cm.

Example 13

A point P moves so that it is always less than 1 cm from the line AB.

Draw the locus.

The dotted line is two lines parallel to AB and two semi-circles, centres A and B, each with a radius of 1 cm. The locus of P is the area **inside** the dotted line.

Example 14

A triangular piece of card has an angle of 60° at its upper vertex. The card is moved so that its two edges always pass through two fixed points.

Draw the locus of the vertex.

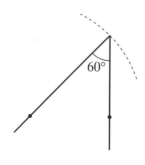

The locus is a major arc of a circle.

Exercise 10F

1   A and B are two fixed points. A point moves so that it
    is always the same distance from A as it is from B.
    Draw the locus and describe it in words.

2   AB and AC are straight lines. A point moves so that it
    is always the same distance from AB as it is from AC.

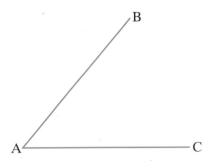

    Draw the locus and describe it in words.

3   The diagram represents a corner of Mrs Jones' garden.
    She wishes to place a washing line so that at any point
    on the line the perpendicular distance from the line to
    the fence is twice the perpendicular distance from the
    line to the wall.

    (a) Sketch where the line should be placed.

    (b) Describe the line.

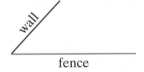

4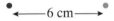

    Black points are drawn so that the distance from each
    black point to the red point is **double** the distance from
    the black to the blue point.

    (a) Find at least 12 positions for the black point.

    (b) Join these black points and describe the figure
    created.

5   A point P lies outside the rectangle and moves so that
    the shortest distance from P to the rectangle is always
    2 cm.

    Draw the locus of P.

6 A and B are two fixed points on a flat surface.
A point P moves such that the angle APB is always 45°.

Hint: You could cut
the corner of a piece
of paper to 45° to
help you.

Draw the locus of P and describe it in words.

7 **(a)** Construct a triangle with sides of length 6 cm, 8 cm
and 10 cm.

(b) A point P lies outside the triangle and moves so
that the shortest distance from P to the triangle is
always 3 cm.
Construct the locus.

8 A point P moves in 3D so that the shortest distance
from P to a fixed point is less than or equal to 5 cm.
What solid shape is formed by this locus?

Summary of key points

1 A pattern of shapes which fit perfectly together
without leaving gaps or overlapping is called a
tessellation.

2 A regular polygon will tessellate if its interior angle
is a factor of 360°.

3 A pattern tessellates if at each point where the
shapes meet the sum of the angles is 360°.

4 A locus is the path of a point which moves
according to a given rule.

11 Decimals

11.1 Working with decimals

You need to be able to work with decimals, both on paper and in your head. In this section you will practise some of the techniques you have already learnt.

Example 1

Work out 4.32×38

$$
\begin{array}{r}
4.32 \\
\times \quad 38 \\
\end{array}
$$

$4.32 \times 8 \longrightarrow \quad 3\,4.5\,6$
$4.32 \times 30 \longrightarrow 1\,2\,9.6\,0$
$4.32 \times 38 \longrightarrow 1\,6\,4.1\,6$

Remember to keep the decimal point in the same place.

So $4.32 \times 38 = 164.16$

Example 2

Without using a calculator, work out $104.72 \div 28$

$(104.72 \div 28 \approx 100 \div 30 = 10 \div 3 \approx 3)$

Line up the decimal points.

$$
\begin{array}{r}
3.74 \\
28\overline{)104.72} \\
-\ 84 \\
\hline
20.7 \\
-\ 19.6 \\
\hline
1.12 \\
-\ 1.12 \\
\hline
0
\end{array}
$$

You can sometimes multiply or divide a decimal by a large whole number by using factors.

Example 3

Using the factors of the whole number, work out:

(a) 4.3×24 (b) $61.38 \div 18$

(a) 4.3×24 is approximately $4 \times 20 = 80$.

$4.3 \times 24 = 4.3 \times 4 \times 6$
$4.3 \times 4 = 17.2$
$17.2 \times 6 = 103.2$

Remember: the results will have 1 decimal place.

So $4.3 \times 24 = 103.2$

$$\begin{array}{r} 172 \\ \times 6 \\ \hline 1032 \\ \hline {\scriptstyle 4\ 1} \end{array}$$

(b) $61.38 \div 18$ is approximately $60 \div 20 = 6 \div 2 = 3$

$61.38 \div 18 = (61.38 \div 3) \div 6$
$61.38 \div 3 = 20.46$
$20.46 \div 6 = 3.41$

So $61.38 \div 18 = 3.41$

$$\begin{array}{r} 2\,0\,.\,4\,6 \\ 3\overline{)6\,1\,.\,{}^1 3\,{}^1 8} \end{array}$$

$$\begin{array}{r} 3\,.\,4\,1 \\ 6\overline{)2\,0\,.\,{}^2 4\,6} \end{array}$$

Hint:
Do these divisions on paper.

Exercise 11A

1 (a) Change $\frac{2}{9}$ to a decimal, giving your answer to 3 d.p.

(b) Change $\frac{3}{15}$ to a decimal giving your answer to 3 d.p.

 Do not use a calculator for questions **2** to **10**.

2 A school buys 32 new computer keyboards.
Each keyboard costs £34.67 and weighs 1.23 kg.
Work out:

(a) the total cost of the 32 keyboards
(b) the total weight of the 32 keyboards.

3 In each question:
- round each number to 1 significant figure to estimate the answer
- calculate the exact answer.

(a) 6.7×31 (b) 8.9×54 (c) 7.8×96
(d) 4.36×23 (e) 7.43×46 (f) 5.42×38
(g) 12.54×34 (h) 75.52×45 (i) 69.37×68

4 Find the answers:

(a) 0.7×0.4 (b) 0.3×0.8 (c) 1.7×0.9

(d) 6.8×5.7 (e) 6.52×3.9 (f) 3.64×2.1

(g) 4.21×3.2 (h) 5.61×0.48 (i) 6.24×3.87

5 In each case, showing all your working:
- estimate the answer by rounding each number to 1 significant figure
- calculate the exact answer.

(a) $36.8 \div 16$ (b) $89.6 \div 32$ (c) $935.9 \div 35$

(d) $88.4 \div 26$ (e) $68.18 \div 16$ (f) $1.734 \div 17$

(g) $0.0342 \div 19$ (h) $29.145 \div 29$ (i) $19.787 \div 47$

6 (a) $8.89 \div 0.7$ (b) $39.54 \div 0.6$ (c) $11.84 \div 0.4$

(d) $27.45 \div 0.9$ (e) $8.271 \div 0.03$ (f) $3.807 \div 0.06$

(g) $114.3 \div 1.8$ (h) $7.263 \div 2.7$ (i) $126.4 \div 0.64$

Hint:
To divide 8.271 by 0.03 multiply both numbers by 100 and then divide by 3.

7 Kate ran 8.96 km in 1.4 hours. Work out her average speed in kilometres per hour. Show all your working.

8 Work these out without writing down any working:

(a) 5.3×3 (b) 7.4×2 (c) 12.2×4

(d) 15.9×5 (e) $12.8 \div 4$ (f) $189.6 \div 3$

(g) $72.9 \div 9$ (h) $36.8 \div 8$

9 Use the factors of the whole number to work out:

(a) 2.3×15 (b) 4.2×14 (c) 5.3×18

(d) $86.1 \div 21$ (e) $61.5 \div 15$ (f) $34.16 \div 28$

10 (a) Given that $437 \times 1.48 = 646.76$, find the value of 4370×0.0148

(b) Given that $\dfrac{2523}{29} = 87$, find the value of $\dfrac{2.523}{0.029}$

11 In parts **(a)** to **(f)**:

- using approximate values, write down a calculation that you could use to estimate the answer
- work out the estimated answer without a calculator
- use a calculator to work out the exact answer.

(a) £28.45 × 3.8

(b) £78.76 ÷ 8.8

(c) 6.076 ÷ 0.4

(d) 0.37 × (9.18 + 28.7)

(e) $\dfrac{62.3 - 21.26}{31.85 - 23.21}$

(f) $\dfrac{8.136 + 29.055}{0.35 \times 2.3}$

11.2 Writing numbers in standard form

Standard form is a way of writing very small or very large numbers to make them easier to use.

Saturn is 1 427 000 000 km from the sun.

In standard form this is 1.427×10^9 km.

The radius of the orbit of the electron in this hydrogen atom is 0.000 000 000 0529 m.

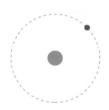

In standard form this is 5.29×10^{-11} m.

■ **A number in standard form is written as $A \times 10^n$, where $1 \leqslant A < 10$ and n is an integer.**

Numbers greater than or equal to 1

Look at these powers of ten:

Ten thousands	Thousands	Hundreds	Tens	Units	
				1	$= 10^0$
			1	0	$= 10^1$
		1	0	0	$= 10^2$
	1	0	0	0	$= 10^3$
1	0	0	0	0	$= 10^4$

Any number to the power of zero is equal to one.

Writing numbers in standard form is just like multiplying by powers of ten:

$$\begin{array}{|c|c|c|c|c|c|} \hline 10^5 & 10^4 & 10^3 & 10^2 & 10^1 & 10^0 \\ \hline & & & 4 & 0 & 0 \\ \hline 3 & 2 & 8 & 6 & 0 & 0 \\ \hline & & & & & 2 \\ \hline \end{array}$$

$= 4 \times 100 = 4 \times 10^2$
$= 3.286 \times 100\,000 = 3.286 \times 10^5$
$= 2 \times 1 = 2 \times 10^0$

You write 3.286×10^5 because the first significant figure is in the 10^5 column.

Example 4

Write in standard form:

(a) 4321 000   **(b)** 2614

Write the numbers in a place value table:

$$\begin{array}{|c|c|c|c|c|c|c|} \hline 10^6 & 10^5 & 10^4 & 10^3 & 10^2 & 10^1 & 10^0 \\ \hline 4 & 3 & 2 & 1 & 0 & 0 & 0 \\ \hline & & & 2 & 6 & 1 & 4 \\ \hline \end{array}$$

Remember that the first column is 10^0 **not** 10^1.

(a) First s.f. is in the 10^6 column so
$$4321\,000 = 4.321 \times 10^6$$

(b) First s.f. is in the 10^3 column so
$$2614 = 2.614 \times 10^3$$

Example 5

Write 4.72×10^3 as an ordinary number.

$10^3 = 1000$ so multiply by 1000:

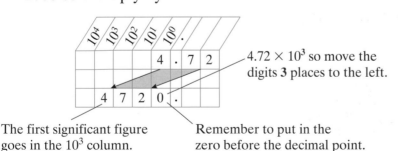

4.72×10^3 so move the digits **3** places to the left.

When a number in standard form has a *positive* power of 10 you move the digits to the *left* to make an ordinary number.

The first significant figure goes in the 10^3 column.

Remember to put in the zero before the decimal point.

So $4.72 \times 10^3 = 4720$

Numbers between 0 and 1

You use negative powers of 10 to write numbers between 0 and 1:

$$0.1 = \tfrac{1}{10} = \frac{10^0}{10^1} = 10^{0-1} = 10^{-1}$$

$$0.01 = \tfrac{1}{100} = \frac{10^0}{10^2} = 10^{0-2} = 10^{-2}$$

There is more on negative powers on page 32.

10^3	10^2	10^1	10^0	.	tenths 10^{-1}	hundredths 10^{-2}	thousandths 10^{-3}	ten thousandths 10^{-4}	ten hundred thousandths 10^{-5}
				.	1				
				.	0	1			
				.	0	0	1		
				.	0	0	0	1	
				.	0	0	0	0	1

You can use a place value diagram to write numbers less than 1 in standard form:

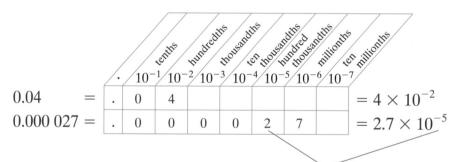

	.	tenths 10^{-1}	hundredths 10^{-2}	thousandths 10^{-3}	ten thousandths 10^{-4}	hundred thousandths 10^{-5}	millionths 10^{-6}	ten millionths 10^{-7}	
0.04 =	.	0	4						$= 4 \times 10^{-2}$
0.000 027 =	.	0	0	0	0	2	7		$= 2.7 \times 10^{-5}$

The first significant figure is in the 10^{-5} column.

The number 0.000 027 is written as 2.7×10^{-5} in standard form. The power of 10 is -5 because the first significant figure (2) is in the 10^{-5} column.

Example 6

Write in standard form:

(a) 0.0024

(b) 0.0561

(c) 0.000 0038

Write the answers in a place value table:

.	10^{-1}	10^{-2}	10^{-3}	10^{-4}	10^{-5}	10^{-6}	10^{-7}
.	0	0	2	4			
.	0	5	6	1			
.	0	0	0	0	0	3	8

(a) First s.f. is in the 10^{-3} column so
$$0.0024 = 2.4 \times 10^{-3}$$

(b) First s.f. is in the 10^{-2} column so
$$0.0561 = 5.61 \times 10^{-2}$$

(c) First s.f. is in the 10^{-6} column so
$$0.000\,0038 = 3.8 \times 10^{-6}$$

Example 7

Write 3.004×10^{-2} as an ordinary number.

$10^{-2} = 0.01$ so multiply by 0.01:

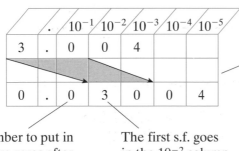

	.	10^{-1}	10^{-2}	10^{-3}	10^{-4}	10^{-5}
3	.	0	0	4		
0	.	0	3	0	0	4

3.004×10^{-2} so move the digits 2 places to the right.

Remember to put in any extra zeros after the decimal point.

The first s.f. goes in the 10^{-2} column.

When a number in standard form has a *negative* power of 10, you move the digits to the *right* to make an ordinary number.

So $3.004 \times 10^{-2} = 0.03004$

Exercise 11B

Use place value diagrams to answer these questions.

1 Write these numbers in standard form:
   (a) 5620   (b) 368 900
   (c) 25.67   (d) 0.004 23
   (e) 0.000 92   (f) 0.000 006
   (g) 354.28   (h) 0.385
   (i) 90 020 000   (j) 52 010
   (k) 0.000 08   (l) 0.0368

2 Write as ordinary numbers:
   (a) 2.4×10^5 (b) 3.69×10^3 (c) 2.146×10^7
   (d) 3.9×10^1 (e) 4.374×10^4 (f) 3.6×10^{-2}
   (g) 4.93×10^{-3} (h) 6.89×10^0 (i) 1.78×10^{-4}
   (j) 6×10^{-8} (k) 5.2×10^{-6} (l) 8.934×10^6

11.3 Prefixes and standard form

Scientists often use prefixes before units when describing quantities that are very large or very small.

For example,

kilo: 1 kilogram = 1000 grams = 10^3 grams

centi: 1 centimetre = $\frac{1}{100}$ metre = 10^{-2} metre

So kilo $\equiv 10^3$ and centi $\equiv 10^{-2}$.

■ **There are several prefixes that represent powers of 10:**

   10^9 **giga** 10^{-2} **centi**
   10^6 **mega** 10^{-3} **milli**
   10^3 **kilo** 10^{-6} **micro**
                        10^{-9} **nano**
                        10^{-12} **pico**

Example 8

Write these quantities using prefixes.

(a) 9×10^6 metres

(b) 1.65×10^{-8} seconds

(a) 9×10^6 metres $= 9$ megametres

(b) 1.65×10^{-8} seconds $= 16.5 \times 10^{-1} \times 10^{-8}$ seconds

$$= 16.5 \times 10^{-9} \text{ seconds}$$

$$= 16.5 \text{ nanoseconds}$$

Note: 1.65×10^{-8} seconds $= 0.0165$ microseconds $= 16.5$ nanoseconds

$$= 16\,500 \text{ picoseconds, etc.}$$

It is often best to write the quantity using a prefix that makes the number greater than 1 but as small as possible. So here you use 16.5 nanoseconds.

Example 9

Write these quantities in standard form.

(a) 2.6 nanolitres   (b) 50.12 megametres

(a) 2.6 nanolitres $= 2.6 \times 10^{-9}$ litres

(b) 50.12 megametres $= 50.12 \times 10^6$ metres

$$= 5.012 \times 10^1 \times 10^6 \text{ metres}$$

$$= 5.012 \times 10^7 \text{ metres}$$

Exercise 11C

1   Write these quantities using prefixes.

(a) 2×10^{-3} metres   (b) 4.5×10^6 seconds

(c) 7.9×10^{-7} litres   (d) 1.86×10^8 grams

(e) 9.1×10^{-1} metres   (f) 3.7×10^{-5} seconds

2   Write these quantities in standard form.

(a) 6 picometres   (b) 10 kilograms

(c) 6000 nanonewtons   (d) 8.6513 gigalitres

(e) 0.05 milliseconds   (f) 501 centimetres

3   Carno Wind Farm in Powys has 56 turbines,
    each generating a maximum of 600 kilowatts.
    The farm produces enough power for 25 000
    homes. Calculate in standard form the maximum
    power generated by the wind farm. Work out
    the power needed to run one household. (Write
    your answers in watts using suitable prefixes.)

4   You can model the Earth as a sphere of
    radius $r = 6.37 \times 10^3$ km. It takes 24 hours to
    turn once about its axis. The speed, v m/s, of a
    point on the surface of the Earth is given by

$$v = \frac{2\pi r}{T}$$

    where r is the radius of the Earth in metres
    and T is the time it takes the Earth to turn
    once about its axis in seconds.
    Work out the value of v in m/s, giving your
    answer to 3 s.f.

E 11.4 Using numbers in standard form

You sometimes need to work out problems involving
numbers written in standard form.

Example 10

Emmet's computer can carry out 2.43×10^8
calculations in one hour. Work out how many
calculations Emmet's computer can carry out
in one second. Give your answer in standard
form.

One hour $= 60 \times 60$ seconds $= 3600$ seconds
$\qquad = 3.6 \times 10^3$

The number of calculations in one second

$= (2.43 \times 10^8) \div (3.6 \times 10^3)$
$= (2.43 \div 3.6) \times (10^8 \div 10^3)$
$= 0.675 \times 10^{8-3}$ ——————— You need to write
$= 6.75 \times 10^{-1} \times 10^5$ 0.675 as a number
$= 6.75 \times 10^4$ between 1 and 10.

$$\frac{2.43 \times 10^8}{3.6 \times 10^3}$$

$$= \frac{2.43}{3.6} \times \frac{10^8}{10^3}$$

So you can divide the
numbers 2.43 and 3.6
and the powers 10^8
and 10^3 separately.

Emmet's computer can do 6.75×10^4 calculations
in one second.

Example 11

Work out $4.75 \times 10^5 + 5.2 \times 10^3$, giving your answer in standard form.

Write as ordinary numbers and add:

	10^6	10^5	10^4	10^3	10^2	10^1	10^0	.	10^{-1}	
4.7×10^5		4	7	5	0	0	0	.		
$+ 5.2 \times 10^3$				5	2	0	0	.		+
Total =		4	8	0	2	0	0	.		

The answer is $480\,200$ or 4.802×10^5.

> If the numbers in the question are in standard form you should give your answer in standard form.

- ■ **You can multiply and divide numbers when they are in standard form in the normal way.**

- ■ **If you add or subtract two numbers in standard form you need to first change them to ordinary numbers.**

Example 12

Work these out, giving your answers in standard form:

(a) $(9.42 \times 10^7) \times (3.6 \times 10^{-3})$ (b) $(5.2 \times 10^6) - (2.4 \times 10^4)$

(a) $(9.42 \times 10^7) \times (3.6 \times 10^{-3})$
$= 9.42 \times 3.6 \times 10^7 \times 10^{-3}$
$= 33.912 \times 10^{7 + -3}$
$= 33.912 \times 10^4$ —————— You need to write 33.912 as 3.3912×10^1.
$= 3.3912 \times 10^1 \times 10^4$
$= 3.3912 \times 10^5$

> You can multiply the numbers 9.42 and 3.6 and the powers 10^7 and 10^{-3} separately.

The answer is 3.3912×10^5

(b) $(5.2 \times 10^6) - (2.4 \times 10^4)$
$= 5\,200\,000 - 24\,000$ ——— Write as ordinary numbers.
$= 5\,176\,000$
$= 5.176 \times 10^6$ ——— Write answer in standard form.

The answer is 5.176×10^6

Exercise 11D

Work these out, giving your answers in standard form.

1 (a) $(5.2 \times 10^4) \times (1.3 \times 10^3)$

(b) $(6.8 \times 10^{-8}) \times (4.3 \times 10^2)$

(c) $(7.3 \times 10^3) + (8.4 \times 10^2)$

(d) $(5.76 \times 10^5) - (3.42 \times 10^4)$

(e) $(4.9 \times 10^{-2}) \times (5.6 \times 10^{-5})$

(f) $(4.2 \times 10^6) + (5.9 \times 10^5)$

2 (a) $\dfrac{6.3 \times 10^{11}}{3.6 \times 10^8}$

(b) $\dfrac{7.2 \times 10^9}{9.6 \times 10^3}$

(c) $(9.5 \times 10^7) \div (2.5 \times 10^{12})$

(d) $(2.1 \times 10^8) \div (7.5 \times 10^{-3})$

3 The mass of the moon is 7.343×10^{19} tonnes. The Earth has a mass 81 times bigger than that of the moon. Work out the mass of the Earth.

4 The Sun is a star. The nearest star to Earth beyond our solar system is *Proxima Centauri*, at a distance of 4.11×10^4 billion kilometres. Light travels at a speed of 3×10^5 km per second.

Remember:
1 billion $= 10^9$.

(a) Work out the time taken, in seconds, for light to travel from *Proxima Centauri* to Earth. Give your answer in standard form.

(b) Taking one year to be 365.25 days, change your answer to part (a) to years, giving your answer as an ordinary number, to 2 decimal places.

E 11.5 Converting recurring decimals to fractions

You can change recurring decimals into exact fractions.

Example 13

Find a fraction which is equivalent to $0.\dot{3}$.

Let $x = 0.\dot{3}$

so $x = 0.333\,333\ldots$ **(1)**

Multiply by 10:

$10x = 3.333\,333\ldots$ **(2)**

Subtract **(1)** from **(2)**

$$10x = 3.333\,333\ldots$$
$$-\quad x = 0.333\,333\ldots$$

so $9x = 3$

$$x = \frac{3}{9} = \frac{1}{3}$$

so $0.\dot{3}$ is equivalent to $\frac{1}{3}$.

> When there is one digit in the repeating pattern, you multiply by 10.

Example 14

Write the recurring decimal $0.\dot{2}\dot{7}$ as a fraction.

Let $x = 0.\dot{2}\dot{7}$

so $x = 0.272\,727\ldots$ **(1)**

Multiply by 100:

$100x = 27.272\,727\ldots$ **(2)**

Subtract **(1)** from **(2)**

$$100x = 27.272\,727\ldots$$
$$-\quad x = 0.272\,727\ldots$$

so $99x = 27$

$$x = \frac{27}{99} = \frac{3}{11}$$

so $0.\dot{2}\dot{7}$ is equivalent to $\frac{3}{11}$.

> When there are two digits in the repeating pattern, you multiply by 100.

Exercise 11E

Convert each recurring decimal to a fraction in its lowest terms.

1 $0.\dot{6}$ **2** $0.\dot{1}$ **3** $0.\dot{9}$

4 $0.0\dot{9}$ **5** $0.7\dot{1}$ **6** $0.\dot{7}$

7 $0.\dot{6}\dot{3}$ **8** $0.\dot{2}3\dot{4}$ **9** $0.7\dot{3}\dot{7}$

10 $0.\dot{1}4285\dot{7}$ (Hint: $\times\ 1\,000\,000$)   **11** $0.\dot{7}1428\dot{5}$

12 $0.\dot{0}7692\dot{3}$ **13** $0.0\dot{6}$ (Hint: $\times\ 10$)

14 $0.41\dot{6}$ **15** $0.4\dot{6}$

Summary of key points

1   A number given in standard form is written as $A \times 10^n$, where $1 \leqslant A < 10$ and n is an integer.

2   There are several prefixes that represent powers of 10:

         10^9 giga 10^{-2} centi

         10^6 mega 10^{-3} milli

         10^3 kilo 10^{-6} micro

                       10^{-9} nano

                       10^{-12} pico

E   You can multiply and divide numbers when they are in standard form in the normal way.

E   If you add or subtract two numbers in standard form you need to first change them to ordinary numbers.

12 Percentages

12.1 Revision

In this section you will revise some of the topics you have already met.

Example 1

Find the new amount when 35 kg is increased by 3%.

New amount $= \left(1 + \frac{3}{100}\right)$ of the original amount

$$= \tfrac{103}{100} \text{ of the original amount}$$
$$= 1.03 \times 35\,\text{kg}$$
$$= 36.05\,\text{kg}$$

Example 2

The human population of the world in 2001 was estimated to be 6.1 billion. It is forecast to increase to 7 billion by 2015. Calculate the forecasted percentage increase in world population between 2001 and 2015.

$$\text{Increase in population} = 7 \times 10^9 - 6.1 \times 10^9$$
$$= 0.9 \times 10^9$$
$$= 9 \times 10^8$$

so

$$\text{Percentage increase} = \frac{9 \times 10^8}{6.1 \times 10^9} \times 100\%$$
$$= 0.15 \times 100\%$$
$$= 15\% \text{ to the nearest } 1\%.$$

Exercise 12A

1 Change these decimals and fractions to percentages:
  (a) 0.12 **(b)** 0.7 **(c)** 0.04 **(d)** 0.382
  (e) $\frac{9}{10}$ **(f)** $\frac{2}{5}$ **(g)** $\frac{7}{25}$ **(h)** $\frac{5}{8}$

2 Find the new amount when:

(a) £575 is increased by 6%

(b) £86 is decreased by 9%

(c) 16 litres is increased by 35%

(d) 5.4 kg is decreased by 5%

(e) £56 is increased by 17.5%

(f) 32.8 kg is decreased by 12.5%

3 Write down the decimal number you should multiply the original amount by when it is:

(a) increased by 2%   (b) decreased by 2%

(c) increased by 13%   (d) decreased by 13%

(e) increased by 8.5%   (f) decreased by 8.5%

(g) increased by 17.5%   (h) decreased by 17.5%

4 Yasmine earns £310 a week working in an office. She is given a 3% pay rise. Work out Yasmine's new weekly wage.

5 In a sale all the usual prices were reduced by 14%. Find the sale price of a CD usually priced at £12.

6 Amelia gained 73 marks out of 80 for the French test and 54 marks out of 60 for the History test.

(a) Change the marks to percentages.

(b) In which test did Amelia do best?

7 In the German test Sean gained 69 marks out of 75, in the Maths test he gained 76 out of 80 and in the Geography test he had 47 out of 50.

(a) Convert Sean's test marks to percentages.

(b) Write down his results in order, starting with the highest.

8 Woody is a painter and decorator. After putting an advert in the newspaper, he notices the number of telephone enquiries he receives rises from 5 per week to 18 per week. What is the percentage increase in the number of calls Woody receives?

9 Bonnie is an art teacher. In April she bought a set of acrylic paints for £32. In September she bought 5 sets at a discounted price for a total of £136. Calculate the percentage discount Bonnie received on each set of paints in September.

10 Estimates suggest that in the next 10–20 years the number of species of living primates will drop from 620 to 500. What percentage of the number of primate species alive today do the estimates suggest will be extinct in 10–20 years?

11 Jochem is paid an annual salary of $35 000. At the time he decides to change jobs the exchange rates are:

£1 = $1.5 = € 1.6

He receives offers for two jobs with salary

(a) £26 000
(b) € 37 000

Calculate the percentage increase or decrease in Jochem's salary in each case.

12.2 Percentages and money

You have already learnt about profit and loss, taxation, buying on credit and simple interest. In this section you will revise these topics.

Example 3

VAT at $17\frac{1}{2}\%$ is added to a telephone bill of £59.26.
Work out the total amount to be paid.

VAT = 17.5% of £59.26 = 0.175 × £59.26 = £10.3705
$\qquad$ = £10.37 (to the nearest penny)

Total cost = £59.26 + £10.37 = £69.63 (to the nearest penny)

Example 4

Mrs Shaw's taxable income for the year 2001–2002 was £31 240.

Calculate the amount of income tax Mrs Shaw paid that year.

For the tax year 6 April 2001–5 April 2002 income tax was paid on taxable income at these rates:

Taxable income	Rate of income tax
Up to £1880	10%
£1881–£29 400	22%
Over £29 400	40%

Step 1:
Tax on the first £1880 of taxable income
at 10% = 10% of £1880 = 0.10×1880 = £188

Step 2:
The amount of taxable income to be taxed at 22% is £29 400 − £1880 = £27 520

Tax on the next £27 520 of taxable income
at 22% = 22% of £27 520 = $0.22 \times 27\,520$ = £6054.40

Step 3:
The amount of taxable income to be taxed at 40% is £31 240 − £29 400 = £1840

Tax on the remaining £1840 of taxable income
at 40% = 40% of £1840 = 0.40×1840 = £736

Total tax = £188 + £6054.40 + £736 = £6978.40

Total tax paid by Mrs Shaw = £6978

Pence are ignored in calculating total income tax!

Example 5

Tina invests £350 for 5 years at an interest rate of 4.5% per annum. Calculate the simple interest she earns.

Interest for 1 year = 4.5% of £350
$= 0.045 \times £350 = £15.75$

Simple interest for 5 years = £15.75 × 5 = £78.75

Per annum (or p.a.) means 'each year'.

Remember:
$4.5\% = \dfrac{4.5}{100} = 0.045$

Exercise 12B

In questions 3, 4, 5 and 6 take the VAT rate to be $17\frac{1}{2}\%$.

1 Michael bough some jeans from a wholesaler for £18.50 a pair. He sold them in his shop and made a 36% profit. What is the selling price of each pair of jeans?

2 Helen bought a bicycle for £372. She later sold it for £250. Calculate her percentage loss, correct to 1 decimal place.

3 Calculate the VAT on a £32.40 bill for a meal for four.

4 Two stores advertise the same computer.
    (a) Which is the cheaper price, including VAT?
    (b) What is the difference in the prices, including VAT?

PC UNIVERSE

£912 +VAT at 17½%

£1036 Inclusive of VAT

STAR computers

5 Matthew's taxable income for 2001–2002 was £14 600. Using the rates for income tax given on page 252 work out how much income tax Matthew paid.

6 Calculate the amount of income tax paid for the year 2001–2002 on these taxable incomes:
    (a) £6580   **(b)** £23 400   **(c)** £42 500

For questions **7** and **8** work out:
(a) the total cost of buying on credit
(b) the difference between the cash price and the cost of buying on credit.

7 A camera costs £140. The credit agreement requires a deposit of 15% and 12 monthly payments of £11.95.

8 A video recorder costs £216. It can be bought on credit with a deposit of 18% followed by 24 monthly payments of £8.69.

9 Robin invested £185 in a savings account at 4.2% per annum. She earned £38.85 simple interest. For how long did Robin invest the £185?

10 Find how much Fred borrowed if the simple interest at a rate of 8.3% p.a. he had to pay after 4 years was £929.60.

12.3 Finding the original amount after a percentage change

You may be told an amount which is the result of a percentage increase or decrease. This section shows how to work out the original amount before the percentage change.

Example 6

The price of a CD player was reduced by 10% to £76.59. What was the original price?

$(100\% - 10\%)$ of the original price $= £76.59$

$\quad\quad$ 90% of the original price $= £76.59$

So $\quad\quad\quad 0.9 \times$ original price $= £76.59$

$\quad\quad\quad\quad$ original price $= £76.59 \div 0.9$

$\quad\quad\quad\quad\quad\quad\quad = £85.10$

$100\% - 10\%$
$= 90\% = \frac{90}{100} = 0.9$

Divide both sides by 0.9

Check:
You would expect this to be more than £76.59.

The original price of the CD player was £85.10

Example 7

The price of a computer is £799 including VAT at 17.5%. Work out the price of the computer excluding VAT.

$(100\% + 17.5\%)$ of the price excluding VAT
$=$ the price including VAT

$100\% + 17.5\%$
$= 117.5\% = \frac{117.5}{100}$
$= 1.175$

So $1.175 \times$ the price excluding VAT $= £799$
$\quad\quad\quad\quad$ original price $= £799 \div 1.175$
$\quad\quad\quad\quad\quad\quad\quad = £680$

Divide both sides by 1.175

Check:
You would expect this to be less than £799.

The price of the computer excluding VAT is £680.

■ **If an original amount is increased by $R\%$ to become a new amount,**

$$\text{the original amount} = \text{the new amount} \div \frac{100 + R}{100}$$

Before working this out, change $\dfrac{100 + R}{100}$ to a decimal.

If $R\% = 4\%$, divide the new amount by 1.04.

■ **If an original amount is decreased by R% to become a new amount,**

the original amount = the new amount ÷ $\dfrac{100 - R}{100}$

Before working this out, change $\dfrac{100 - R}{100}$ to a decimal.

If $R\% = 24\%$, divide the new amount by 0.76.

Exercise 12C

1 Dan's weekly wage has increased by 3% to £247.20. Work out his weekly wage before the increase.

2 The price of a jacket is £33 after a reduction of 25%. What was the price before the reduction?

3 The cost of a train ticket has risen by 5% to £16.80. What was the original price of the ticket?

4 Rezena sold her motorbike for £1554, making a loss of 16% of the price she paid. Work out the price Rezena paid.

5 A piece of elastic was stretched by 28% to a length of 32 cm. Calculate its unstretched original length.

6 The weight of a cake was 760 g after Jade had eaten 20% of it. What was the original weight of the cake?

7 The price of a printer is £305.50 including VAT at $17\frac{1}{2}\%$. Work out the price of the printer excluding VAT.

8 The price of a sleeping bag has been reduced by $12\frac{1}{2}\%$ to £42 in a sale. What was the original price?

9 The price of a television has increased by $6\frac{1}{4}\%$ to £382.50. Work out the price of the television before the increase.

10 Rachel bought a train ticket using a railcard and was given a discount of 32.5%. She paid £30.24 for her ticket. Calculate the usual price of the ticket, without the discount.

11 Work out the missing values and complete the table.

	Original price	New price	Increase %
(a)	£65		14%
(b)		£47.70	6%
(c)	£80	£96	

12 Calculate the missing values and complete the table.

	Original weight	New weight	Loss %
(a)		244.8 kg	4%
(b)	92 kg		12.5%
(c)	64 kg	61.92 kg	

E ## 12.4 Repeated percentage change

When there is a repeated percentage change over several years, a more complex method is often used to calculate the final amount. The gain (or loss) is worked out for the first year and added to (or subtracted from) the original amount. The gain (or loss) for the second year is then worked out as a percentage of the new amount and added to (or subtracted from) the new amount, and so on.

Example 8

Kerry bought a car for £8950. Each year the car depreciates by 12% of its value at the beginning of the year. Calculate the value of the car after 3 years.

Loss in value = 12% each year
so the value after one year is 100% − 12% = 88% of £8950
$$= £8950 \times 0.88$$
$$= £7876$$

The value after two years   = 88% of the value after one year
$$= £7876 \times 0.88$$
$$= £6930.88$$

The value after three years $= 88\%$ of the value after two years

$$= \pounds6930.88 \times 0.88$$

$$= \pounds6099.1744$$

$$= \pounds6099.17 \text{ (to the nearest penny)}$$

Compound interest

Usually when you invest or borrow money you earn or pay **compound interest**.

- **The compound interest for any year is interest paid on the total of the sum of money invested and the interest earned in previous years.**
  The compound interest over several years is the total of the compound interest earned for each year.

Example 9

Calculate the compound interest earned when £350 is invested for 2 years at an interest rate of 4.5% p.a. The interest is paid every year.

Interest for first year $\quad = 4.5\%$ of £350

$$= 0.045 \times \pounds350$$

$$= \pounds15.75$$

Amount after one year $\quad = \pounds350 + \pounds15.75$

$$= \pounds365.75$$

Interest for second year $= 4.5\%$ of £365.75

$$= 0.045 \times \pounds365.75$$

$$= \pounds16.458\,75$$

The total compound interest earned $= \pounds15.75 + \pounds16.458\,75$

$$= \pounds32.208\,75$$

The compound interest $= \pounds32.21$ (to the nearest penny)

Here is an alternative way of finding the answer to Example **9**.

The interest is 4.5% each year
so the amount after one year $= 104.5\%$ of £350

$$= 1.045 \times £350$$
$$= £365.75$$

The amount after two years $= 104.5\%$ of £365.75
$$= 1.045 \times £365.75$$
$$= £382.208\,75$$

Total compound interest $=$ the amount after 2 years $-$ original amount invested
$$= £382.208\,75 - £350$$
$$= £32.20875$$
$$= £32.21 \text{ (to the nearest penny)}$$

Exercise 12D

1   A clarinet is bought for £320. If its value increases each year by 15% of its value at the beginning of the year, what will its value be after two years?

2   The value of a secondhand car is £8000. Each year the value decreases by 10% of the value at the beginning of the year. Calculate the value of the car in three years' time.

3   A new hedge trimmer costs £84. With depreciation, its value falls each year by 15% of its value at the beginning of the year. Work out the value of the hedge trimmer after two years.

4   £350 is invested for 2 years at 6% per annum compound interest, paid yearly. Work out the total interest earned.

5   £6000 is invested for 3 years at 5% per annum compound interest, paid annually. What is the total interest earned?

6   £1000 is borrowed for 4 years at 10% p.a. compound interest, charged annually. Calculate the total interest paid.

7 £800 is borrowed for 2 years at $9\frac{1}{2}\%$ p.a. compound interest, charged yearly. Work out the total interest charged.

8 £250 is invested for 3 years at 6.4% per annum compound interest, paid annually. Calculate the total interest earned, giving your answer to the nearest penny.

Summary of key points

1 If an original amount is increased by $R\%$ to become a new amount,

the original amount = the new amount $\div \dfrac{100 + R}{100}$

Before working this out, change $\dfrac{100 + R}{100}$ to a decimal.

2 If an original amount is decreased by $R\%$ to become a new amount,

the original amount = the new amount $\div \dfrac{100 - R}{100}$

Before working this out, change $\dfrac{100 - R}{100}$ to a decimal.

E The compound interest for any year is interest paid on the total of the sum of money invested and the interest earned in previous years.
The compound interest over several years is the total of the compound interest earned for each year.

13 Pythagoras' theorem

Pythagoras' theorem tells you about the lengths of the sides of a right-angled triangle. This is useful because right-angled triangles appear everywhere in the world around you.

13.1 Right-angled triangles

In any triangle, the longest side is the side opposite the largest angle.

In a right-angled triangle the right angle is the largest angle. So the longest side is the side opposite the right angle. This is called the **hypotenuse**.

Exercise 13A

1   The diagram shows a right-angled triangle with squares drawn on each of its sides.

   (a) Find the number of small squares inside the red square drawn on the hypotenuse.

   (b) Find the number of small squares inside each of the squares drawn on the other two sides.

   (c) Find a relationship between your answers to **(a)** and **(b)**.

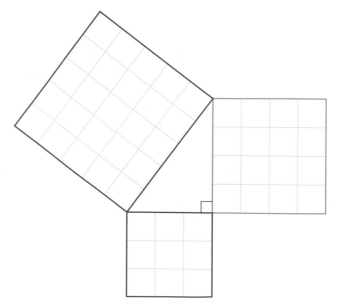

2   Repeat Question **1** for this right-angled triangle.

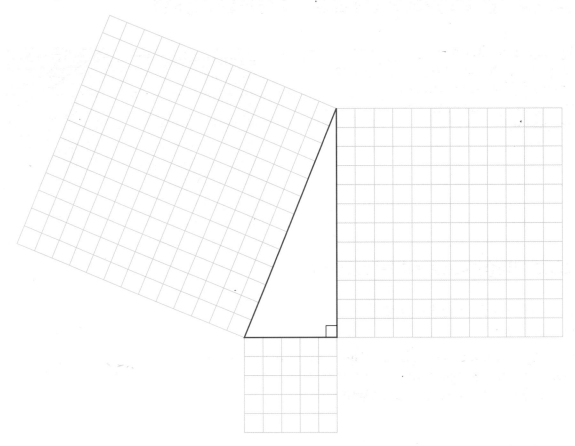

3   The diagrams show two tiling patterns. The red triangles are right-angled and isosceles. Squares have been drawn on each of their sides.

(**i**) Find the number of small triangles inside each of the squares.

(**ii**) Find a relationship between your answers to (**i**).

(**a**)

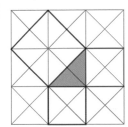

(**b**)

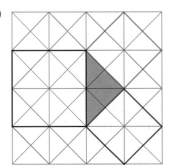

13.2 Pythagoras' theorem

In Exercise 13A, you found this result:

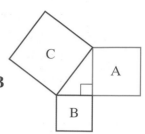

■ **In a right-angled triangle, the area of the square drawn on the hypotenuse is equal to the sum of the areas of the squares drawn on the other two sides.**

   area of square C = area of square A + area of square B

   This result is Pythagoras' theorem.

Pythagoras was a Greek mathematician, who lived in the sixth century BC. The theorem, or rule, which bears his name was known to the Egyptians over a thousand years before his time but it is possible that Pythagoras, or one of his followers, was the first to *prove* it.

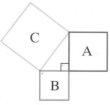

Example 1

The area of square A is 21 cm^2 and the area of square C is 33 cm^2.

Work out the area of square B:

Using Pythagoras' theorem,

   area of square C = area of square A + area of square B

   33 = 21 + area of square B

so area of square B = 33 − 21

   = 12 cm^2

Exercise 13B

1   Copy and complete the table.

Area of square A	Area of square B	Area of square C
17 cm²	8 cm²	
11 cm²		24 cm²
	7 cm²	19 cm²
13 cm²	20 cm²	
	15 cm²	29 cm²

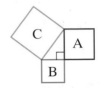

2   Three squares have areas of 6 cm², 17 cm² and 11 cm².
   (a) Will the squares exactly surround a right-angled triangle?
   (b) Explain your answer.

3   Three squares have areas of 13 cm², 10 cm² and 22 cm².
   (a) Will the squares exactly surround a right-angled triangle?
   (b) Explain your answer.

4   The area of a square drawn on the hypotenuse of a right-angled, isosceles triangle is 24 cm². Work out the areas of the squares drawn on each of the other two sides.

5   Three squares exactly surround a right-angled triangle. The areas of two of the squares are 5 cm² and 12 cm². Work out the **two** possible areas of the third square.

6   (a) Measure the lengths of the sides of these squares and find their areas.
   (b) Will the squares exactly surround a right-angled triangle?

13.3 Finding lengths using Pythagoras' theorem

Pythagoras' theorem is mainly used for finding the length of the third side of a right-angled triangle if the lengths of the other two sides are known. For this, it is more useful if the theorem is stated in terms of the lengths of the sides of the triangle.

Consider a right-angled triangle with sides of lengths a, b and c, where c is the length of hypotenuse.

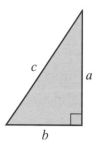

Draw squares on each of its sides.

These squares have areas a^2, b^2 and c^2.

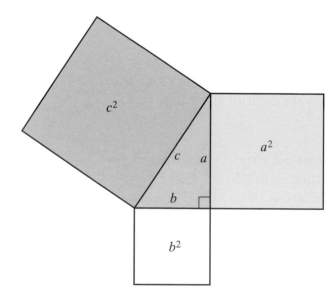

■ **For any right-angled triangle with sides of length a, b and c, where c is the length of the hypotenuse**

$$c^2 = a^2 + b^2$$

This is often the most useful way of writing Pythagoras' theorem.

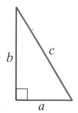

Example 2

Calculate the length x in this right-angled triangle.

Using Pythagoras' theorem,

$$x^2 = 8^2 + 5^2$$
$$x^2 = 64 + 25$$
$$x^2 = 89$$
$$x = \sqrt{89}$$
$$x = 9.43 \text{ cm (to 3 s.f.)}$$

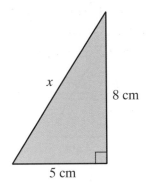

If you need to find the length of the hypotenuse or the length of one of the other sides, always start by writing down the square of the hypotenuse, whether it is a letter or a number, and then write down an equals sign.

Example 3

Calculate the length y in this right-angled triangle.

Using Pythagoras' theorem,

$$8^2 = 5^2 + y^2$$
$$64 = 25 + y^2$$
$$y^2 = 64 - 25$$
$$y^2 = 39$$
$$y = \sqrt{39}$$
$$y = 6.24 \text{ cm (to 3 s.f.)}$$

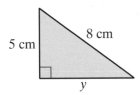

Example 4

Calculate the vertical height of this isosceles triangle.

Let D be the mid-point of BC.
AD bisects the base BC, i.e. $BD = CD = 6$ cm

Using Pythagoras' theorem,

$$AB^2 = AD^2 + BD^2$$
$$10^2 = AD^2 + 6^2$$
$$100 = AD^2 + 36$$
$$AD^2 = 100 - 36$$
$$AD^2 = 64$$
$$AD = \sqrt{64}$$
$$AD = 8 \text{ cm}$$

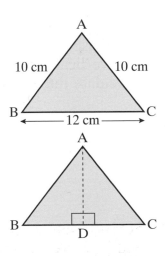

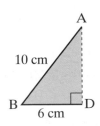

Exercise 13C

1   Calculate the length of each of the sides marked with a
    letter.

(a)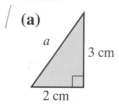
a 3 cm 2 cm

(b)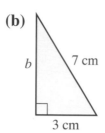
b 7 cm 3 cm

(c)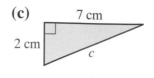
7 cm 2 cm c

(d)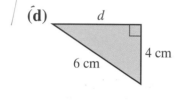
d 4 cm 6 cm

(e)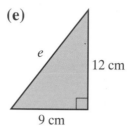
e 12 cm 9 cm

(f)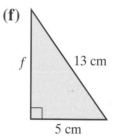
f 13 cm 5 cm

(g)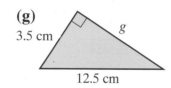
3.5 cm g 12.5 cm

(h)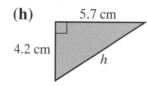
5.7 cm 4.2 cm h

(i)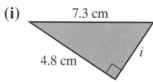
7.3 cm 4.8 cm i

2   A rectangle is 8 cm long and 4 cm wide.
    Calculate the length of a diagonal.

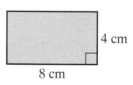
4 cm

8 cm

3   In the isosceles triangle PQR, PQ = PR = 9 cm.
    The vertical height, PS, of the triangle is 7 cm.
    Calculate the length of the base, QR.

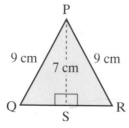

P

9 cm 7 cm 9 cm

Q S R

4   The sides of an equilateral triangle are 8 cm long.
    Calculate the vertical height of the triangle.

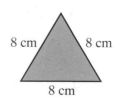
8 cm 8 cm

8 cm

5 The diagram shows a right-angled triangle DEG.
F is a point on EG.
DE = 5 cm, FG = 9 cm and DG = 13 cm.
(**a**) Calculate the length of EF.
(**b**) Calculate the length of DF.

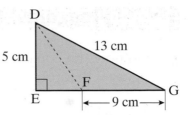

6 The diagram shows a rhombus ABCD.
The length of the diagonal AC is 32 cm.
The length of the diagonal BD is 24 cm.
Calculate the length of a side of the rhombus.
(The diagonals of a rhombus bisect each other and
intersect at right angles.)

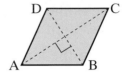

7 The diagram shows a kite JKLM.
JK = JM = 4 cm. KL = LM = 8 cm.
The length of the diagonal KM is 6 cm.
Calculate the length of the other diagonal JL.

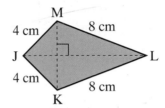

8 The diagram shows a trapezium ABCD.
AB = 10 cm, CD = 6 cm and AD = 5 cm.
Calculate the length of BC.

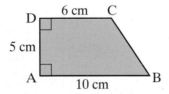

9 The diagram shows a circle, centre O.
The radius of the circle is 9 cm.
XY is a chord and XY = 14 cm.
M is the mid-point of the chord XY.
Calculate the perpendicular distance, OM, from the
chord to the centre of the circle.

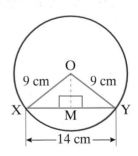

10 The diagram shows an isosceles trapezium.
PS = QR and PQ is parallel to SR.
PQ = 13 cm and SR = 7 cm. The vertical height
of the trapezium is 4 cm.
Calculate the perimeter of the trapezium.

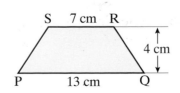

13.4 Pythagoras' theorem and coordinates

If you know the coordinates of two points, you can use Pythagoras' theorem to find the distance between them.

Example 5

P is the point with coordinates $(2, 1)$ and Q is the point with coordinates $(9, 5)$.

Calculate the length of the line PQ.

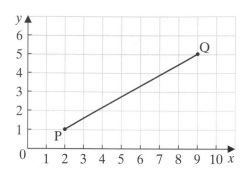

First construct triangle PQR, where the angle at R is $90°$.

Now you need to find the lengths of the lines PR and QR.

PR is parallel to the x-axis so you subtract the x-coordinate of P from the x-coordinate of R:

$$PR = 9 - 2 = 7 \text{ units.}$$

QR is parallel to the y-axis so you subtract the y-coordinate of R from the y-coordinate of Q:

$$QR = 5 - 1 = 4 \text{ units.}$$

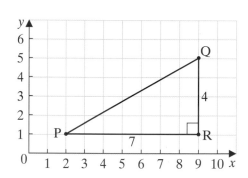

Using Pythagoras' theorem,

$$PQ^2 = PR^2 + QR^2$$
$$PQ^2 = 7^2 + 4^2$$
$$PQ^2 = 49 + 16$$
$$PQ^2 = 65$$

So $PQ = 8.06$ units (to 3 s.f.)

This result can be generalised:

■ **The distance between two points with coordinates (x_1, y_1) and (x_2, y_2) is**
$$\sqrt{(x_2 - x_1)^2 + (y_2 - y_1)^2}$$

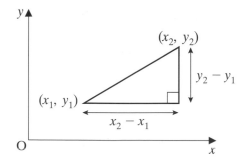

It is easy to make mistakes when using this formula with negative coordinates. To help avoid errors you should sketch a diagram of the points in their relative positions (it need not be on squared paper). Then sketch a right-angled triangle so you can use Pythagoras' theorem.

Example 6

Calculate the distance between the points with coordinates $(4, 2)$ and $(-5, 6)$.

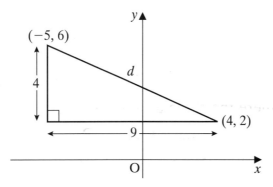

Using Pythagoras' theorem,

$$d^2 = 4^2 + 9^2$$
$$d^2 = 16 + 81$$
$$d^2 = 97$$
$$d = 9.85$$

The distance between the two points is 9.85 units (to 3 s.f.)

Example 7

A is the point with coordinates $(3, 2)$ and
B is the point with coordinates $(11, 8)$.
The line AB is a diameter of a circle.

(a) Calculate the length of AB.
(b) Find the coordinates of the centre of the circle.

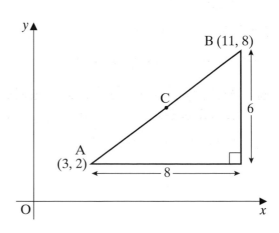

(a) Using Pythagoras' theorem

$$AB^2 = 8^2 + 6^2$$
$$AB^2 = 64 + 36$$
$$AB^2 = 100$$
$$AB = 10 \text{ units}$$

(b) The mid-point, C, of AB, is the centre of the circle.

x-coordinate of C $= 3 + \dfrac{8}{2} = 3 + 4 = 7$

The midpoint of the line is half way along and half way up.

y-coordinate of C $= 2 + \dfrac{6}{2} = 2 + 3 = 5$

The centre of the circle is at (7, 5).

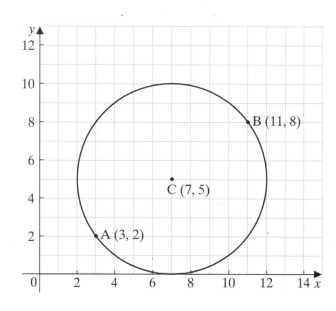

Notice that $7 = \dfrac{11 + 3}{2}$, i.e. the x-coordinate of the mid-point of AB, is the mean of the x-coordinate of A and the x-coordinate of B.

Similarly, $5 = \dfrac{8 + 2}{2}$, i.e. the y-coordinate of the mid-point of AB, is the mean of the y-coordinate of A and the y-coordinate of B.

■ **If a line joins two points with coordinates (x_1, y_1) and (x_2, y_2), the coordinates of the mid-point of the line are $\left(\dfrac{x_1 + x_2}{2}, \dfrac{y_1 + y_2}{2}\right).$**

Exercise 13D

1 Calculate the distance between each pair of points.

(a) $(3, 4)$ and $(8, 7)$ (b) $(1, 5)$ and $(7, 2)$
(c) $(-3, 1)$ and $(2, 5)$ (d) $(-4, 2)$ and $(2, -3)$
(e) $(-5, -1)$ and $(3, 2)$ (f) $(1, -6)$ and $(5, -2)$

Remember:
Always draw a
diagram.

2 P is the point with coordinates $(2, 1)$ and Q is the point with coordinates $(14, 17)$. The line PQ is a diameter of a circle.

(a) Calculate the length of PQ.
(b) Find the coordinates of the centre of the circle.

3 Find the coordinates of the mid-point of the line joining each pair of points.

(a) $(4, 3)$ and $(8, 7)$ (b) $(8, 5)$ and $(-2, 3)$
(c) $(4, 9)$ and $(-4, -3)$ (d) $(6, 7)$ and $(-8, 1)$
(e) $(3, 1)$ and $(-5, -7)$ (f) $(-3, -7)$ and $(0, -8)$

4 The centre of a circle is at $(2, 6)$. The point with coordinates $(5, 10)$ lies on the circumference of the circle. Calculate the radius of the circle.

5 The centre of a circle is at $(3, 1)$. The radius of the circle is 6 units. Work out whether each of these points lie inside, outside or on the circle.

(a) $(7, 6)$ (b) $(3, 7)$ (c) $(5, 3)$ (d) $(9, 1)$

E 13.5 Perigal's dissection

There are over 200 different proofs of Pythagoras' theorem. Some of them are based on 'dissections', where one or two of the squares are cut into pieces, which are then rearranged. One of the most famous of these is Perigal's dissection.

Exercise 13E Perigal's dissection

You will need a piece of plain paper or card and scissors.

(a) Draw a right-angled triangle.
(b) Draw squares on each of its sides.
(c) Find the centre of the second largest square by drawing its diagonals.
(d) Draw two lines, shown dotted, through the centre, one parallel to the hypotenuse of the triangle and the other one perpendicular to it.
(e) Cut out the second largest square and cut it into four pieces along the dotted lines.
(f) Cut out the smallest square.
(g) Reassemble the five pieces you have cut out to make the largest square.

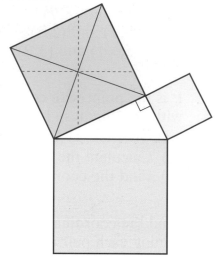

E 13.6 Problems

You can now solve problems involving Pythagoras' theorem. Example **8** lists the steps in solving a typical problem.

Example 8

A ladder 7 m long leans against a wall so that the top of the ladder is 5 m from the ground. How far is the foot of the ladder from the wall?

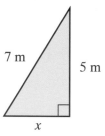

Draw a diagram showing the information in the question. You can use a letter to represent the distance you need to find.

Using Pythagoras' theorem,

$$7^2 = x^2 + 5^2$$
$$49 = x^2 + 25$$
$$x^2 = 49 - 25$$
$$x^2 = 24$$
$$x = \sqrt{24}$$
$$x = 4.90$$

Use Pythagoras' theorem.

State your answer, including the units.

The foot of the ladder is 4.90 m (to 3 s.f.) from the wall.

Exercise 13F

1   A ladder 7 m long leans against a wall so that the foot of the ladder is 3 m from the wall. How far is the top of the ladder above the ground?

2   The foot of a ladder is 2 m from a wall and the top of the ladder is 6 m above the ground. Calculate the length of the ladder.

3   A man walks 4 km East and 5 km North. Calculate his distance from his starting point.

4   In a right-angled triangle, the hypotenuse is 8 cm long. One of the other sides is 3 cm long. Calculate the length of the third side.

5   A badminton court is a rectangle 13.4 m long and 6.1 m wide. Calculate the distance between opposite corners.

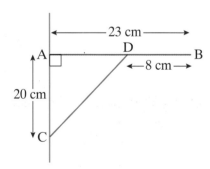

6   The lengths of two of the sides of a right-angled triangle are 3 cm and 4 cm. Calculate the two possible lengths of the third side.

7   A rope 10 m long is stretched from the top of a flag pole, which is 9 m high, to a peg in the ground. How far is the peg from the foot of the pole?

8   The diagram shows a horizontal shelf AB. The shelf is fixed to a vertical wall at A. The support CD is fixed to the wall at C and to the shelf at D. AB = 23 cm, AC = 20 cm and BD = 8 cm. Calculate the length of CD.

9   The diagram shows a support strut for a roof. XZ = YZ = 6 m. XY = 10 m. M is the mid-point of XY. Calculate the length of MZ.

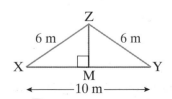

10   ABCD represents one end of a garden shed.
     AB = 2.30 m, AD = 2.25 m and BC = 3.15 m.
     Calculate

     (a) the length of CD,
     (b) the perimeter of ABCD.

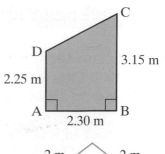
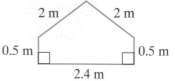

11   The diagram shows the cross-section of a tent.
     Calculate the height of the top of the tent above
     the ground.

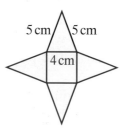

12   The diagonals of a square are 10 cm long. Calculate the
     length of the sides of the square.

13   ABC is a triangle.
     Name the type of angle at *C* if
     (a) $c^2 = a^2 + b^2$
     (b) $c^2 < a^2 + b^2$
     (c) $c^2 > a^2 + b^2$

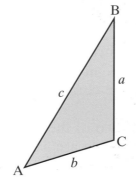

14   The diagram shows the net of a square-based pyramid.
     It consists of a square with sides 4 cm long and four
     isosceles triangles whose equal sides are 5 cm long.
     Calculate the total area of the net.

15   The lengths of the diagonals of a rhombus are 8 cm and
     10 cm. Calculate the length of the sides of the rhombus.

16   The diagram shows the plan of a room.
     Calculate the perimeter of the room.

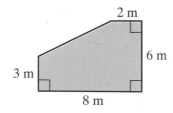

E 13.7 Pythagorean triples

The three **whole** numbers 3, 4 and 5 satisfy Pythagoras' theorem because

$$3^2 + 4^2 = 5^2$$

For this reason, [3, 4, 5] is called a **Pythagorean triple**.

$$\begin{aligned} 3^2 + 4^2 &= 9 + 16 \\ &= 25 \\ &= 5^2 \end{aligned}$$

■ **A Pythagorean triple is three distinct, positive integers that satisfy Pythagoras' theorem. The numbers are written in square brackets in ascending order of size.**

'Distinct' means 'different'.

Example 9

Show that [12, 16, 20] is a Pythagorean triple.

$$\begin{aligned} 12^2 + 16^2 &= 144 + 256 \\ &= 400 \end{aligned}$$

so $\quad 12^2 + 16^2 = 20^2$

therefore [12, 16, 20] is a Pythagorean triple.

Exercise 13G

1 Show that each of these is a Pythagorean triple.
   (a) [6, 8, 10]   **(b)** [5, 12, 13]   **(c)** [8, 15, 17]   **(d)** [9, 40, 41]

2 Each of the following is a Pythagorean triple.
   Work out the value of x in each case.
   (a) [7, 24, x]   **(b)** [x, 30, 34]   **(c)** [11, x, 61]

3 The expressions
   $$2nm, n^2 - m^2, n^2 + m^2$$
   where n and m are positive integers and $n > m$ generate Pythagorean triples.
   Work out the Pythagorean triple generated when
   (a) $n = 2, m = 1$ **(b)** $n = 5, m = 3$ **(c)** $n = 8, m = 5$

   The positive integers are 1, 2, 3, 4, ...

   In each case check your results by substituting into Pythagoras' formula.

   (d) Generate two more Pythagorean triples by substituting you own values of m and n.

4 You already know that [3, 4, 5] and [6, 8, 10] are Pythagorean triples.

(a) Show that [9, 12, 15] and [12, 16, 20] are also Pythagorean triples.

(b) What do you notice about these four sets of integers?

(c) Show that [15, 20, 25] is a Pythagorean triple.

You are told that $[x, y, z]$ is a Pythagorean triple.

(d) Write down an equation involving x, y and z.

(e) Investigate the numbers nx, ny and nz where n is a positive integer.

(f) What can you say about multiples of Pythagorean triples? Check your answer with some examples.

Summary of key points

1 In a right-angled triangle, the area of the square drawn on the hypotenuse is equal to the sum of the areas of the squares drawn on the other two sides.

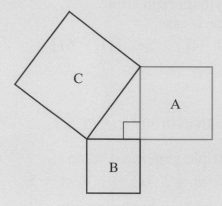

area of square C = area of square A + area of square B

This result is Pythagoras' theorem.

2 For any right-angled triangle with sides of length a, b and c, where c is the length of the hypotenuse

$$c^2 = a^2 + b^2$$

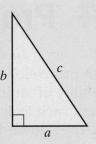

3 The distance between two points with coordinates (x_1, y_1) and (x_2, y_2)

is $\sqrt{(x_2 - x_1)^2 + (y_2 - y_1)^2}$

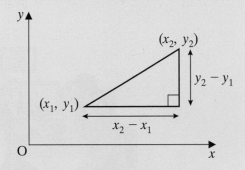

4 If a line joins two points with coordinates (x_1, y_1) and (x_2, y_2), the coordinates of the mid-point of the line are $\left(\dfrac{x_1 + x_2}{2}, \dfrac{y_1 + y_2}{2} \right)$.

E A Pythagorean triple is three distinct, positive integers that satisfy Pythagoras' theorem. The numbers are written in square brackets in ascending order of size.

14 Probability

Health professionals use research results to model the probability of an individual developing a particular health problem such as lung cancer. The professional can then advise the patient how they could reduce the risk of the disease, for example by giving up smoking.

14.1 Calculating probabilities

You will remember the following from your earlier work in probability.

■ **The probability that something will happen is:**

$$P(\text{event}) = \frac{\text{number of successful outcomes}}{\text{total number of possible outcomes}}$$

■ **The probabilities of all the possible outcomes of an event add up to 1.**

■ **P(event not happening) = 1 − P(event happening)**

Example 1

A card is chosen at random from an ordinary deck of playing cards.

Write the probability as a fraction that:
(a) a diamond is chosen,
(b) a Jack is chosen,
(c) a red three is chosen.

(a) P(diamond) $= \frac{13}{52} = \frac{1}{4}$

(b) P(Jack) $= \frac{4}{52} = \frac{1}{13}$

(c) P(red three) $= \frac{2}{52} = \frac{1}{26}$

> Remember:
> Write fractions in
> their simplest form.

Example 2

(a) Write the probability of getting each of the colours on the spinner as a fraction, decimal and percentage.

(b) What should you change so that the probability that you will not get red is 0?

(a)

Colour	Fraction	Decimal	Percentage
red	$\frac{2}{4} = \frac{1}{2}$	0.5	50%
yellow	$\frac{1}{4}$	0.25	25%
blue	$\frac{1}{4}$	0.25	25%

> Remember:
> Probabilities can be
> written as fractions,
> decimals or
> percentages.

(b) If you want P(not red) = 0, then P(red) = 1 so the spinner must be completely red.

Exercise 14A

1   Paul chooses a member for his team from the group shown. Each person is equally likely to be chosen. What is the probability that:

(a) he chooses a person with black hair?

(b) he chooses a boy?

(c) he does not choose a boy?

(d) he chooses a girl in a white T-shirt?

(e) he does not choose someone in shorts?

Paul's friend Katie joins the group.

(f) What is the probability now that Paul chooses a boy?

2   A ten-sided spinner is spun. Its sides are numbered
    1 to 10. What is the probability of:
    (a) getting an odd number?
    (b) getting a prime number?
    (c) not getting a multiple of 3?

3   Mary needs to decide how to stock the petfood shelves
    in a supermarket. In the table you can see the
    probabilities of customers choosing a particular brand
    based on the total sales of cat food in a year.

Brand	Probability it is chosen
Miaow Munch	0.25
Kitty-Bites	0.42
Mr Tom	0.28
Sam's Scrum	0.05

(a) What is the percentage probability that Sam's
        Scrum is chosen?

(b) What is the probability that Mr Tom is not chosen?

(c) Which do you think is the most popular cat food
        and why?

14.2 Combined events

When two events happen at the same time, you can use
sample space diagrams to show all the possible outcomes.

Example 3

(a) Draw a sample space to show all the possible
        outcomes when these two spinners are spun.

(b) How many possible outcomes are there?

(c) What is the probability of getting two
        identical numbers?

(d) What is the probability of getting a total less
        than 5 if the scores are added?

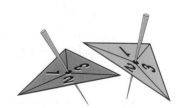

(a)

Green spinner	3	(1, 3)	(2, 3)	(3, 3)
	2	(1, 2)	(2, 2)	(3, 2)
	1	(1, 1)	(2, 1)	(3, 1)
		1	2	3

Red spinner

The outcomes are like coordinates. (3, 2) means the score was 3 on the red and 2 on the green.

(b) There are 9 possible outcomes.

(c) P(two identical numbers)

$$= \frac{\text{number of cases of two identical numbers}}{\text{total number of possible outcomes}} = \frac{3}{9} = \frac{1}{3}$$

(d) There are six outcomes where the sum of the scores is less than 5 so

$$P(\text{total score less than } 5) = \frac{6}{9} = \frac{2}{3}$$

For **(d)** the outcomes (1, 1) (1, 2) (1, 3) (2, 1) (2, 2) (3, 1) give a total score of less than 5.

■ **When two events happen independently you can show all the possible outcomes on a sample space diagram.**

Independently means the outcome of one event doesn't affect the outcome of the other.

Exercise 14B

1 Eva is choosing her after-school activities. She wants to choose one for Monday and one for Wednesday.

Monday	Wednesday
Football	Art
Hockey	Drama
Swimming	Music
Netball	

(a) Draw a sample space to show all the possible combinations she could choose.

(b) Find the probability that she will choose hockey and music if all combinations are equally likely.

Hint: To save writing, use 'F' for football, 'H' for hockey, and so on.

2   Robbie is having a break. He can choose one drink and one snack.

   (a) Use a sample space to show all the possible choices he could make.
   (b) Find the probability that he will choose a hot drink with cake.

3   Chloe is playing a word game and chooses a vowel and a consonant at random from her letters.

   (a) Show all the possible choices she can make on a sample space diagram.
   (b) What is the probability of choosing A and R?
   (c) What is the probability of choosing I and L?
   (d) What is the probability of choosing I and not choosing L?

4   Two fair six-sided dice are thrown. The scores are added.
   If the total is even, you win.
   If it is odd, you lose.
   Is this a fair game? Draw a sample space diagram to check.

5   Two fair six-sided dice are thrown as in question **4**, but this time the scores are multiplied. If the result is even, you win. Is this a fair game? Explain your answer.

14.3 Estimating probabilities

The theoretical probability that something will happen is

$$\frac{\text{the number of successful outcomes}}{\text{the total number of possible outcomes}}$$

The theoretical probability is found by saying all events are equally likely.

On normal dice there are six equally likely outcomes and one of them is 5. The theoretical probability of rolling a 5 would be $P(5) = \frac{1}{6}$.

Sometimes you need to estimate the probability that an event will happen.

If you count the number of times a certain event happens and the total number of trials, you can find the **relative frequency** of the event. This is an estimate of the probability that the event will happen.

Example 4

Ollie dropped a drawing pin 10 times. It landed pin-up 7 times and pin-down 3 times. Estimate the probability of the drawing pin landing pin-down.

Out of 10 trials the drawing pin landed pin-down 3 times. So the relative frequency of this event is $\frac{3}{10}$ so $P(\text{pin-down}) = \frac{3}{10}$.

■ **The estimated or experimental probability that an event will happen is:**

$$\text{relative frequency} = \frac{\textbf{number of successful trials}}{\textbf{total number of trials}}$$

■ **Theoretical probability is used when you know the total number of possible outcomes and that they are all equally likely. Otherwise you use relative frequency to estimate the probability of an event happening. To calculate relative frequencies you use data collected from experiments (such as surveys or observations).**

■ **The experimental probability may vary from one experiment to the next. The theoretical probability is always the same.**

Example 5

Jemima asked her class how they each got to school that morning. She displayed her results in a frequency table.

Type of transport	Tally	Frequency
car	⊬⊬1	5
walk	⊬⊬1 ⊬⊬1	10
bus	⊬⊬1 ⊬⊬1 ||	12
bicycle	|||	3
train		0

(a) How many people did she ask?

(b) Estimate the probability that a person in the class walks to school on a school day.

(c) What is the estimated probability that a person in the class does not walk to school on a school day?

(d) What is the estimated probability that a person in the class takes the train to school on a school day?

(a) $5 + 10 + 12 + 3 + 0 = 30$ so she asked 30 people.

(b) 10 people walked to school so the estimated probability is $P(\text{walk}) = \frac{10}{30} = \frac{1}{3}$

(c) $P(\text{did not walk}) = 1 - P(\text{walk}) = 1 - \frac{1}{3} = \frac{2}{3}$

(d) $P(\text{train}) = 0$

Example 6

Colour	Frequency in 1000 trials
red	240
blue	260
green	300
yellow	200

The spinner is spun 1000 times.
The results are shown in the table above.

(a) Using these results, calculate the estimated probabilities of getting each colour as a fraction, decimal and percentage.

(b) From these results, write down as a decimal the experimental probability of getting:
(i) not green, **(ii)** not blue.

(c) The spinner is fair. What is the theoretical probability of getting red?

(a)

Colour	Estimated probability as a fraction	Estimated probability as a decimal	Estimated probability as a percentage
red	$\frac{240}{1000} = \frac{6}{25}$	0.24	24%
blue	$\frac{260}{1000} = \frac{13}{50}$	0.26	26%
green	$\frac{300}{1000} = \frac{3}{10}$	0.3	30%
yellow	$\frac{200}{1000} = \frac{1}{5}$	0.2	20%

(b) **(i)** $P(\text{green}) = \frac{3}{10} = 0.3 = 30\%$
$P(\text{not green}) = 1 - P(\text{green})$
so $P(\text{not green}) = 1 - 0.3 = 0.7$

(ii) $P(\text{not blue}) = 1 - P(\text{blue})$
$P(\text{not blue}) = 1 - 0.26 = 0.74$

(c) As the spinner is fair, each colour is equally likely. The theoretical probability is:
$P(\text{red}) = \frac{1}{4} = 0.25 = 25\%$

Exercise 14C

1 An insurance salesperson told Sheila: 'You have a 10% chance of a house burglary in your area.'
For each of the following methods of estimating probability, explain why you think this method was used or was not used:

(a) equally likely outcomes
(b) an experiment
(c) checking past data
(d) personal judgement based on the salesperson's experience

2 Sally keeps a record of the position her horse, Lucky Lady, achieves in each race.

Position in last 40 races	
1, 2, 2, 3, 4, 1, 3, 5, 1, F, 1, 2, 3, 4, 5, 3, 2, 3, 3, 2, 5, 2, 3, 3, 4, 2, P, 1, 2, 3, 4, 5, 6, P, 4, 3, 2, 2, 1, 1	1 first 2 second 3 third 4 fourth 5 fifth 6 sixth F fell P pulled up by jockey

Use these results to estimate the probability that in the next race Lucky Lady will:

(a) come first,   **(b)** come second,
(c) will not come first,   **(d)** will fall.
(e) Sally thinks there is a strong chance that Lucky Lady will be in the first three. Is she right? Explain your answer.

3 A simulation of throwing a dice 6000 times was carried out. The following results were found.

What is the estimated probability of getting:

No. on dice	Frequency
1	600
2	1800
3	1000
4	800
5	850
6	950

(a) a 6?
(b) an even number?
(c) a prime number?
(d) not a prime number?
(e) Do you think the simulation was for a fair dice? Explain your answer.

4 Activity

Choose one of these questions to carry out a survey with your class. You will need to design a data collection sheet.

> For more on data collection see Chapter 9.

(a) How do pupils travel to school?
Find out from your survey the probability of someone walking to school.

(b) What is the favourite colour of pupils in your class?
Find out from your survey the probability of someone liking blue most.

(c) Which type of music do pupils like best? (Limit the choices they can make.) Find out from your survey the probability of someone liking classical music best.

14.4 Expected number of outcomes

You can sometimes use the theoretical probability to work out how many times you would expect a particular outcome to happen in an experiment. You can then compare this expected number with what actually happened.

> Remember:
> When using decimal probabilities you will need to round your answers.

■ **Expected number of outcomes = P(event) × number of trials**

Example 7

(a) If you toss a fair coin 20 times, how many tails would you expect?

(b) Imran claimed a coin was unfair. It gave only 5 tails in 20 tosses. Was he correct?

(a) The probability of getting a tail on a coin is 0.5. So if you toss the coin 20 times you would expect
$0.5 \times 20 = 10$ tails

(b) Although 5 tails in 20 tosses is less than the expected 10, you would need to toss the coin a lot more, recording the result each time, to test whether the coin is fair or not.

Exercise 14D

1 (a) The probability of taking out a red counter from this bag is 0.3.

You take out a counter 10 times, always replacing it each time. How many red counters would you expect?

(b) P(blue) = 40%
You take out a counter, note the colour, then replace the counter. You do this 100 times. How many blue counters would you expect to get?

(c) You know P(red) = 0.3 and P(blue) = 40%. If there are only red, green and blue counters in the bag, what is P(green)?

(d) How many of each colour would you expect to take out after 30 trials, replacing the counter each time?

2 You choose a card at random from a normal pack of playing cards.

(a) What is the probability of choosing a red card?

(b) You choose a card at random, replace it and repeat this 20 times. How many red cards would you expect to have chosen?

(c) How many kings would you expect in 13 trials?

(d) How many cards that are not kings would you expect in 52 trials?

Would you expect to see **exactly** this number if you carried out the experiment?

3 A fair 12-sided dice is thrown. Its sides are numbered 1 to 12.

(a) What is P(even)?

(b) How many even numbers would you expect after 50 throws of the dice?

(c) What is P(prime)?

(d) How many primes would you expect after 400 throws of the dice?

E 14.5 Relative frequency and theoretical probability

Remember:

- The estimated probability or relative frequency that an event will happen is:

    number of successful trials
    ————————————————
      total number of trials

- The theoretical probability that something will happen is:

    number of successful outcomes
    ————————————————————
    total number of possible outcomes

Exercise 14E

1   Mary and Tom tossed a coin 100 times. They kept a running total of the number of heads. This table shows their results.

P(head) is the relative frequency of getting a head.

No. of trials	No. of heads so far	P(head) as a fraction	P(head) as a decimal
10	7	$\frac{7}{10}$	0.7
20	12		
30	15		
40	18	$\frac{18}{40}$	
50	26		
60	30		
70	35		0.5
80	44		
90	45		
100	51		

Use a calculator to work out the decimals.

(a) Copy the table on page 289 and complete it.

(b) Draw axes on graph paper. Put 'No. of trials' on the horizontal axis, from 0 to 100.
Put 'P(head)' on the vertical axis, using a scale of 1 cm to 0.2.
Plot the values of P(head) as a decimal from your table.

This type of graph is sometimes called a **graph of relative frequency**.

(c) What is the theoretical probability of getting a head with a fair coin?
Draw a line across your graph at this value.
What do you notice?

2   Carry out your own experiment with an ordinary six-sided dice. First, choose a number on the dice and record it: $n = \ldots$

(a) Do the following experiment 12 times altogether.
Throw the dice 10 times and record the number of times your chosen number comes up. Put the results in a table.

Experiment	Tally	Frequency of n in 10 throws
1		
2		
and so on up to		
12		

(b) Now analyse your results. Use a table like this.

No. of throws so far	Frequency of n so far	Relative frequency of n
10		
20		
and so on up to		
120		

Relative frequency
$$= \frac{\text{frequency of } n \text{ so far}}{\text{no. of throws so far}}$$

(c) Draw axes on graph paper. Put 'No. of throws' on the horizontal axis, numbered from 0 to 120. Put 'Relative frequency' on the vertical axis, using a scale of 1 cm to 0.2. Plot the points from your table in part **(b)**.

(d) What is the theoretical probability of throwing your chosen number with a fair dice? Draw a line across your graph at this value. Write about what you notice.

(e) Do you think this graph would be the same for all six numbers on the dice? Explain your answer.

E **14.6 Using relative frequency**

If there is a large number of trials you would expect the relative frequency to be close to the theoretical probability. In this way you can test if an experiment is fair. For example, you would expect to get an even number on an ordinary dice half the times you throw it.

So the experimental probability (or relative frequency) of rolling an even number on an ordinary, fair dice tends to a limit of $\frac{1}{2}$ as the number of times you throw the dice increases.

■ **With repeated trials, experimental probability (or relative frequency) tends to a limit.**

Exercise 14F

1 Paul throws an eight-sided dice.

(a) What is the theoretical probability of getting a number 1?

(b) If the dice is thrown 80 times, how many times would you expect Paul to get the number 1?

(c) These results are recorded after 1000 trials.

Number on dice	Frequency
1	120
2	110
3	135
4	125
5	138
6	122
7	128
8	122

Can you tell if this dice is biased? Explain your answer.

(d) After 5000 trials these results are recorded.

Number on dice	Frequency
1	620
2	630
3	625
4	610
5	635
6	630
7	610
8	640

Find the relative frequencies for each of the numbers. Are they close to the theoretical probability for a fair eight-sided dice?

(e) Plot your answers to part **(d)** on a graph of number on dice against relative frequency. Draw a line of best fit. What do you notice?

Summary of key points

1   The theoretical probability that something will happen is:

$$P(event) = \frac{number\ of\ successful\ outcomes}{total\ number\ of\ possible\ outcomes}$$

2   The probabilities of all the possible outcomes of an event add up to 1.

3   P(event not happening) = 1 − P(event happening)

4   When two events happen independently you can show all the possible outcomes on a sample space diagram.

5   The estimated or experimental probability that an event will happen is:

$$relative\ frequency = \frac{number\ of\ successful\ trials}{total\ number\ of\ trials}$$

6   Theoretical probability is used when you know the total number of possible outcomes and that they are all equally likely. Otherwise you use relative frequency to estimate the probability of an event happening. To calculate relative frequencies you use data collected from experiments (such as surveys or observations).

7   The experimental probability may vary from one experiment to the next. The theoretical probability is always the same.

8   Expected number of outcomes = P(event) × number of trials

E   With repeated trials, experimental probability (or relative frequency) tends to a limit.

15 Transformations

This pattern was designed on a computer.

Start with a square and apply a
   . . . rotation
   . . . reflection
   . . . translation

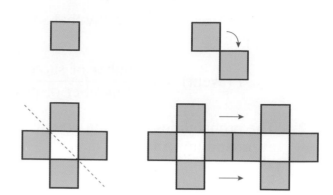

15.1 Translations using distance and direction

The boat needs to reach the lighthouse before dark.

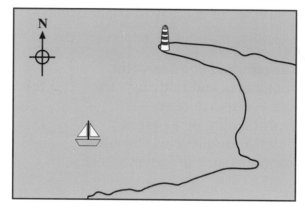

The captain should:

set her course East and then North:

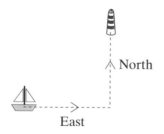

set her course North-East:

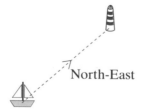

Hint:
The direction is
always given as a
bearing.
There is more on
bearings on p. 138.

North-East would be much quicker!

■ **You can describe a translation by giving a distance and
a direction (as a bearing).**

Example 1

Describe this translation using
a distance and a direction:

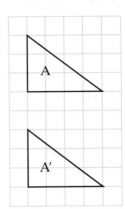

Each point on shape A has moved
5 units South (or 180°).

The translation can be written as [5, 180°].

Exercise 15A

1   For each diagram, describe the translation using
    distance and direction.

(a)

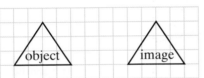

(b)

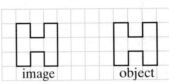

(c)

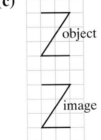

2   Copy this diagram and for each of (a)–(f):
    - Plot and label the point.
    - Describe the point as a translation
      of P, using a distance and direction.

    (Hint: You may need Pythagoras' theorem
    to work out the distance)

    (a) Q (1, 4)   (d) T (3, 8)
    (b) R (5, 6)   (e) U (7, 4)
    (c) S (3, 0)   (f) V (1, 2)

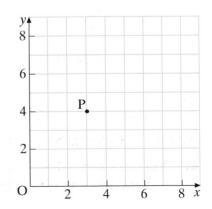

15.2 Reflection and rotation

You can find lines of reflection using perpendicular lines.

Example 2

Find the line of reflection between ABCD and A'B'C'D'.

You label the image of point A as A' (you say 'A prime').

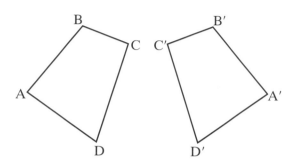

First draw lines between one of the points A, B, C or D and its image, say AA'. The perpendicular bisector of this line is the line of reflection.

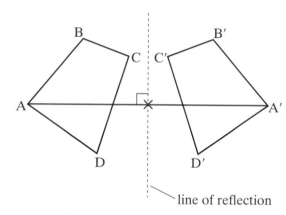

line of reflection

There is more on constructing perpendicular bisectors in Chapter 10.

This is true for all reflections.

■ **The line of reflection is the perpendicular bisector of the line between any point on the object and its image.**

You can also find centres of rotation using perpendicular bisectors.

Example 3

ABC is rotated to form A'B'C'.

Find the centre of rotation.

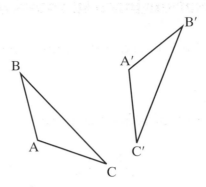

Join any two points with their
corresponding images:

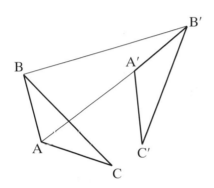

Draw the perpendicular
bisectors:

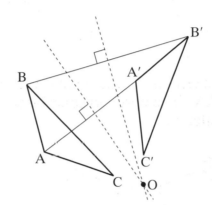

The point O where the perpendicular bisectors cross is the
centre of rotation.

■ **The point where the perpendicular bisectors of the
lines joining any two points and their corresponding
images cross is the centre of rotation.**

Exercise 15B

1   Draw a pair of axes labelled from −8 to 8. On the axes plot:
   • triangle ABC: A(−2, 6), B(−2, 2), C(−4, 5)
   • triangle DEF: D(−2, −2), E(−2, −6), F(−4, −5)
   • triangle GHI: G(6, 5), H(7, 3), I(3, 3)
   Draw the line of reflection when:
   (a) ABC is the object and DEF is the image.
   (b) DEF is the object and GHI is the image.

2 Copy this diagram. In each part draw the image after the given rotation about P. The first one has been done for you.

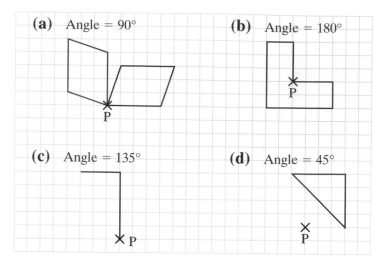

(a) Angle = 90°

(b) Angle = 180°

(c) Angle = 135°

(d) Angle = 45°

Remember:
Always measure
rotations anticlockwise

3 For each object and image, give the coordinates of the centre of rotation.
In each case the object is blue and the image is red.

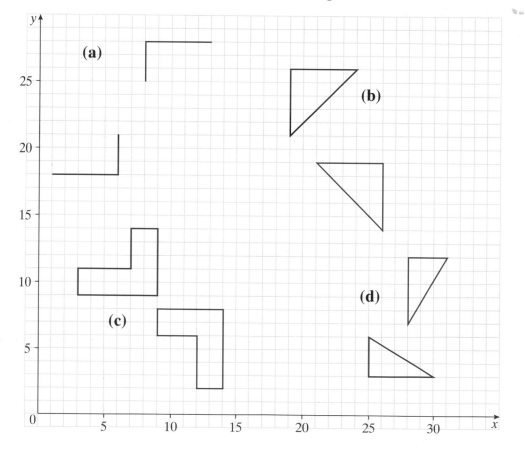

For questions **4**, **5**, and **6**, copy the diagrams onto squared paper.

4 (a) Reflect shape A in the *y*-axis. Label the image B.

    (b) Rotate shape B 270° about the origin. Label the image C.

    (c) Describe the single transformation that moves shape A to shape C.

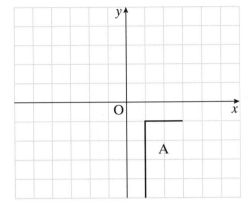

5 (a) Reflect shape R in the *x*-axis. Label the image S.

    (b) Reflect shape S in the *y*-axis. Label the image T.

    (c) Describe the single transformation that moves shape R to shape T.

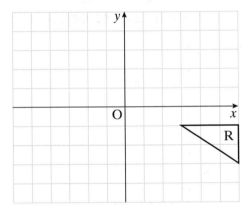

6 (a) Reflect shape L in the line $y = x$. Label the image M.

    (b) Reflect shape M in the *y*-axis. Label the image N.

    (c) Describe the single transformation that moves shape L to shape N.

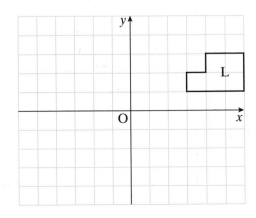

15.3 Enlargement and the centre of enlargement

Each of these shapes has been enlarged by a scale factor of 2. The **centre of enlargement** positions the image.

✕ = centre of enlargement

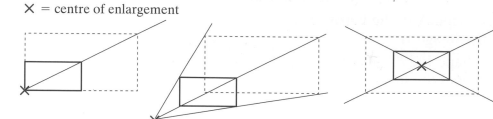

- ■   **You describe an enlargement by giving the scale factor and the centre of enlargement.**

- ■   scale factor $= \dfrac{\textbf{length of image}}{\textbf{corresponding length of object}}$

Example 4

Enlarge triangle ABC by a scale factor of 2 from point P.

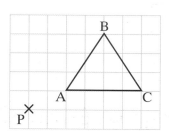

Imagine lines joining P and each corner of ABC:

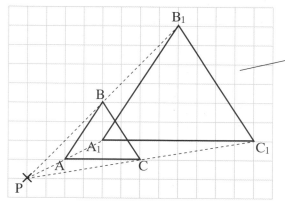

The corners of $A_1 B_1 C_1$ are on those lines, but twice as far from P.

Notice that the lengths of the Lines PA_1, PB_1 and PC_1 depend on the scale factor:

$PA_1 = 2 \times PA$

$PB_1 = 2 \times PB$

$PC_1 = 2 \times PC$

Example 5

On the diagram show these enlargements of triangle ABC:

(a) $A_1B_1C_1$: scale factor (s.f.) $\frac{1}{3}$, centre of enlargement O

(b) $A_2B_2C_2$: scale factor (s.f.) $1\frac{1}{3}$, centre of enlargement O

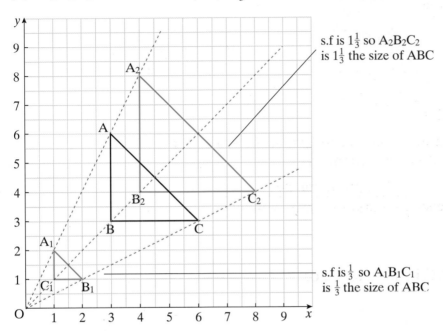

s.f is $1\frac{1}{3}$ so $A_2B_2C_2$ is $1\frac{1}{3}$ the size of ABC

s.f is $\frac{1}{3}$ so $A_1B_1C_1$ is $\frac{1}{3}$ the size of ABC

Exercise 15C

1 Copy each diagram onto squared paper and enlarge it by the given scale factor. Use the red dot as the centre of enlargement.

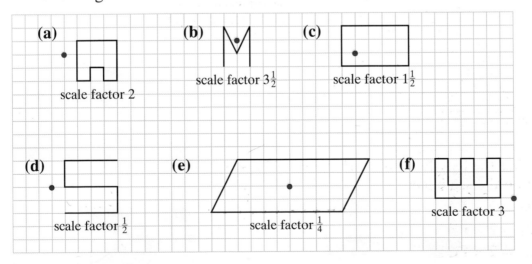

(a) scale factor 2

(b) scale factor $3\frac{1}{2}$

(c) scale factor $1\frac{1}{2}$

(d) scale factor $\frac{1}{2}$

(e) scale factor $\frac{1}{4}$

(f) scale factor 3

2 Find the scale factor for each enlargement.

(a)

object

image

(b)

object

image

(c)

(d)

object

image

3 Copy this diagram onto squared paper.

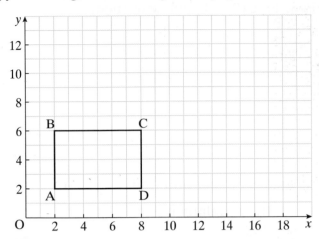

(a) Draw an enlargement with a scale factor of 2 and centre of enlargement O. Label the image $A_1 B_1 C_1 D_1$.

(b) Draw an enlargement with a scale factor of $\frac{1}{2}$ and centre of enlargement O.
Label the image $A_2 B_2 C_2 D_2$.

4 Draw axes on squared paper from -8 to 16 in the y-direction and -6 to 18 in the x-direction. Copy this square onto your axes and using P as the centre of enlargement draw the image when the scale factor is:

(a) 3   (b) $1\frac{1}{2}$ (c) $\frac{1}{4}$

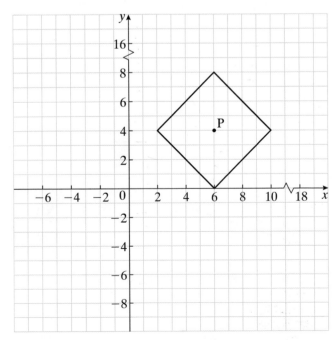

5 Draw an *x*-axis from 0 to 10 and a *y*-axis from −4 to 4.
Plot the points A(1, 1), B(3, 1), C(2, −1) and join them
to form a triangle.

Draw an enlargement of triangle ABC, with a scale
factor of 3 and the origin as the centre of enlargement.
Label this triangle A'B'C'.

6 Copy these diagrams onto squared paper and find

- the coordinates of the centre of enlargement
- the scale factor.

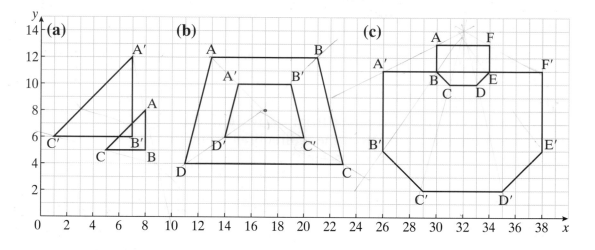

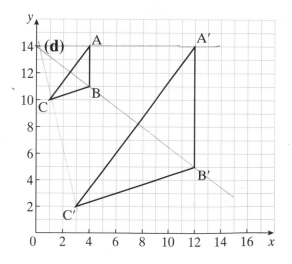

15.4 Congruence

These vases are identical: they are exactly
the same shape and size.

- ■ **Shapes that are exactly the same shape and size are
  congruent.**

You can see that two triangles are congruent by using one of the following
combinations:

Combination	Picture	Description
SSS (side, side, side)		Three pairs of equal sides
SAS (side, angle, side)		Two pairs of equal sides and a pair of equal angles
AAS (angle, angle, side)		Two pairs of equal angles and a pair of corresponding sides that are equal
RHS (right angle, hypotenuse, side)		A pair of right angles, a pair of equal hypotenuses and a pair of equal sides

Example 6

For **(a)**–**(c)** compare the two triangle and say whether they are congruent, not congruent or if there is not enough information to tell.

If triangles are congruent, list the reasons and label the matching vertices.

(a)   **(b)**   **(c)**

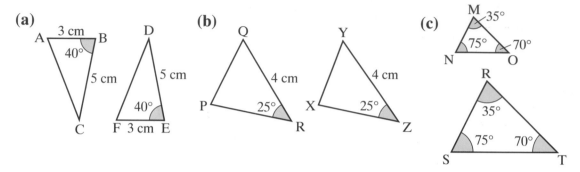

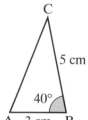

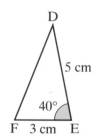

(a) These triangles are congruent using the SAS combination. This is easier to see when you rotate and reflect triangle ABC: $BC = ED$, $AB = FE$, $\angle ABC = \angle FED$. The vertices are $ABC = FED$.

(b) Not enough information.

(c) The two triangles have the same angles but triangle RST is an enlargement of triangle MNO. Enlargements are never congruent.

Exercise 15D

1   Write down the pairs of congruent shapes.

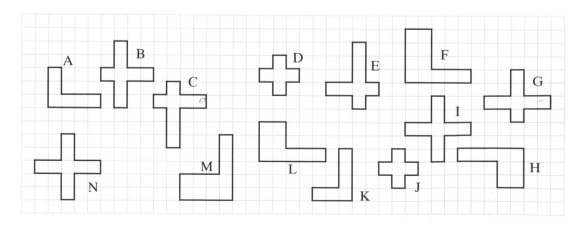

2   State whether the following pairs of triangles are congruent, give reasons for the congruence and match the vertices.

(a)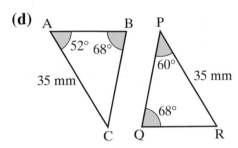

(b)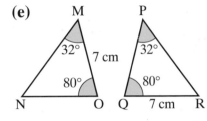

(c)

(d)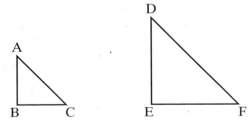

(e)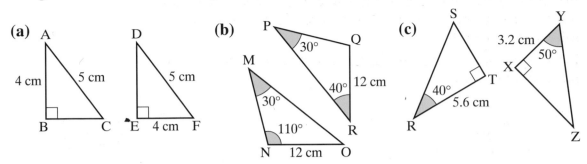

15.5 Similar shapes

In maths, the word similar has a more exact meaning.

■   **Two shapes are mathematically similar if one shape is an enlargement of the other.**

These dolls all look similar.

These triangles are mathematically similar: they have the same shape, but are different sizes.

As they have the same shape, they will also have the same angles.

■   **In similar triangles the angles at corresponding vertices are equal.**

Look at the two triangles below.

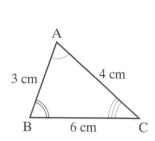
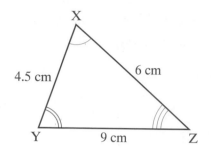

Triangle ABC is similar to triangle XYZ, because

$$\widehat{A} = \widehat{X}, \quad \widehat{B} = \widehat{Y}, \quad \widehat{C} = \widehat{Z}$$

$\widehat{A}$ means 'angle A'.

The ratios of the corresponding sides are the same:

$$\frac{XY}{AB} = \frac{YZ}{BC} = \frac{XZ}{AC}$$

$$\frac{9}{6} = \frac{6}{4} = \frac{4.5}{3} = 1\frac{1}{2}$$

You can work out these ratios using any two of these cards:

... and this is the scale factor of the enlargement.

For any similar triangles:

■ **If triangle ABC is similar to triangle XYZ, then**

$$\frac{XY}{AB} = \frac{YZ}{BC} = \frac{XZ}{AC} = \text{scale factor of enlargement.}$$

Example 7

Show that triangle MNO is similar to triangle OPQ.

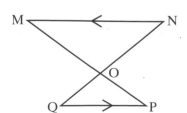

$\angle QOP = \angle NOM$ (opposite angles)

$\angle OMN = \angle OPQ$ (alternate angles)

$\angle OQP = \angle ONM$ (alternate angles)

There are three pairs of equal angles, therefore the triangles are similar.

Example 8

(a) Show that triangle ABC is similar to triangle EFG.

(b) Find the length of side FG.

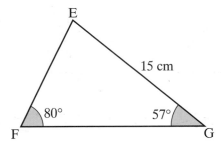

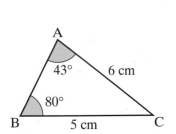

(a) Find the missing angles:

$$\angle ACB = 180° - 80° - 43° = 57°$$

$$\angle FEG = 180° - 80° - 57° = 43°$$

Therefore:

$$\angle ABC = \angle EFG = 80°$$

$$\angle BAC = \angle FEG = 43°$$

$$\angle BCA = \angle FGE = 57°$$

... and the two triangles are similar.

(b) Using the ratio for the scale factor:

$$\frac{EG}{AC} = \frac{15}{6} = 2.5$$

So: $FG = BC \times 2.5$

$$= 5 \times 2.5 = 12.5\,\text{cm}$$

Exercise 15E

1 Show that triangle ABC
is similar to triangle ADE.

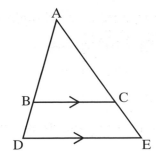

2 Show that triangle POQ is similar to triangle MON.

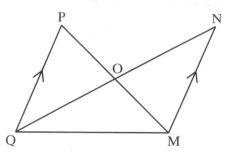

3 Show that triangle PQR is similar to triangle STU.

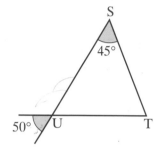

4 For each pair of triangles show that they are similar and find the length of side x.

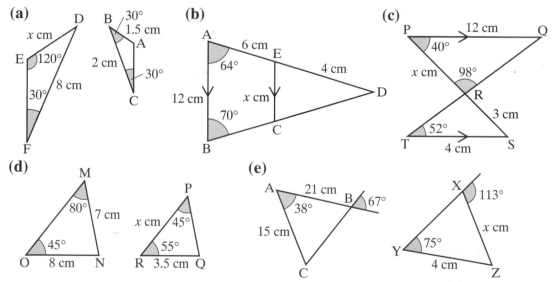

15.6 Similar shapes and area

In section 15.5 you learned that similar shapes have corresponding sides in the same ratio.

In this section, you will investigate the ratio of the areas of similar shapes.

Exercise 15F

1   Bob is laying a patio in his garden. He has a number of
1 m square slabs. Some are red and some are blue.

Bob has decided to make a square patio.

He lays the first slab and thinks about
the pattern he will make:

The area of this patio is 1 m².

Bob places three blue slabs to make
another square. The side of this
square is twice the length of the
original square:

(a) How much fencing would Bob need to go around
the perimeter of this patio?

(b) What is the area of this patio?

Bob places more slabs to
make a larger square:

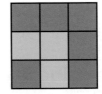

(c) What length of perimeter fence
would he need now?

(d) What is the area of this patio?

(e) Continue the pattern of Bob's patio – he has 36
slabs in total. Copy the table and fill in the missing
values from your pattern.

Patio	Square	Perimeter	Area
■	1 m × 1 m	4 m	1 m²
▦	2 m × 2 m	...	...
▦	3 m × 3 m	...	...
	...	...	...
	...	...	...
	...	...	...

(f) Look carefully at your results. What do you notice?

2 Bob has bought some equilateral triangular slabs to make a patio in his friend's garden.

The final patio will be an equilateral triangle with sides 6 m long.

The diagrams show the early stages of building:

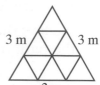

Bob has noticed a link between the length of side, the perimeter and the number of triangular slabs in each patio.

Bob draws a table to record his results:

Length of side, l (m)	Perimeter, p (m)	Number of triangles, t
1	3	1
2		
3		9
4	12	
5		
6		

(a) Copy and complete Bob's table.

(b) Write down a relationship between p and l.

(c) Write down a relationship between t and l.

(d) Write down the values for p and t for a patio with sides of length 8 metres.

3 Bob is really interested in how the perimeter of the patio and the number of slabs he needs changes with the length of the side of the patio, so he redraws his table:

Length of side, l (m)	Perimeter, p (m)	Number of triangles, t
1	1×3	1
2		
3		3^2
4	4×3	
5		
6		

(a) Using your answers to parts **(b)** and **(c)** of question **2**, copy and complete Bob's table.

(b) Use your table to work out what happens to the number of slabs Bob needs if the length of the side of the patio is

(i) doubled   (ii) trebled   (iii) multiplied by *n*.

(c) Would your answer to **(b)** change if Bob used square slabs?

E 15.7 Similar shapes and volume

In this section you will investigate the ratio of the volumes of similar solids.

Example 9

Sarah has a large box of unit cubes. She uses these to build larger cubes and to investigate their properties

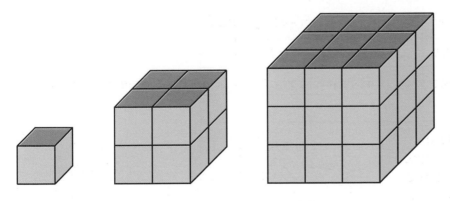

Write down the scale factor of enlargement between the unit cube and the cubes with edges of length 2 units and 3 units.

$$\text{scale factor} = \frac{\text{length of image}}{\text{corresponding length of original}}$$

so the scale factors of enlargement are 2 and 3 respectively.

Exercise 15G

1 Sarah draws a table to record her results:

Length of edge, l	Area of face, A	Volume, V
1	1	1
2	4	
3		
4		64
5		

(a) Copy and complete Sarah's table.

(b) Write down a relationship between A and l.

(c) Write down a relationship between V and l.

(d) Write down the values for A and V for a cube with edges of length 17 units.

2 Sarah redraws her table:

Length of edge, l	Area of face, A	Volume, V
1	1	1
2	2^2	
3		
4		4^3
5		

(a) Using your answers to parts (b) and (c) of question 1, copy and complete her table.

(b) Use your table to work out what happens to the area and volume of a unit cube if its length of edge is
(i) doubled (ii) trebled (iii) multiplied by n.

E **15.8 Rules for area and volume of similar shapes**

In section 15.6, you should have noticed a relationship between the length of side, perimeter and area of square and triangular patios.

As the length of side of a patio increased the perimeter and area increased by different scale factors.

Change in length of side	Scale factor for length	Scale factor for perimeter	Scale factor for area
1 m to 2 m	2	2	4
1 m to 3 m	3	3	9
1 m to 4 m	4	4	16
⋮	⋮	⋮	⋮
1 m to x m	x	x	x^2

This rule is true for all similar shapes:

■ **If you increase the length of side by scale factor N**
  • **the perimeter increases by scale factor N,**
  • **the area increases by scale factor N^2.**

Example 10

These two shapes are similar.
What is the area of shape B?

The length of side of shape B is twice as big as the corresponding side of shape A.

This means that the length of side has changed by scale factor 2.

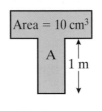

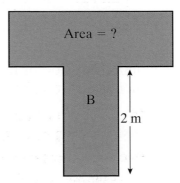

Because the shapes are similar, you know that the area increases by scale factor 2^2.

$2^2 = 4$ so the area of shape B will be 4 times the area of shape A.

$4 \times 10\,\text{cm}^2 = 40\,\text{cm}^2$ so the area of shape B is $40\,\text{cm}^2$.

In section 15.7, you should have noticed that a relationship also exists between the length of side of a 3D shape and its volume.

As the length of side of Sarah's cube increased the area of each face and the volume of the cube increased by different scale factors.

Scale factor for length	Scale factor for area	Scale factor for volume
2	4	8
3	9	27
$\vdots$	$\vdots$	$\vdots$
x	x^2	x^3

This rule is true for all similar solids:

■ **If you increase the length of side of a solid by scale factor N**

  • **the area of each face increases by scale factor N^2,**
  • **the volume increases by scale factor N^3.**

Example 11

These two pyramids are similar. What is the surface area and volume of pyramid B?

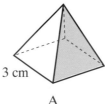

3 cm

A
Area = 16.2 cm^2
Volume = 5 cm^3

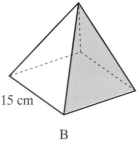

15 cm

B
Area = ?
Volume = ?

The length of side of the square base has increased from 3 cm to 15 cm, a scale factor of N = 5.

Because the pyramids are similar solids,

  • the area increases by scale factor N^2, or 5^2
  • the volume increases by scale factor N^3, or 5^3

So area of B $= 16.2\,\text{cm}^2 \times 5^2$ and volume of B $= 5\,\text{cm}^3 \times 5^3$

$\qquad\qquad\quad = 16.2\,\text{cm}^2 \times 25$ $\qquad\qquad\qquad\qquad = 5\,\text{cm}^3 \times 125$

$\qquad\qquad\quad = 405\,\text{cm}^2$ $\qquad\qquad\qquad\qquad\qquad = 625\,\text{cm}^3$

Exercise 15H

1   Bob is making a patio in his neighbour's
    garden using red and blue slabs.
    The pattern is based on the letter L.

    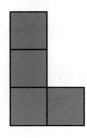

    The perimeter of the first stage is 10 m
    and the area is 4 m^2:

    (a) The second stage will be enlarged
        by scale factor 2. Show that the
        perimeter will be 20 m and the area
        will be 16 m^2.

    (b) How many extra slabs will Bob need to put down?

    (c) If the lengths of the original L are tripled, what will
        the new perimeter and area be?

2   These rectangles are similar:

    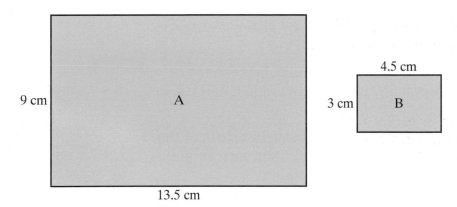

    B is an enlargement of A.

    (a) What is the scale factor of enlargement?

    (b) What is the scale factor of enlargement for
        area?

    (c) What is the area of rectangle A?

    (d) Use the scale factor of enlargement for area to
        work out the area of B.

    (e) Check your answer to (d) by calculating the area
        of rectangle B.

3   Eva has been given an arts council grant for a new sculpture at her local gallery.

She decides to make a giant house brick out of real house bricks.

She uses a scale factor of enlargement of 50.

(a) What will the length, width and height of her sculpture be?

(b) What will the scale factors for area and volume be?

(c) How many real house bricks will she need?

(d) If each brick weighs 1.25 kg, will the mass of the sculpture be less than the floor safety limit of 150 tonnes?

Remember:
1 tonne = 1000 kg

Summary of key points

1 You can describe a translation by giving a distance and a direction (as a bearing).

2 The line of reflection is perpendicular bisector of the line between any point on the object and its image.

3 The point where the perpendicular bisectors of the lines joining any two points and their corresponding images cross is the centre of rotation.

4 You describe an enlargement by giving the scale factor and the centre of enlargement.

5 scale factor = $\dfrac{\text{length of image}}{\text{corresponding length of object}}$

6 Shapes that are exactly the same shape and size are congruent.

7 Two shapes are mathematically similar if one shape is an enlargement of the other.

8 In similar triangles the angles at corresponding vertices are equal.

9 If triangle ABC is similar to triangle XYZ, then

$$\frac{XY}{AB} = \frac{YZ}{BC} = \frac{XZ}{AC} = \text{scale factor of enlargement.}$$

E If you increase the length of side by scale factor N
- the perimeter increases by scale factor N,
- the area increases by scale factor N^2.

E If you increase the length of side of a solid by scale factor N
- the area of each face increases by scale factor N^2,
- the volume increases by scale factor N^3.

16 Number sequences

Number sequences are everywhere in nature from plants' root systems to galaxies. The picture opposite shows a fractal, which is generated from a sequence of numbers.

16.1 Number sequences

Each number in a sequence is called a **term**.

5, 9, 13, 17, 21, 25, ..., ..., ...

This is term number 1, the **first term**.

This is term number 6, the **sixth term**.

An unknown number in the sequence is called term number *n* or the *n*th term.

■ **When investigating number sequences you can find:**

- **a rule to find the next term, called a term-to-term rule.**

- **a general rule to find the *n*th term, sometimes called the general term.**

Using the sequence

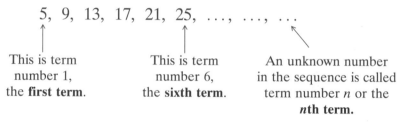

5, 9, 13, 17, 21, 25, ..., ..., ...

+4   +4   +4   +4   +4   +4

The difference between consecutive terms is +4

The next term is 29 (= 25 + 4)

The term-to-term rule is 'add 4'.

■ **A sequence is linear (or arithmetic) if the difference between any two consecutive terms is the same.**

If you know the first term and the difference you can generate a linear sequence of any length.

Example 1

Jaya and Dan are playing a sequence game.

Dan turns over 3 number cards and an operation card.

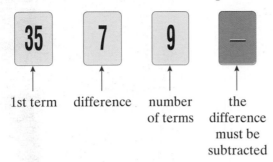

| 1st term | difference | number of terms | the difference must be subtracted |

Jaya uses the cards to generate a linear sequence.

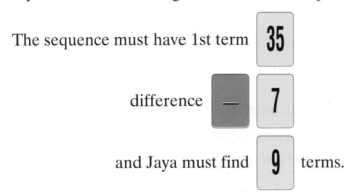

The sequence must have 1st term 35

difference $-$ 7

and Jaya must find 9 terms.

She records her sequence in a table:

Position	Term
1	35
2	$35 - 7 = 28$
3	$28 - 7 = 21$
4	$21 - 7 = 14$
5	$14 - 7 = 7$
6	$7 - 7 = 0$
7	$0 - 7 = -7$
8	$-7 - 7 = -14$
9	$-14 - 7 = -21$

The first 9 terms in the sequence are:

$35, 28, 21, 14, 7, 0, -7, -14, -21$

Exercise 16A

1 For each sequence write down:
   - the next two terms
   - the rule you used.

   (a) 25, 22, 19, 16, . . .   **(b)** 51, 62, 73, . . .
   (c) 9, 18, 27, 36, 45, . . .   **(d)** $\frac{1}{2}$, 1, $1\frac{1}{2}$, 2, $2\frac{1}{2}$, . . .
   (e) 1, 3, 9, 27, . . .   **(f)** 6.5, 8, 9.5, 11, . . .
   (g) 2000, 1000, 500, . . .   **(h)** 0.25, 1, 4, . . .
   (i) 57, 44, 31, . . .   **(j)** 1, $\frac{1}{2}$, $\frac{1}{4}$, . . .
   (k) 1, −1, 1, −1, 1, −1, . . .   **(l)** 1, −2, 4, −8, 16, . . .

2 Use these number and operation cards to generate sequences.

   - The **1st card** gives the **1st term**.
   - The **2nd card** gives the **difference number**.
   - The **3rd card** tells you **how many terms to find**.
   - The **operation card** tells you **what to do with the difference number**.

   (a) 19 5 6 +   **(b)** 37 12 7 +

   (c) 3 5 4 ×   **(d)** 63 7 9 −

   (e) 56 2 4 ÷   **(f)** 9 3 5 ×

3 For each sequence:
   - find the missing terms
   - write down the rule you used.

   (a) 3, 10, 17, . . . , 31, . . . , . . .   **(b)** 8, 20, . . . , . . . , 56, 68, 80
   (c) 90, 84, 78, . . . , . . . , . . .   **(d)** 15, . . . , 45, 60, . . . , 90
   (e) 8, . . . , 4, . . . , 0, −2, . . .   **(f)** 3, 9, 15, . . . , . . . , 33, 39, . . .

4   Dr Jones is exploring an ancient temple. He comes to a locked door upon which are engraved four puzzles:

A sequence has first term *b* and term-to-term rule 'add *a*'. Find *a* and *b* such that

(a) each term in the sequence is even.

(b) each term is a multiple of 7.

(c) every other term is an integer.

(d) the first three terms are negative, the fourth term is zero and every other term is a multiple of 3.

Dr Jones answers the four puzzles correctly and the door opens. What are his answers?

16.2 Finding the *n*th term

You can use algebraic rules to help find any number in a sequence. These rules are called **general rules**.

You use them to find the **general** or **nth term**.

Example 2

Find the general rule, the nth term and the 99th term in this sequence:

   7, 14, 21, 28, 35, …

Using a table is always a good idea:

Position	Term
1 ——×7——→	7
2 ——×7——→	14
3 ——×7——→	21
4 ——×7——→	28
5 ——×7——→	35
6 ——×7——→	42
⋮	⋮
n ——×7——→	$7n$

Look for a **link** between the term number and the term.

+7 is called the **constant difference** between terms

The general rule for this sequence is 'multiply the position number by 7'.

The nth term is $7n$.

You can use the nth term to find any term:

The 99th term is

   $7 \times 99 = 693$.

Exercise 16B

For each sequence find:
- the general rule
- the *n*th term.

1

Position	Term
1	20
2	21
3	22
4	23
5	24
⋮	⋮
n	

2

Position	Term
1	8
2	16
3	24
4	32
5	40
⋮	⋮
n	

3

Position	Term
1	20
2	40
3	60
4	80
5	100
⋮	⋮
n	

4

Position	Term
1	−5
2	−4
3	−3
4	−2
5	−1
⋮	⋮
n	

5

Position	Term
1	−2
2	−4
3	−6
4	−8
5	−10
⋮	⋮
n	

6

Position	Term
1	70
2	140
3	210
4	280
5	350
⋮	⋮
n	

16.3 Using the difference to find the general rule

The sequence

6, 11, 16, 21, 26, 31, ...

can be written in a table:

Position	Term
1 — ×5 + 1 →	6
2 — ×5 + 1 →	11
3 — ×5 + 1 →	16
4 — ×5 + 1 →	21
5 — ×5 + 1 →	26
6 — ×5 + 1 →	31
⋮	
10 — ×5 + 1 →	51
⋮	
100 — ×5 + 1 →	501
⋮	
n — ×5 + 1 →	$5n + 1$

+5
+5
+5
+5
+5

The constant difference between terms is +5...

... so the first part of the general rule is $5n$.

The constant difference between consecutive terms gives you the first part of the general rule.

To complete the general rule for this sequence you need to add 1.

So the general rule is $5n + 1$.

You can write this as $T(n) = 5n + 1$.

$T(n)$ is the nth term.

■ **The nth term, $T(n)$, of any linear sequence can be written as**

$$T(n) = An + B$$

where A and B are numbers.

Example 3

Find T(n) for the linear sequence

$-8, \ -14, \ -20, \ -26, \ -32, \ \ldots$

Write the sequence in a table:

Position	Term
1 $\xrightarrow{\times -6 - 2}$	-8
2 $\xrightarrow{\times -6 - 2}$	-14
3 $\xrightarrow{\times -6 - 2}$	-20
4 $\xrightarrow{\times -6 - 2}$	-26
5 $\xrightarrow{\times -6 - 2}$	-32
$\vdots$	$\vdots$
10 $\xrightarrow{\times -6 - 2}$	-62
$\vdots$	$\vdots$
100 $\xrightarrow{\times -6 - 2}$	-602
$\vdots$	$\vdots$
n $\xrightarrow{\times -6 - 2}$	$-6n - 2$

-6
-6
-6
-6

Because the constant difference is -6, the first part of T(n) is $-6n$.

To complete the general rule for this sequence you need to subtract 2.

1st term

$n = 1$ so T(1) $= 1 \times -6 - 2 = -8$

T(1) is the 1st term

2nd term

$n = 2$ so T(2) $= 2 \times -6 - 2 = -14$

T(2) is the 2nd term

so, for the nth term T(n) $= n \times -6 - 2 = -6n - 2$

so   T(n) $= -6n - 2$ for $n = 1, 2, 3, 4, \ldots$

■   **The difference between terms in the sequence gives the number by which you multiply n in the general rule. You may need to add or subtract a number to complete the general rule.**

If the nth term of a linear sequence is

$\quad$ T(n) $= An + B$

then A is the constant difference between consecutive terms of the sequence.

If A is a positive number, the terms in the sequence increase

e.g.   from Example 2, $A = 7$ $(B = 0)$

    7, 14, 21, 28, 35, ...

so the sequence is **ascending**.

If A is a negative number, the terms in the sequence decrease

e.g.   from Example 3, $A = -6$ $(B = 1)$

    -5, -11, -17, -23, -29, ...

so the sequence is **descending**.

Exercise 16C

1   For each sequence decide if it is ascending or descending and find:

- the 10th and 100th terms
- the nth term.

(a)

Position	Term
$1 \xrightarrow{\times 3 + 1} 4$	
$2 \xrightarrow{\times 3 + 1} 7$	
$3 \xrightarrow{\times 3 + 1} 10$	
$4 \xrightarrow{\times 3 + 1} 13$	
$5 \xrightarrow{\times 3 + 1} 16$	
⋮	⋮
10	
⋮	⋮
100	
⋮	⋮
n	

(b)

Position	Term
1	7
2	9
3	11
4	13
5	15
⋮	⋮
10	
⋮	⋮
100	
⋮	⋮
n	

Hint: × then +

(c)

Position	Term
1	-1
2	1
3	3
4	5
5	7
⋮	⋮
10	
⋮	⋮
100	
⋮	⋮
n	

Hint: × then −

(d)

Position	Term
1	−1
2	−3
3	−5
4	−7
5	−9
⋮	⋮
10	
⋮	⋮
100	
⋮	⋮
n	

(e)

Position	Term
1	−6
2	−10
3	−14
4	−18
5	−22
⋮	⋮
10	
⋮	⋮
100	
⋮	⋮
n	

(f)

Position	Term
1	6
2	9
3	12
4	15
5	18
⋮	⋮
10	
⋮	⋮
100	
⋮	⋮
n	

(g)

Position	Term
1	2
2	8
3	14
4	20
5	26
⋮	⋮
10	
⋮	⋮
100	
⋮	⋮
n	

(h)

Position	Term
1	11
2	13
3	15
4	17
5	19
⋮	⋮
10	
⋮	⋮
100	
⋮	⋮
n	

(i)

Position	Term
1	−2
2	−9
3	−16
4	−23
5	−30
⋮	⋮
10	
⋮	⋮
100	
⋮	⋮
n	

2 For each sequence, state whether it is ascending or descending and find
- the general term
- the 20th term
- the 200th term.

(a) 3, 5, 7, 9, ... **(b)** −7, −9, −11, −13, −15. ...

(c) −1, 3, 7, 11, 15, ... **(d)** −3, −7, −11, −15, −19, ...

(e) 0, 3, 6, 9, 12, ... **(f)** 9, 15, 21, 27, 33, ...

(g) −2, 0, 2, 4, 6, ... **(h)** $-\frac{1}{2}, 0, \frac{1}{2}, 1, 1\frac{1}{2}, \ldots$

3 Below are the *n*th terms of some linear sequences. Describe in words the term-to-term rule for each sequence and say whether the sequence is ascending or descending.

(a) $T(n) = 2n + 1$ **(b)** $T(n) = 10n - 7$

(c) $T(n) = -2n + 3$ **(d)** $T(n) = -8n + 3$

(e) $T(n) = 56n + 12$ **(f)** $T(n) = -107n + 1$

(g) $T(n) = -107n - 1$ **(h)** $T(n) = 3$

16.4 Mappings

Look at these number machines

When you input a number you multiply it by 2 and subtract 1

so x becomes $2x - 1$

You can write this as $x \rightarrow 2x - 1$

This is called a mapping.

Example 4

Write as a mapping.

Put a number x into the number machines:

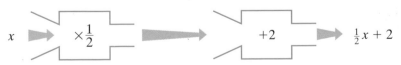

so this is the same as the mapping $x \rightarrow \frac{1}{2}x + 2$

■ **A number machine maps one number onto another.
You can write number machines as mappings.**

is the same as $x \rightarrow 12(x + 3)$

You can represent a mapping on a mapping diagram.

Example 5

Represent these mappings on separate mapping diagrams.

(a) $x \rightarrow \frac{1}{2}x + 2$

(b) $x \rightarrow 2x - 1$

(a) $x \rightarrow \frac{1}{2}x + 2$

so $0 \rightarrow \frac{1}{2} \times 0 + 2 = 2$

$1 \rightarrow \frac{1}{2} \times 1 + 2 = 2\frac{1}{2}$

$2 \rightarrow \frac{1}{2} \times 2 + 2 = 3$

$3 \rightarrow \frac{1}{2} \times 3 + 2 = 3\frac{1}{2}$

$4 \rightarrow \frac{1}{2} \times 4 + 2 = 4$

etc.

You can represent this on a mapping diagram as

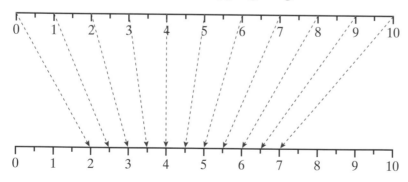

You could also mark where fractions are mapped (e.g. $\frac{1}{2} \rightarrow 2\frac{1}{4}$) but you should show only where the whole numbers from 0 to 10 are mapped unless asked otherwise.

(b) The mapping diagram for $x \rightarrow 2x - 1$ is

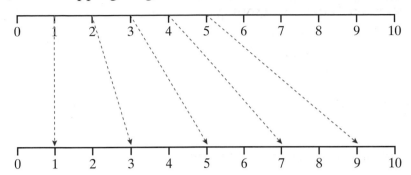

Note:
$0 \rightarrow -1$ is off the lower scale so you cannot draw it on this diagram.

Exercise 16D

1 Write these number machines as mappings:

(a)

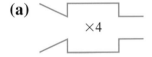

$\times 4$

(b)

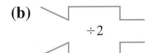

$\div 2$

(c)

$\times \frac{1}{2}$ $+3$

(d)

$+1$ $\div 3$

(e)

-2 $\times 2$

(f)

$\times 3$ $+8$ $\div 2$

2 Draw mapping diagrams, with scales marked from 0 to 10, for the mappings in question **1**.

3 Draw a diagram for the mapping $x \rightarrow x$. Describe this mapping in words.

$x \rightarrow x$ is called the identity mapping.

16.5 Inverse mappings

You can find the inverse of a linear mapping by finding the inverse of its number machines.

Linear mappings are mappings of the form $x \rightarrow ax + b$ where a and b are numbers.

Example 6

(a) Find the inverse of the mapping $x \rightarrow 2x - 1$.
(b) Draw a diagram to show that the inverse mapping outputs the original number.

(a) You can write this mapping using number machines:

When you input x, the number machines output $2x - 1$.

The inverse of these number machines is

When you input x, the number machines output $(x + 1) \div 2$ or $\frac{1}{2}(x + 1)$.

So the inverse of the mapping $x \rightarrow 2x - 1$ is $x \rightarrow \frac{1}{2}(x + 1)$

(b) Draw three scales, each labelled from 0 to 10:

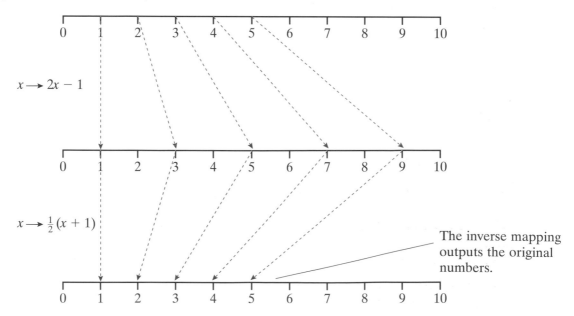

The inverse mapping outputs the original numbers.

■ **A mapping tells you what happens to x as it goes through the number machines.**

The inverse mapping tells you what happens to x as it goes through the inverse number machines.

Exercise 16E

1 Find the inverse mapping of

(a) $x \rightarrow 2x$ (b) $x \rightarrow 2 - x$

(c) $x \rightarrow \frac{1}{2}x + 1$ (d) $x \rightarrow 3x - 6$

(e) $x \rightarrow 4 + x$ (f) $x \rightarrow 2 - \frac{3}{2}x$

2 Draw mapping diagrams for the mappings and their inverses in question **1**.

3 What do you notice about the inverse of the mapping $x \rightarrow 2 - x$ in part **(b)** of question **1**?
Find the inverse mapping of

(a) $x \rightarrow 1 - x$

(b) $x \rightarrow 8 - x$

> A mapping that is the same as its inverse is called a self-inverse mapping.

4 George writes down a linear sequence

$$T(n) = 4n + 1$$

He notices that this general rule maps the position n onto the term $4n + 1$ and so he writes

$$n \rightarrow 4n + 1$$

Find the position of the term
(a) 17
(b) 265
(c) 10 697

in George's sequence.

(Hint: Find the inverse of George's mapping.)

5 Find the position of the term in each of the following sequences.

(a) $T(n) = 6n - 2$, term $= 52$

(b) $T(n) = 10n - 11$, term $= 879$

(c) $T(n) = 385n - 183$, term $= 2512$

16.6 Non-linear sequences

Sequences are not always linear.

For example the sequence $T(n) = 3n^2 - 1$ is quadratic.

Example 7

Generate the first 5 terms of the sequence described by $T(n) = 3n^2 - 1$.

n	$T(n)$
1	$3 \times 1^2 - 1 = 3 - 1 = 2$
2	$3 \times 2^2 - 1 = 12 - 1 = 11$
3	$3 \times 3^2 - 1 = 27 - 1 = 26$
4	$3 \times 4^2 - 1 = 48 - 1 = 47$
5	$3 \times 5^2 - 1 = 75 - 1 = 74$

The first five terms are 2, 11, 26, 47 and 74.

Exercise 16F

Find the first 5 terms of the following sequences:

1 n^2 **2** $n^2 - 2$ **3** $2n^2 + 1$

4 $-2n^2 + n$ **5** $-n^2 + 4$ **6** $2n^2 - n + 1$

E 16.7 Finding the general rule for a quadratic sequence

Sometimes the difference between terms in a sequence is not constant.

Then you have to look at the *second difference* – the difference between differences.

If this has a constant value you can still find a general rule.

Look at the sequence   6,   11,   18,   27,   38,   ...

Writing the first five terms of the sequence in a table:

Position	Term
1	6
2	11
3	18
4	27
5	38

+5, +7, +9, +11 (1st differences); +2, +2, +2 (2nd differences)

The difference between terms changes. But the second difference is constant at 2.

This means that there is a general rule.

Because you have to go to a second difference you will need a term in n^2.

2 for 2nd
2 for squared

Instead of having the form $T(n) = An + B$

it will have the form $T(n) = An^2 + Bn + C$
(where A, B and C are numbers)

■ **When the first difference in a sequence is not constant but the second difference is constant, the general rule has the form $T(n) = An^2 + Bn + C$ where A, B and C are numbers. This is called a quadratic sequence.**

■ **In quadratic sequences the second difference equals $2A$.**

Example 8

Find the general rule of the quadratic sequence
6, 11, 18, 27, 38,...

Because second difference $= 2A$

$$2A = 2$$
$$A = 1$$

so $$T(n) = n^2 + Bn + C$$

Now substitute $n = 1$ and $n = 2$ into $T(n) = n^2 + Bn + C$:

$$T(1) = 6 \qquad\qquad T(2) = 11$$

so $\quad 1 + B + C = 6 \qquad$ so $\quad 4 + 2B + C = 11$

$$B + C = 5 \quad \textbf{(1)} \qquad\qquad 2B + C = 7 \quad \textbf{(2)}$$

Now solve the simultaneous equations **(1)** and **(2)**.

Subtract **(1)** from **(2)**: $\quad B = 2$

Substitute into **(1)**: $\qquad C = 5 - 2 = 3$

so $\qquad\qquad T(n) = n^2 + 2n + 3$

Check:

The term $T(3)$ should be 18

$$3^2 + 2 \times 3 + 3 = 18 \quad \checkmark$$

Example 9

Find the general term of the sequence

$$4, \ 7, \ 12, \ 19, \ 28, \ \ldots$$

Writing the sequence in a table:

n	$T(n)$
1	4
2	7
3	12
4	19
5	28

1st difference: $+3, +5, +7, +9$

2nd difference: $+2, +2, +2$

The second difference is constant at 2.

So the general term is

$$T(n) = An^2 + Bn + C$$

where A, B and C are numbers.

Because second difference $= 2A$

$$2A = 2$$

$$A = 1$$

so $T(n) = n^2 + Bn + C$

Substitute $n = 1$ and $n = 2$ into $T(n) = n^2 + Bn + C$:

$$T(1) = 4 \qquad \text{and} \qquad T(2) = 7$$

so $\quad 1 + B + C = 4 \qquad$ so $\quad 4 + 2B + C = 7$

$$B + C = 3 \quad \textbf{(1)} \qquad\qquad 2B + C = 3 \quad \textbf{(2)}$$

Now solve the simultaneous equations **(1)** and **(2)**.

Subtract **(1)** from **(2)**: $B = 0$

Substitute into **(1)**: $C = 3$

So the general term, $T(n) = n^2 + 0n + 3 = n^2 + 3$

Check:

The 4th term should be 19

$$n^2 + 3 = 4^2 + 3 = 16 + 3 = 19 \quad \checkmark$$

Exercise 16G

1 Find the first 5 terms ($n = 1, 2, 3, 4, 5$) of the sequences with these general terms:

(a) $n^2 + 5$

(b) $n^2 - 1$

(c) $2n^2 + n + 1$

(d) $2n^2 + 3n - 1$

(e) $3n^2 - 4$

(f) $4n^2 + 2n - 1$

(g) $n^2 - n + 1$

(h) $n^2 - 3n + 4$

2 Find the 10th, 20th and 100th terms of the sequences with these general terms:

(a) $n^2 - 5$

(b) $2n^2 + 4$

(c) $3n^2 - 4$

(d) $n^2 + 2n - 4$

(e) $3n^2 + 4n - 5$

(f) $n^2 - 9$

(g) $n^2 + 100$

(h) $2n^2 + 5n - 9$

3 The first 5 terms of a sequence are:

$$5, \ 8, \ 13, \ 20, \ 29, \ \ldots$$

(a) Copy this table, showing the 1st and 2nd differences.

n	$T(n)$
1	5
2	8
3	13
4	20
5	29

1st difference

2nd difference

$+3$ $+2$

$+5$ $+2$

$+7$ $+2$

$+9$

(b) Write down the form of the general term.

(c) Write down the value of A.

(d) Substitute $n = 1$ and $n = 2$ into the general term to get two simultaneous equations.

(e) Find B and C and write down the general term.

(f) Check your answer by substituting $n = 4$ into your general term.

4   Find the general term for this sequence:

n	$T(n)$
1	4
2	10
3	20
4	34
5	52

1st difference

2nd difference

$)+6$ $+4$

$)+10$ $+4$

$)+14$ $+4$

$)+18$

5   Find the general terms of these sequences.

   (a) $-4, -1, 4, 11, 20, \ldots$ **(b)** $7, 10, 15, 22, 31, \ldots$

   (c) $3, 9, 19, 33, 51, \ldots$ **(d)** $1, 7, 17, 31, 49, \ldots$

E 16.8 Investigating number sequences

Number sequences appear often in mathematics. You can now investigate number sequences using what you have learnt.

Example 10

Find an expression for the nth triangular number.

You can find the triangular numbers by drawing diagrams:

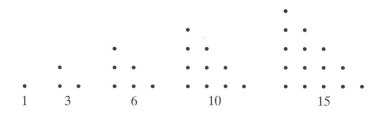

1   3   6   10   15

Put the first five terms into a table:

n	$T(n)$
1	1
2	3
3	6
4	9
5	15

1st difference

2nd difference

$+2$ $+1$
$+3$ $+1$
$+4$ $+1$
$+5$

The second differences are constant so $T(n)$ must be of the form $An^2 + Bn + C$.

Because second difference $= 2A$

this means $\qquad\qquad 2A = 1$

so $\qquad\qquad\qquad A = \frac{1}{2}$

So the rule is of the form $\qquad T(n) = \frac{1}{2}n^2 + Bn + C$

Now $\quad T(1) = 1$ so $\qquad \frac{1}{2} + B + C = 1$

$\qquad\qquad\qquad$ so $\qquad\qquad B + C = \frac{1}{2}$ $\qquad$ **(1)**

and $\quad T(2) = 3$ so $\quad \frac{1}{2} \times 2^2 + 2B + C = 3$

$\qquad\qquad\qquad$ so $\qquad\qquad 2B + C = 1$ $\qquad$ **(2)**

Subtracting **(1)** from **(2)**: $\quad B = \frac{1}{2}$

$B = \frac{1}{2}$ in **(1)** gives $\quad \frac{1}{2} + C = \frac{1}{2}$

$\qquad\qquad\qquad$ so $\qquad C = 0$

Therefore $\quad T(n) = \frac{1}{2}n^2 + \frac{1}{2}n$

The nth triangular number is $\frac{1}{2}n^2 + \frac{1}{2}n$.

The sequence of triangular numbers is actually the sum of the whole numbers:

$\qquad$ 1 $\qquad\qquad$ $1+2$ $\qquad\qquad$ $1+2+3$ $\qquad\qquad$ $1+2+3+4$

so the sum of the first n whole numbers is $\frac{1}{2}n^2 + \frac{1}{2}n$.

Exercise 16H

1 Look again at the diagram at the start of Example 10.
Find an expression in terms of n for $T(n) + T(n - 1)$.
(Hint: square numbers.)

2 Find an expression for the nth hexagonal number.

3 This table shows the sum of the interior angles of polygons of different sizes. Use this sequence to find the sum of the interior angles of an n-sided polygon.

n	Sum of interior angles of n-sided polygon
3	180
4	360
5	540
6	720
7	900

4 Jude takes a piece of paper and draws straight lines across it, such that at each stage the paper is divided into the maximum number of regions possible.

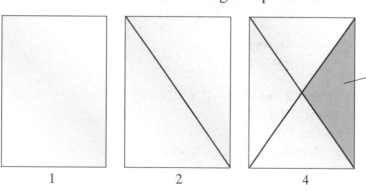

This is one region.

1   2   4

After drawing each line he records his results in a table:

Number of lines, n	Maximum number of regions

Copy and complete the table for $n = 0, 1, 2, 3, 4, 5$ and find the nth term of the sequence.

Summary of key points

1 When investigating number sequences you can find:
   - a rule to find the next term, called a term-to-term rule
   - a general rule to find the nth term, sometimes called the general term.

2 A sequence is linear (or arithmetic) if the difference between any two consecutive terms the same.

3 The nth term, $T(n)$, of any linear sequence can be written as

   $$T(n) = An + B$$

   where A and B are numbers.

4 The difference between terms in the sequence gives the number by which you multiply n in the general rule. You may need to add or subtract a number to complete the general rule.

5 A number machine maps one number onto another. You can write number machines as mappings.

   $+3$ ⟶ $\times 12$ ⟶ is the same as $x \longrightarrow 12\,(x + 3)$

6 A mapping tells you what happens to x as it goes through the number machines.
   The inverse mapping tells you what happens to x as it goes through the inverse number machines.

E When the first difference in a sequence is not constant but the second difference is constant, the general rule has the form $T(n) = An^2 + Bn + C$ where A, B and C are numbers. This is called a quadratic sequence.

E In quadratic sequences the second difference equals $2A$.

E 17 Trigonometry

Trigonometry is a branch of mathematics that brings together geometry, measure, arithmetic and algebra. Many professionals, such as surveyors, engineers, navigators and scientists, make regular use of trigonometry in their work.

E 17.1 Right-angled triangles

One of the most common uses of trigonometry is in working out lengths and angles in right-angled triangles.

First, you need to look at how the sides of a right-angled triangle are labelled:

The abbreviations **hyp**, **adj** and **opp** are used for 'hypotenuse', 'adjacent' and 'opposite'.

hypotenuse – the longest side, opposite the right angle

opposite – the side opposite the angle

adjacent – the side next to the angle

θ

The greek letter θ (pronounced 'theta') is often used to represent angles.

■ **The sides of a right-angled triangle can be labelled like this:**

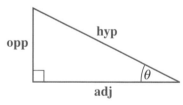

Exercise 17A

Sketch each of these triangles. Label each side 'opp', 'adj' and 'hyp' with respect to the marked angle θ.

1

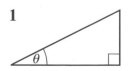

2

3

4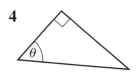

5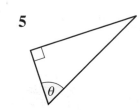

6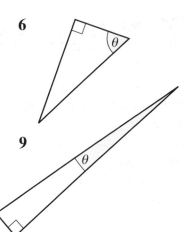

7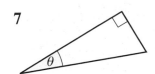

8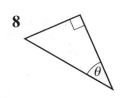

9

E 17.2 The trigonometric ratios

■ **The three trigonometric ratios for a right-angled triangle are:**

$$\sin \theta = \frac{\text{opp}}{\text{hyp}} \qquad \cos \theta = \frac{\text{adj}}{\text{hyp}} \qquad \tan \theta = \frac{\text{opp}}{\text{adj}}$$

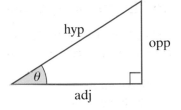

In this section you will investigate these ratios.

Exercise 17B – an investigation

Choose an angle θ between 30° and 70°.

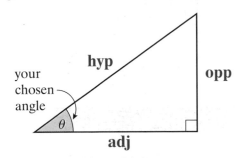

On graph paper, draw a 10 cm horizontal line. Draw a right angle at one end. At the other end, carefully measure out your chosen angle to complete a right-angled triangle.

Draw perpendiculars from the adjacent side to meet the hypotenuse (using graph paper makes this easy to do).

For triangle 5:

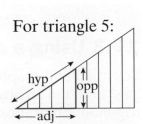

Measure each side and complete a table like this:

Angle $\theta =$ Write the size of your angle here.

Triangle	Adjacent (cm)	Opposite (cm)	Hypotenuse (cm)
1	1		
2	2		
and so on up to			
10	10		

Now use a calculator to work out these ratios, correct to two decimal places, for each triangle:

$$\frac{\text{opp}}{\text{hyp}} \qquad \frac{\text{adj}}{\text{hyp}} \qquad \frac{\text{opp}}{\text{adj}}$$

Put your results in a table like this:

Angle $\theta = \ldots$

Triangle	$\dfrac{\text{opp}}{\text{hyp}}$	$\dfrac{\text{adj}}{\text{hyp}}$	$\dfrac{\text{opp}}{\text{adj}}$
1			

What do you notice?

Do others in your class get similar results?

The values of the ratios $\dfrac{\text{opp}}{\text{hyp}}, \dfrac{\text{adj}}{\text{hyp}}$ and $\dfrac{\text{opp}}{\text{adj}}$ are constant for a given angle, θ.

They have special names:

$$\frac{\text{opp}}{\text{hyp}} = \sin\theta \qquad \frac{\text{adj}}{\text{hyp}} = \cos\theta \qquad \frac{\text{opp}}{\text{adj}} = \tan\theta$$

sin is short for 'sine'   cos is short for 'cosine'   tan is short for 'tangent'

The triangles are similar – there is more about similarity in Chapter 15.

E ## 17.3 Using a calculator 1

Scientific and graphical calculators have keys labelled 'sin', 'cos' and 'tan'. These make it easy to find the value of the trigonometric ratios of any angle.

Example 1

Use a calculator to find sin 52°, cos 52° and tan 52°, correct
to three decimal places.

On a **scientific calculator**

Press   sin 5 2 Ans

On some calculators
you press

 5 2 sin

On a **graphical calculator**

Press   sin 5 2 EXE

In both cases the display shows 0.788 010 75 . . .
You can find cos 52° and tan 52° in the same way, using the
'cos' and 'tan' keys.

   sin 52° = 0.788   cos 52° = 0.616   tan 52° = 1.280

■ **You can use the** sin **,** cos **and** tan **keys on a**
   calculator to find trigonometric ratios.

Exercise 17C

1   Use your calculator to find the values of:
    (a) cos 23°   **(b)** tan 45°
    (c) sin 78°   **(d)** cos 81°

2   **(a)** Copy and complete the table below, giving values
        to 3 significant figures.

Angle x	$\sin x$	$\cos x$	$\tan x$	$\dfrac{\sin x}{\cos x}$
0°	0	1	0	0
10°	0.174	0.985	0.176	. . .
20°				
30°				
and so on up to				
90°	1	0	–	–

    (b) Look at the two right-hand columns. What do
        you notice? Can you prove it?

Hint: Think about
how sine and cosine
are defined.

3 **(a)** On graph paper, draw axes from 0 to 1, using a scale of 0.1 to 1 cm. Label the horizontal axis 'cos *x*' and the vertical axis 'sin *x*'.

Plot the points (cos *x*, sin *x*), using the values in your table for question **2**.

Join the points with a smooth curve. What do you notice?

(b) Draw a line from the origin to the curve. Measure the angle between the horizontal axis and the line – call it *y*.

(i) Use a calculator to find the values of cos *y* and sin *y*. Plot the point (cos *y*, sin *y*). What do you notice?

(ii) Work out the gradient of the line. Work out the value of tan *y*. What do you notice?

(iii) Explain your answer to part **(ii)**.

4 Use your calculator to find the values of: tan 89°, tan 89.9°, tan 89.99°, tan 89.999°, tan 89.9999° and so on. What do you notice?

E 17.4 Finding unknown lengths in right-angled triangles

If you are given the length of one side and an angle, you can use trigonometric ratios to work out unknown lengths.

Example 2

In the triangle PQR, PR = 20 cm and angle PRQ = 52°.

Work out the length of PQ.

PR is the hypotenuse and, for the given angle, PQ is opposite.

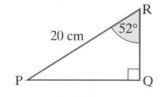

Since $\quad \sin \theta = \dfrac{\text{opp}}{\text{hyp}}$

then $\quad \sin 52° = \dfrac{PQ}{20}$

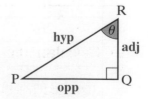

θ and hyp are known, opp is wanted. So choose the trigonometric ratio that links them.

So $PQ = 20 \times \sin 52°$

$\qquad = 20 \times 0.788\ldots$ (using a calculator)

$\qquad = 15.76\,\text{cm}$ (to 2 d.p.)

You can think of this as using $\sin\theta$ as a multiplier:

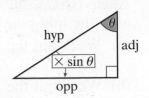

Exercise 17D

1 In this question all of the lengths are in cm. Work out the length of each side marked with a letter. Give your answer in cm and correct to 2 d.p.

(a)
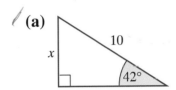

(b)
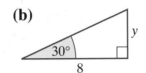

(c)
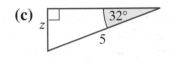

(d)
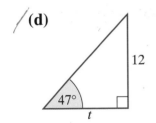

(e)
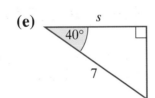

(f)
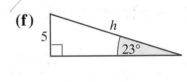

(g)
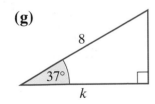

(h)
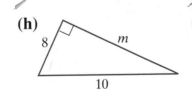

(i)
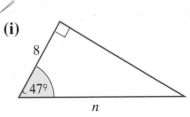

2 **(a)** Calculate the perimeter of triangle RST.
   (b) Calculate the shortest distance from S to the line RT.

Hint: The shortest distance from a point to a line is the perpendicular to the line that goes through the point.

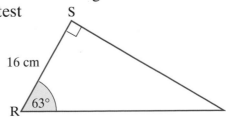

3 ABC is an isosceles triangle.
AB = AC = 12 cm
Angle BAC = 40°
M is the mid-point of BC.

(a) Work out the length of AM.

(b) Work out the area of the triangle ABC.

State the units and degree of accuracy for each answer.

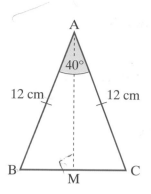

Remember:
area of triangle
$= \frac{1}{2} \times$ base × height

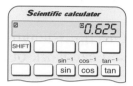

E **17.5 Using a calculator 2**

Sometimes you might be given the value of a trigonometric ratio and be asked to work out the angle. You can do this using a calculator.

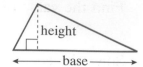

Example 3

Find the value of angle θ in each of these cases.
Give your answers correct to one decimal place.

(a) $\tan \theta = 0.625$ (b) $\cos \theta = 0.906$ (c) $\sin \theta = 0.6$

Once again, different calculators may use different key presses. Check how to work out $\tan^{-1}(0.625)$ on your calculator.

$\tan \theta = 0.625$ is sometimes rewritten

as $\theta = \tan^{-1}(0.625)$

You might see this form on your calculator.

The display shows 32.005 3832…

Using your calculator you should get these answers:

(a) $\theta = 32.0°$ (b) $\theta = 25.0°$ (c) $\theta = 36.9°$

Exercise 17E

1 Find the value of angle A when:

(a) $\sin A = 0.1$ (b) $\tan A = 1.333\,333$ (c) $\cos A = 0.6$

(d) $\tan A = 1$ (e) $\sin A = 0.75$ (f) $\cos A = 0.453$

(g) $\cos A = 0.234$ (h) $\tan A = 2.3$ (i) $\sin A = 0.1234$

(j) $\tan A = \frac{5}{6}$ (k) $\sin A = 0.95$ (l) $\cos A = 0.345$

2   Find the value of angle θ if
$$2\sin\theta = 1$$

3   Find the value of angle A if:
$$5\cos A = 2$$

4   Find the value of angle B if:
$$2\tan B = 1$$

5   Solve the equation:
$$5\sin x = 3$$

> Hint:
> $2\sin\theta = 1$ means
> $2 \times \sin\theta = 1$
> so $\sin\theta = \frac{1}{2}$
> or $\sin\theta = 0.5$

E 17.6 Finding unknown angles in right-angled triangles

Given the lengths of two sides of a right-angled triangle,
you can work out the size of the angles.

Example 4

Work out the size of the angle marked θ.

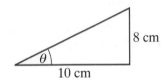

In the triangle you are given:

opposite $= 8\,\text{cm}$ adjacent $= 10\,\text{cm}$

From the three trigonometric ratios, the one using opp
and adj is:

$$\tan\theta = \frac{\text{opp}}{\text{adj}}$$

so $\tan\theta = \dfrac{8}{10} = 0.8$

Using a calculator:

$$\theta = 38.7° \text{ (to 1 d.p.)}$$

Remember:

$$\sin\theta = \frac{\text{opp}}{\text{hyp}}$$

$$\cos\theta = \frac{\text{adj}}{\text{hyp}}$$

$$\tan\theta = \frac{\text{opp}}{\text{adj}}$$

Exercise 17F

1   In this question all the lengths are in centimetres.
Work out the size of each angle labelled with a letter.
Give your answers in degrees and correct to one
decimal place.

(a)
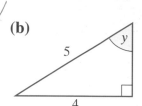

(b)
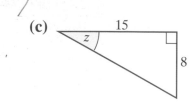

(c)

(d)
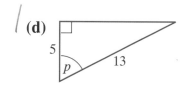

(e)
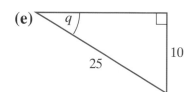

(f)
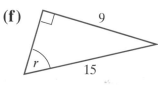

(g)
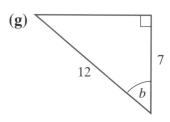

(h)
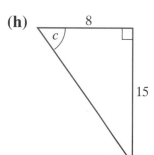

(i)
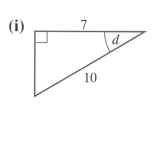

2   In the diagram BCD is a straight line,
AB = 12 cm,   angle ABC = 43°,
AC is perpendicular to BD,
CD = 20 cm.

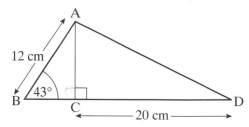

Work out:

(a) the length of AC,

(b) the size of angle ADC.

E 17.7 Using trigonometry to solve problems

You can use trigonometry to solve problems involving bearings and angles of elevation and depression.

Example 5

The diagram shows the positions of four towns.

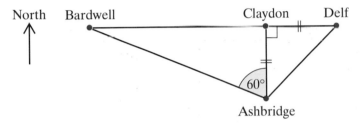

Claydon is directly North of Ashbridge.

Bardwell is directly West of Claydon.

Delf is directly East of Claydon.

The distance from Claydon to Delf is the same as the distance from Claydon to Ashbridge.

(a) Work out the bearing of Delf from Ashbridge.

(b) Work out the bearing of Bardwell from Ashbridge.

(c) Work out the bearing of Ashbridge from Delf.

(a) Since DA = DC, triangle ADC is an isosceles right-angled triangle, and so angle CAD = 45°

So the bearing of Delf from Ashbridge is 045°

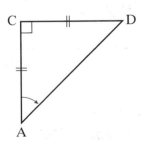

(b) Angle BAC = 60° so the reflex angle BAC = 360° − 60° = 300°

So the bearing of Bardwell from Ashbridge is 300°

(c) The angle from North, around D (Delf) to A (Ashbridge) is 180° + 45° = 225°

So the bearing of Ashbridge from Delf is 225°

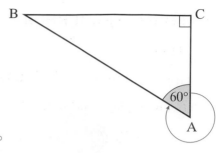

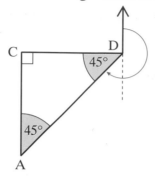

Remember:
Bearings are always measured **clockwise** from North.

Example 6

The diagram shows the relative positions of the three landmarks P, Q and R.

R is 8 kilometres East of Q.
Q is North of P.
The distance from P to R is 17 kilometres.

Work out

(a) the distance from P to Q   **(b)** the size of the angle *r*

(c) the bearing of R from P to the nearest degree.

(a) Using Pythagoras' theorem:

$$PQ^2 + QR^2 = PR^2$$
$$PQ^2 + 8^2 = 17^2$$
$$PQ^2 = 289 - 64 = 225$$
$$PQ = \sqrt{225} = 15 \text{ km}$$

(b) PR (hyp) and QR (adj) are known, so use the formula for cos *r*.

$$\cos r = \frac{8}{17} = 0.4706\ldots$$
$$r = 61.9° \text{ (to 1 d.p.)}$$

Remember:

$$\cos r = \frac{\text{adj}}{\text{hyp}}$$

(c) Let the angle at $P = p$.

Then

$$p + 90 + r = 180 \text{ (angle sum of triangle)}$$

So $p = 180 - 90 - 61.9$

$$= 28.1°$$

So the bearing of R from P is $028°$ (to the nearest degree).

Angles of elevation and depression

Imagine that you are standing on flat ground looking straight ahead. You look up at the top of a tree. The angle you turn your eyes through is the **angle of elevation** of the top of the tree from where your head is.

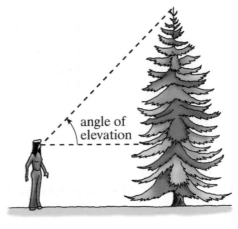

Here is a picture of a boat out at sea.

The angle between the line from the top of the cliff to the boat and the horizontal line across from the top of the cliff is 50°.

The **angle of depression** of the boat from the top of the cliff is 50°.

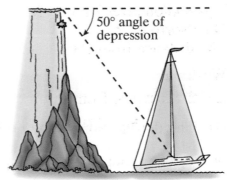

■ **This diagram shows the angle of elevation of A from B.**

■ **This diagram shows the angle of depression of X from Y.**

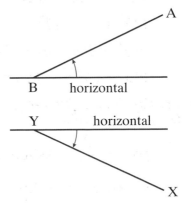

Example 7

The diagram shows a vertical mast of height 12 metres.

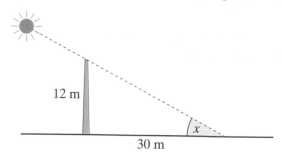

The length of the mast's shadow on horizontal ground is 30 metres.

Calculate the angle of elevation of the sun.

Let the angle of elevation be x.

You know the lengths of the opposite and adjacent sides, so use the formula for $\tan x$.

So $\tan x = \dfrac{12}{30} = 0.4$

Using a calculator,

$x = 21.8°$ (correct to 1 d.p.)

Remember:

$$\tan x = \frac{\text{opp}}{\text{adj}}$$

Exercise 17G

1   The diagram shows the positions of three radio masts.
    Mast A is South of mast B and 9 km from mast C.
    Mast C is 5 km West of mast B.

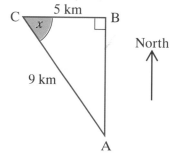

(a) Calculate the distance from mast A to mast B.
    Give your answer correct to three significant
    figures.

(b) Calculate the size of the angle marked x.
Give your answer in degrees correct to 1 d.p.

(c) Work out the bearing of C from A.

Remember:
Bearings are
measured clockwise
from North.

2 A vertical flag-pole of height 15 metres casts a shadow of length 40 metres on horizontal ground.

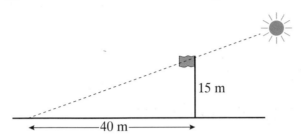

15 m

40 m

Calculate the angle of elevation of the sun.

3 As it comes into land, an aeroplane descends at a constant angle. It travels 4 kilometres and descends 200 metres.

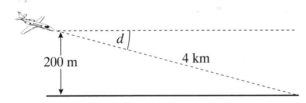

d

200 m

4 km

Calculate the aeroplane's angle of descent, d.

4 The diagram represents the cross-section of a valley.

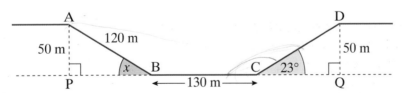

A

D

120 m

50 m

50 m

x B

C 23°

P

130 m

Q

Calculate:

(a) the angle x

(b) the distance PB

(c) the distance CQ

(d) the distance PQ

(e) the distance CD

(f) the distance straight across the valley from D to A

(g) the angle of elevation of A from C

(h) the angle of depression of P from D.

5 The diagram shows the relative positions of three towns. A is South of B, and C is East of B. AB = 40 km and BC = 9 km.

(a) Calculate the distance AC.

(b) Calculate the bearing of C from A.

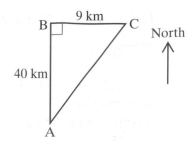

E **17.8 Puzzles and problems**

You can now use what you have learnt to tackle these puzzles and problems.

Exercise 17H

1 (a) Work out the lengths of
  (i) BM
  (ii) BC

(b) Write down the values of
  (i) $\cos x$
  (ii) $\tan z$
  (iii) $\sin y$

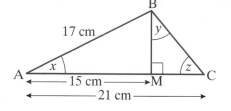

2 The diagram shows three towns: A, B and C.

(a) Calculate the distance between town B and town C.

(b) Work out the bearing of town C from town B.

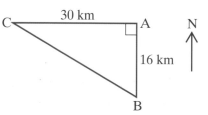

3 ABCDE is a regular pentagon, centre O. The perimeter of the pentagon is 100 cm.

(a) Work out the area of the triangle AOB.

(b) Work out the area of the pentagon ABCDE.

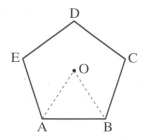

4   The angle θ is acute and

$$\cos \theta = \tfrac{5}{13}$$

without using a calculator, write down the value of $\sin x$
as a fraction.
(Hint: You looked at Pythagorean triples in Chapter 13.)

5   A ship travels East from the lighthouse L to the
lighthouse M.

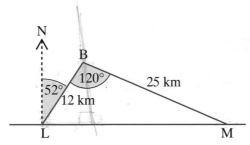

A second ship travelling from L to M is forced to take
a detour via the marker buoy B.
Work out the difference in the distances travelled by
the two ships.

6   ABCD is a rectangle.

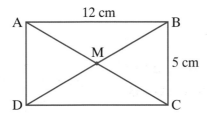

The diagonals AC and BD meet at M.
Work out

(a) the length AC,

(b) the size of the angle DMC.

7   Work out the angle that the graph of $2y = 3x - 4$
makes with the x-axis.

8 Work out

(a) the length AD

(b) the angle DAC.

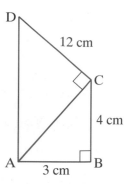

9 Calculate the area of a regular hexagon with perimeter 1200 cm.

10 The diagram shows the path taken by a ship.

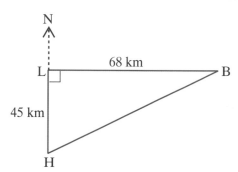

The ship left a harbour H and travelled 45 km North to a lighthouse L.

At L the ship turned East and travelled a further 68 km to a marker buoy B.

At B the ship turned again and travelled in a straight line back to H.

(a) Calculate the total distance travelled by the ship.

(b) Calculate the bearing of B from H.

(c) Calculate the shortest distance between the ship and the lighthouse L on the ship's return journey from B to H.

11 The angle y is acute and

$$\tan y = 0.75$$

Without using a calculator, work out the value of $\sin y$.

12 A road has a gradient of 20%. Find the angle that the road makes with the horizontal.

(*Hint*: Write the percentage as a fraction.)

You have looked at gradients in Chapter 7.

13 The total angle of swing of a particular
pendulum is 40° (20° each way).
Work out the difference in height of
the bottom of the pendulum at the
lowest and highest point in its swing.

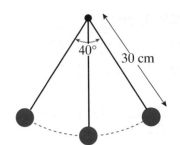

14 Solve the equation

$$\sin x = \cos x$$

Explain how you found your solution.

Summary of key points

E The sides of a right-angled triangle
can be labelled like this:

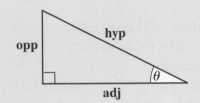

E The three trigonometric ratios for a right-angled triangle are:

$$\sin \theta = \frac{\text{opp}}{\text{hyp}} \qquad \cos \theta = \frac{\text{adj}}{\text{hyp}} \qquad \tan \theta = \frac{\text{opp}}{\text{adj}}$$

E You can use the `sin`, `cos` and `tan` keys on a calculator to find
trigonometric ratios.

E This diagram shows
the angle of elevation
of A from B.

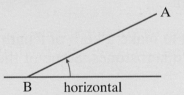

E This diagram shows
the angle of depression
of X from Y.

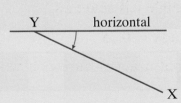

18 Using and applying mathematics

Introduction

This chapter is about the **problem-solving process**. In the chapter you will learn more about how to use and apply mathematics to **investigate** a problem-solving situation.

18.1 The problem

This problem is about making kerbs of various lengths from kerbstones of different length.
At the start we just have two different kerbstones:

white kerbstones

which are of length 1 unit

red kerbstones

which are of length 2 units.

Suppose that we wanted to make a kerb of length 10 units using these white and red kerbstones. Some of the different ways of doing this are:

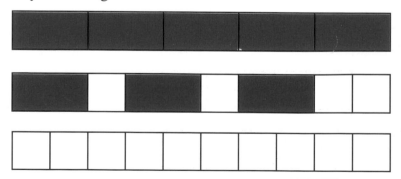

There are a lot of different ways and we would probably get mixed up if we tried to list them all.

Solving the problem means that if you need a kerb of a particular length, you can state how many different ways there are of making that length of kerb. You should also be able to explain why your answer is true.

Understand the problem

The first thing you need to do is make sure that you understand the problem.

In this problem you have a selection of:

white kerbstones ☐ of length 1 unit

and red kerbstones ▮ of length 2 units

You are going to investigate the **number of different ways** of making a kerb of any length.

For instance, if the kerb is of length 5 units then some of the different ways of making it are:

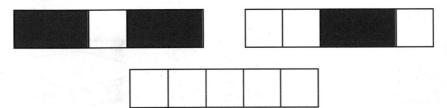

Exercise 18A

Here are four different ways of making a kerb of length five units using the white and red kerbstones:

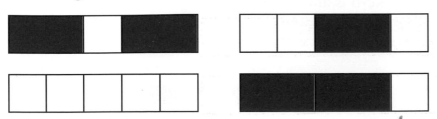

Find at least **two other ways** of making a kerb of length five units.

18.2 Simplify the problem

The first stage of the problem-solving process is to make the problem as simple as you can.

Start by looking at some kerbs of very short lengths, such as 1, 2 and 3 units.

The simplest case is when the kerb is of length 1 unit.

A very simple case is called a **trivial** case.

It can be made in only **one way**. by using a single white kerbstone:

When the length of the kerb is two units it can be made in two ways:

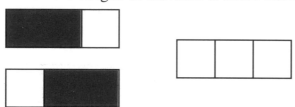

and

When the length of the kerb is three units it can be made as:

So when the length of the kerb is three units, it can be made in three ways.

Now you have three simple results:

Length of kerb	Number of ways
1	1
2	2
3	3

At this stage you might start to think that the number of different ways of making a kerb is always equal to the length of the kerb – but you would be wrong, as the next exercise shows.

Exercise 18B

Show that there are five different ways of making a kerb of length four units.

18.3 Developing strategies

One of the most important parts of the problem-solving and investigation process is developing a strategy.

An efficient strategy for the kerbstones problem would be to use letters to represent the kerbstones:

w to represent white [ ]   *r* to represent ,red

You can now represent your kerbs using the letters *r* and *w* in different orders. The five different kerbs of length 4 units look like this:

r r 2 red and 0 white

r w w
w r w 1 red and 2 white (in any order)
w w r

w w w w 0 red and 4 white

You only use three different combinations of blocks to make the five different kerbs.

There are three different kerbs that use one red block and two white blocks.

There is a pattern where it seems as if the red (or *r*) *slides* down a diagonal

r w w
w r w
w w r

You now have three strategies that are helpful in solving the problem:

1 using letters to represent the kerbstones

2 separating the different combinations of blocks such as 1 red and 2 white, etc.

3 the *sliding* of a single letter down a diagonal.

Strategy 3 is an example of writing your results in a **systematic** way.
If you had written:

w w r
r w w
w r w

you might not have spotted a pattern.

Example 1

Use the strategies to find all eight ways of making a kerb of length five units.

A kerb of length 5 units can be made as:

2 red and 1 white	*w r r* *r w r* *r r w*	3 ways
1 red and 3 white	*r w w w* *w r w w* *w w r w* *w w w r*	4 ways
0 red and 5 white	*w w w w w*	1 way

This gives a total of $3 + 4 + 1 = 8$ ways.

Recording results and making observations

You now have five results. It is a good idea to record your results in a table:

Length of kerb	Number of different ways of making the kerb
1	1
2	2
3	3
4	5
5	8

You need to be able to make observations based on your results.

For instance, quite simply you might see that:

As the length of the kerb increases then the number of ways of making it also increases.

You might also notice that:

The pattern for the number of ways of making a kerb goes

odd	even	odd	odd	even
1	2	3	5	8

You should try to find a rule:

The pattern for the number of ways of making a kerb, that is, the numbers:

1,   2,   3,   5,   8

is generated by the following rule.

The next number is the sum of the previous two numbers

$$3 + 5 = 8$$

1,   2,   3,   5,   8

$$2 + 3 = 5$$

Making and testing a prediction

You now have a possible rule for finding the next number in the sequence. This is called a **conjecture**. It is a statement about **what you think is happening**. The conjecture is:

The next number is the sum of the previous two numbers.

You can use your conjecture to make a **prediction**. You can add your prediction to your table of results:

Length of kerb	Number of different ways of making the kerb
1	1
2	2
3	$2 + 1 = 3$
4	$3 + 2 = 5$
5	$5 + 3 = 8$
6	$8 + 5 = 13$

Using your conjecture, you can predict that there are 13 different ways of making a kerb of length 6 units.

You now need to **test your prediction**. You can use your strategies to find the number of different kerbs of length 6 units:

3 red and 0 white	*r r r*	1 way

	r r w w	
	r w r w	
2 red and 2 white	*r w w r*	6 ways
	w w r r	
	w r w r	
	w r r w	

	r w w w w	
	w r w w w	
1 red and 4 white	*w w r w w*	5 ways
	w w w r w	
	w w w w r	

0 red and 6 white	*w w w w w w*	1 way

There are $1 + 6 + 5 + 1 = 13$ ways to make a kerb of length 6.

You now have 6 definite results:

Length of kerb	Number of different ways of making the kerb
1	1
2	2
3	3
4	5 $\Big\rangle +$
5	8
6	13 $=$

You have made a prediction, tested it and found it to be true. You can be **very confident** that the general rule is true.

However, there is far more to establishing truth in mathematics than the confidence that comes from predicting and testing. Later on in this chapter you will explain **why the rule works**.

Exercise 18C

Using the general rule:

1 **(a)** make a prediction for the number of different ways of making a kerb of length 7 units.
(b) test that prediction.

2 Make predictions for the number of different ways of making a kerb of length:
(a) 8 units   **(b)** 9 units   **(c)** 10 units

18.4 Using symbols

In section 18.3 you used letters to represent the kerbstones. It will be useful to be able to write the general rule using letters and symbols.

The general rule for the kerbstones problem is:

The next number in the sequence is the sum of the previous two numbers.

One way to write this in symbols would be to call the next number the nth number. Then you could write the rule as:

$$n\text{th} = (n-1)\text{th} + (n-2)\text{th}$$

This is a better way of writing the rule, but it is still not very elegant. You could use the symbol U_n to mean the nth term of the sequence.

You couldn't just write

$$n = (n-1) + (n-2)$$

This is an equation which can be solved to give $n = 3$.

Example 2

Write down U_5 for the sequence given by the kerbstones problem.

The sequence is:

$$1, \quad 2, \quad 3, \quad 5, \quad 8, \quad 13, \quad \ldots$$

                  ↑
The 5th term is 8

$$U_5 = 8$$

Example 3

Write down the general rule for the kerbstone problem using U_n to represent the nth term of the sequence.

The rule is:

$$n\text{th} = (n-1)\text{th} + (n-2)\text{th}$$

You can write this:

$$U_n = U_{n-1} + U_{n-2}$$

Exercise 18D

1   For the kerbstone sequence:

$$1, \quad 2, \quad 3, \quad 5, \quad 8, \quad 13, \quad \ldots$$

write down the values of:
   (a) U_1 **(b)** U_4 **(c)** U_7 **(d)** $U_8 + U_9$

2   Write these rules using U_n to represent the nth term of the sequence.
   (a) The next number in the sequence is twice the previous number.
   (b) The next number in the sequence is the previous number plus three.
   (c) The next number in the sequence is the product of the previous two numbers.

Remember:
the product of a and b is $a \times b$ or ab.

18.5 Have you seen it before?

At any stage in the problem solving or investigative process you should ask yourself, *'Have I seen this or something like this before?'*

You might have seen the sequence

$$1, \quad 2, \quad 3, \quad 5, \quad 8, \quad 13, \quad \ldots$$

before.

The sequence is known as the **Fibonacci sequence**. It was first developed by an Italian mathematician called Leonardo of Pisa in the thirteenth century.

Example 4

For the Fibonacci sequence:

   1,   2,   3,   5,   8,   13,   21,   ...

Work out the value of $\dfrac{U_5}{U_4}$

$U_5 = 8, U_4 = 5$

So $\dfrac{U_5}{U_4} = \dfrac{8}{5} = 1.6$

Exercise 18E

For the Fibonacci sequence, work out these values:

1 $\dfrac{U_6}{U_5}$

2 $\dfrac{U_{n+1}}{U_n}$ for values of n from 1 to 9

3   Draw axes on graph paper. Put n along the horizontal axis from 0 to 9. Put $\dfrac{U_{n+1}}{U_n}$ on the vertical axis from 0 to 3, using a scale of 1 cm to 0.25.
Plot your values from question **2**. What do you notice?

4   Without working out any values, write down what you think $\dfrac{U_{100}}{U_{99}}$ might be to one decimal place.

18.6 Why does it work?

You should now be confident that the solutions to the kerbstone problem are like this:

Length of kerb	1	2	3	4	5	6	7	8	9	10
Number of ways	1	2	3	5	8	13	21	34	55	89

You also know that the rule for the number sequence is:

The next number is the sum of the previous two numbers

and that this rule can be written in symbols as:

$$U_n = U_{n-1} + U_{n-2}$$

The next stage of the process is to **justify** this rule. You need to say **why it works**.

A self-justifying system

Go back and look at the original problem.

The ways of making a kerb of length 3 are:

The ways of making a kerb of length 4 are:

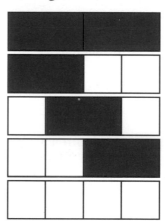

There are two ways of making a kerb of length five:

Take a kerb of length three and add a single red block to the end:

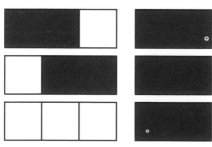

Take a kerb of length four and add a single white block to the end:

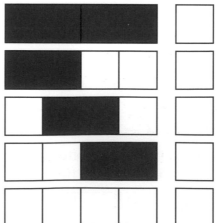

These are all eight ways of making a kerb of length five.

You now have a very powerful system for making a kerb of a particular length from your knowledge of the kerbs of the two previous lengths.

You can use the same argument to show why the general rule must be true.

There are two ways to make a kerb of length n units:

Take a kerb of length $n - 1$ units and add a single white block to the end:

Take a kerb of length $n - 2$ units and add a single red block to the end:

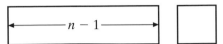   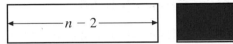

There are U_{n-1} kerbs of length $n - 1$ units, so you make U_{n-1} kerbs in the first way.

There are U_{n-2} kerbs of length $n - 2$ units, so you make U_{n-2} kerbs in the second way.

This is all the kerbs of length n:

$$U_n = U_{n-1} + U_{n-2}$$

This way of constructing kerbs is called a **self-justifying system**. It not only tells you how to make all the kerbs of a certain length, but it also shows you **why the rule is true**.

You have now correctly established a general rule, expressed it in symbols and said why it works.

You have successfully **solved the original problem**.

Extending the problem

Mathematical problems can always be extended – one problem can lead to another.

In the original problem you made kerbs from:

white kerbstones of length 1 unit:

red kerbstones of length 2 units:

The general rule for a kerb of length n units is:

$$U_n = U_{n-1} + U_{n-2}$$

where U_n is the number of ways of making a kerb of length n units.

Changing variables

Having solved the problem with the white and red kerbstones a good mathematical question to ask is:

What will happen if we change the problem to making kerbs when we use:

white kerbstones of length 1 unit:

green kerbstones of length 3 units:

You could start again with some simple lengths of kerbs and list the ways a certain length can be made.

For example, using white and green and writing:

w for ☐ and *g* for ▭

a kerb of length 6 units can be made as:

g g

g w w w
w g w w
w w g w
w w w g

w w w w w w

So using white (of length 1 unit) and green (of length 3 units), a kerb of length 6 units can be made in 6 ways.

But if you repeat the process of listing all the possibilities, as you did before, then you have not learnt from your previous experience.

The key to solving the original problem was making kerbs of a particular length from your knowledge of kerbs of previous lengths.

Using white and green blocks, you can make a kerb of length *n* units in two ways:

Take a kerb of length $n - 1$ units and add a single white block to the end:

Take a kerb of length $n - 3$ units and add a single green block to the end:

$\longleftarrow n - 1 \longrightarrow$

$\longleftarrow n - 3 \longrightarrow$

The general rule for the number of kerbs of length n units, or U_n, with green and white blocks is:

$$U_n = U_{n-1} + U_{n-3}$$

You can test this rule by checking some cases.

Example 5

(a) Show that by using white (of length 1) and green (of length 3) kerbstones, a kerb of length 6 units can be made in $U_6 = 6$ different ways.

(b) Confirm that $U_6 = U_5 + U_3$

(a) 6 units: g g
　　　　　　g w w w
　　　　　　w g w w
　　　　　　w w g w
　　　　　　w w w g
　　　　　　w w w w w w   so $U_6 = 6$

(b) 5 units: g w w
　　　　　　w g w
　　　　　　w w g
　　　　　　w w w w w   so $U_5 = 4$

　　3 units: g
　　　　　　w w w   so $U_3 = 2$

$U_5 + U_3 = 4 + 2 = 6 = U_6$

Exercise 18F

You are making kerbs using white and green kerbstones.

1 Work out the values of:
   (a) U_7
   (b) U_8

2 Confirm that:
   (i) $U_7 = U_6 + U_4$
   (ii) $U_8 = U_7 + U_5$

18.7 Further extensions

The problem using white and green kerbstones is now solved, but that does not stop you going further.

Suppose you want to make kerbs of various lengths using:

white kerbstones of length 1 unit:

purple kerbstones of length 4 units:

You can use your previous experience to make a **conjecture** straight away.

This is the third problem you've looked at. It is useful to be able to label the problems in an easy way.

The first problem used white and red kerbstones, of lengths 1 and 2. You can call this the $(1, 2)$ problem.

The second problem used white and green kerbstones of lengths 1 and 3. This was the $(1, 3)$ problem.

The general rules are:

$(1, 2)$ problem: $U_n = U_{n-1} + U_{n-2}$
$(1, 3)$ problem: $U_n = U_{n-1} + U_{n-3}$

The new problem uses white and purple blocks of lengths 1 and 4. Your conjecture is:

$(1, 4)$ problem: $U_n = U_{n-1} + U_{n-4}$

This is still only a conjecture.
You haven't shown why it is true yet.

Exercise 18G

1   Copy and complete this table for making kerbs using white (of length 1) and purple (of length 4) kerbstones.

Length of kerb	1	2	3	4	5	6	7	8	9	10
Number of ways	1									

2 Confirm that in all cases

$$U_n = U_{n-1} + U_{n-4}$$

3 Explain why

$$U_n = U_{n-1} + U_{n-4}$$

E 18.8 Extending and generalising

This exercise offers some further opportunities to extend the problem.

Exercise 18H

1 Kerbs of varying lengths are to be made from:

white kerbstones of length 1 unit:

yellow kerbstones of length 5 units:

Write down and justify the general relationship for U_n.

2 A kerb of any length is to be made from:

red kerbstones of length 2 units: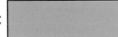

green kerbstones of length 3 units:

Write down and justify the general relationship for U_n.

3 A kerb of any length is to be made from:

red kerbstones of length 2 units:

yellow kerbstones of length 5 units:

Write down and justify the general relationship for U_n.

4 A kerb of any length is to be made from kerbstones of length:

x units

y units

(a) Write down the general result for U_n.

(b) Justify this result.

(c) Investigate these cases:
  (i) $x = 2, y = 4$
  (ii) $x = 6, y = 9$
  (iii) x and y have a common factor
  (iv) x and y are co-prime

Two numbers are co-prime if they have no common factor other than 1.

5 A kerb of any length is to be made from these kerbstones:

white (length 1)

red (length 2)

green (length 3)

Establish and justify a general relationship for U_n, the number of ways of making a kerb of length n units.

Summary of key points

In any problem-solving or investigative situation you should

1 Make sure that you understand the problem.

2 Ask yourself if you have seen the problem or something like it before. You may be able to benefit from that experience.

3 Simplify the problem.

4 Develop strategies to deal with the problem.

5 Record results and make observations.

6 Make and test predictions.

7 Make a generalisation.

8 Use symbols wherever appropriate.

9 Justify the results – explain why they work.

10 Extend the problem or investigation by changing some variables.

11 Reflect on what you have done to solve the extended problem.

12 Justify or prove any results to your extended problems.

19 Calculators and computers

This unit shows you ways of using scientific calculators, graphical calculators and computer software to help build on and extend the work you have been studying in the other units of this book.

Some of the activities are designed to work on Casio calculators. Your teacher will tell you if you need to do anything differently.

19.1 Investigating π

Many mathematicians, both professional and amateur, have attempted to find good approximations for π.

There is more about π on page 38.

Computers are often used to find good decimal approximations to π. The largest number of decimal places ever calculated on a PC is 6442 450 944.

Over 206 158 430 208 decimal digits is the 1999 world record, generated on a super computer. Below are the first 38 decimal places.

$\pi = 3.14159265358979323846243383279502884197$

View the first 10 000 decimal digits of π at www.heinemann. co.uk/hotlinks (express code: PIDIGITS)

Exercise 19A Scientific calculator

1   Measure the length of the 38 decimal digits in the approximation for π above and estimate the number of times 206 158 430 208 digits will wrap round the equator. (Use a radius of 6400 km for the Earth.)

2   The Indian mathematician Srinivasa Aiyangar Ramanujan found the following approximations for π. Find the value of each one and list them in ascending order.

(a) $\dfrac{19\sqrt{7}}{16}$

Find out about Ramanujan's amazing life at www. heinemann.co.uk/ hotlinks (express code: SAR1)

(b) $\dfrac{7}{3}\left(1+\dfrac{1}{5}\sqrt{3}\right)$

(c) $\dfrac{9}{5}+\sqrt{\dfrac{9}{5}}$

(d) $\dfrac{63}{25}\left(\dfrac{17+15\sqrt{5}}{7+15\sqrt{5}}\right)$ _____

(e) $\dfrac{355}{113}\left(1-\dfrac{0.0003}{3533}\right)$

Hint: In this approximation you should add brackets around both the numerator and denominator:

$\dfrac{63}{25}\left(\dfrac{(17+15\sqrt{5})}{(7+15\sqrt{5})}\right)$

3 What do you notice about these Ramanujan approximations for π?

$$\left(102-\dfrac{2222}{22^2}\right)^{\frac{1}{4}}, \quad \left(9^2+\dfrac{19^2}{22}\right)^{\frac{1}{4}}, \quad \left(97+\dfrac{1}{2}-\dfrac{1}{11}\right)^{\frac{1}{4}}$$

(Remember to include brackets around the power $\frac{1}{4}$.)

Find out what Ramanajun observed about the number 1729 at www.heinemann.co.uk/hotlinks (express code: SAR2)

4 Work out the following approximation for π, which uses all of the digits from 1 to 9.

$$\sqrt{\sqrt{3^4+\dfrac{19^2}{78-56}}}$$

5 Which is the more accurate of the following two approximations for π?

$$\left(\dfrac{1700^3+82^3-10^3-9^3-6^3-3^3}{69^5}\right)$$

$$\left(100-\dfrac{2125^3+214^3+30^3+37^2}{82^5}\right)^{\frac{1}{4}}$$

There is more about indices and roots on pages 10 to 16.

19.2 Bearings, polygons and loci

You can draw bearings, constructions and loci on a computer using *WinLogo*.

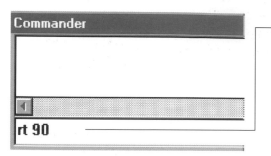

Type your instructions here and then press the Enter key before typing your next set of instructions.

In *WinLogo* you must provide instructions to move the 'turtle' around the screen.

The turtle begins this way round:

rt 90

will turn it 90° clockwise.

fd 100

will move it forward '100' places and draw a line '100' units long.

Example 1

Draw on screen:

(a) a bearing of 070°

(b) a bearing of 330°

(a) Type:
fd 100 label ″N bk 100
rt 70 fd 100

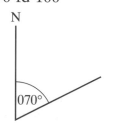

(b) Type:
cs fd 100 label
″N bk 100
rt 330 fd 100

You will find the following instructions useful in this section:

bk 100
will move it back '100' places and draw a line '100' units long.

lt 90
will turn it 90° anticlockwise.

pu
will pick the pen up and you will not be able to draw again until you enter:

pd
which puts the pen down again.

cs
clears the screen and places the turtle back at the origin [0 0].

Label "Alice
to put the word 'Alice' on screen

Exercise 19B WinLogo

1 Use *WinLogo* to draw:

  (a) a bearing of 060°   **(b)** a bearing of 120°

  (c) a bearing of 210°   **(d)** a bearing of 290°

  (e) a journey of 200 kilometres on a bearing of 230°, using a scale of 20 logo units to represent 50 km.

  (f) the following journey

In parts (a) to (d) make the 'arms' of your bearing 100 units long.

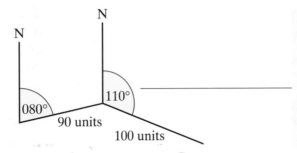

Hint:
After moving forward 90 units on the first leg of your journey, you will need to turn left through 80° before heading North again.

2 Use *WinLogo* to construct:

  (a) angle BAC and its bisector, where angle BAC is 50°

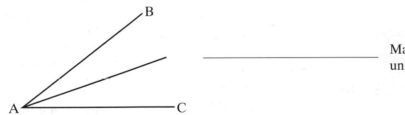

Make each line 100 units long

  (b) the line EF and its perpendicular bisector, GH

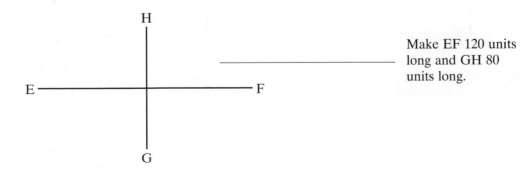

Make EF 120 units long and GH 80 units long.

3 Use *WinLogo* to construct the following set of nested regular polygons:

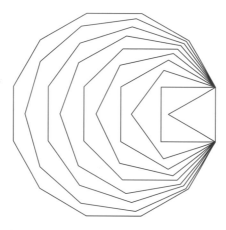

Hint: For the heptagon, a polygon with 7 sides, and the 11-gon, you need to use the decimal point in *WinLogo* for the left turn.

Each polygon has a side of size 40 units.

The code for the octagon is:
repeat 8[fd 40 lt 45]

the number of sides, *n*

$$\frac{360°}{n}$$

4 Use *WinLogo* to draw:

(a) the locus of a point which is always the same distance from a given point

(b) the locus of a point which is always the same distance from AB as it is from AC in the diagram below

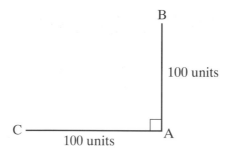

Hint:
Think of a circle as a polygon with a lot of sides, say 360.

There is more about the locus of a point on page 231.

B

100 units

C ──────── A
   100 units

(c) the locus of a point which is always the same distance from the line EF below

E

150 units

F

5   Use *WinLogo* to recreate the following image:

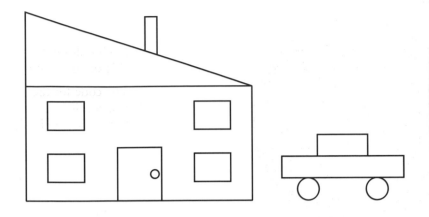

You will need your knowledge of trigonometry from Chapter 17 to help you draw the roof.

19.3 Cumulative frequencies

You can use a spreadsheet to create cumulative frequency curves and use them to *estimate* the median average, lower quartile and upper quartile for a set of data.

Exercise 19C Spreadsheet

1   The heights in millimetres of 60 shrubs were measured to the nearest mm. The results are shown in the table.

Height in mm	Frequency	Cumulative frequency
50–59	9	9
60–69	11	20
70–79	6	26
80–89	14	40
90–99	8	48
100–109	12	60

There is more about grouped continuous data and cumulative frequency curves in Chapter 4.

In a spreadsheet:

- Write labels in cells A1, B1 and C1 as shown in the diagram.
- Enter 59 in cell A2.
- Enter the formula =A2+10 in cell A3 and copy it down to cell A7.
- Enter the frequencies from the table into cells B2 to B7.
- Enter the number 9 in cell C2.
- Enter the formula =B3+C2 in cell C3 and copy it down to cell C7.
- Highlight the cells A1 to A7 and *while holding down the Ctrl key on your keyboard*, highlight cells C1 to C7.
- Use the chart wizard to draw a cumulative frequency curve, similar to the one below:

You use the end of the range when plotting the cumulative frequencies.

	A	B	C
1	Height in mm	Frequency	Cumulative frequency
2	59	9	9
3	69	11	=B3+C2
4	79	5	
5	89	14	

Drag this square down to cell C7 to copy the formula down

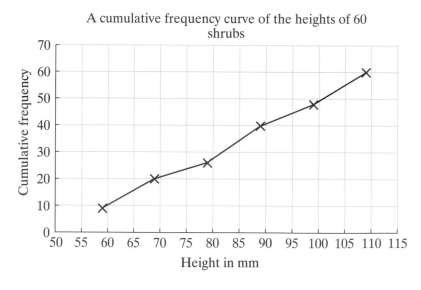

A cumulative frequency curve of the heights of 60 shrubs

Choose the *XY* (*Scatter*) graph option at stage 1 of the wizard.

Use a printout of your curve to *estimate*:

(a) the median height of the shrubs, ──────────

(b) the number of shrubs with a height between 65 mm and 70 mm,

(c) the lower quartile and upper quartile.

2 The resting pulse rates of 100 athletes were measured and the results are shown in the frequency table below:

Pulse rate (beats per minute)	Number of athletes
41-45	7
46–50	11
51–55	23
56–60	26
61–65	14
66–70	9
71–75	7
75–80	3

In a new sheet:

- Enter 'Pulse rate' in cell A1 and the *end of range* data with the aid of a formula in cells A2 to A9.

- Enter 'Number of athletes' in cell B1 and the frequencies from the table in cells B2 to B9.

- Enter 'Cumulative frequency' in cell C1.

- Enter the number 7 in cell C2.

- Enter formula =C2+B3 in cell C3 and copy it down to cell C9.

- Create a cumulative frequency curve and print out a hard copy of your curve.

- Use your printout to find estimates for
  (i) the median pulse rate
  (ii) the interquartile range. ──────────

There are 60 shrubs.
$\frac{60}{2} = 30$
On your graph find the 30th shrub on the vertical axis and draw a horizontal line until you meet the curve. Draw a vertical line down from this point to the horizontal axis to find your estimate for the median.
Use
$\frac{60}{4} = 15$ and
$3 \times \frac{60}{4} = 45$
on the vertical axis to help you find the quartiles.

For more accuracy before you print:
- Place your chart as a new sheet at step 4 of the wizard.
- Double click each axis in turn, click the scale tab and change the major unit to 1.

Remember to place the chart as a new sheet at stage 4 of the wizard and to change the major unit of each axis.

The interquartile range is the value of the upper quartile minus the value of the lower quartile.

19.4 Simultaneous equations

You can solve simultaneous equations on a graphical calculator.

After you have switched on the calculator select the **GRAPH** icon using the arrow keys and then press the EXE key to display a window similar to this:

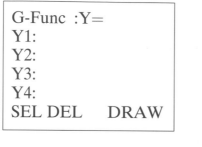

```
G-Func :Y=
Y1:
Y2:
Y3:
Y4:
SEL DEL    DRAW
```

Press SHIFT F3 to bring up the V-Window

```
V-Window
Xmin:        −10
max:          10
scl:           1

INIT  TRIG  Sto  Rcl
```

Change the size of the x-axis to a minimum of −10 and a maximum of 10, using the EXE key to confirm each entry.

Use a scale of 1.

Press the down arrow key to produce a similar window for y and change the y-axis from −10 to 10, using a scale of 1, again.

When finished press EXE to bring up the G-Func menu again.

Exercise 19D Graphical calculator

To begin question **1**, press X, T + 1 EXE to store the equation $Y1 = X + 1$.

Then press 3 − X, T EXE to store the equation $Y2 = 3 − X$.

Press F4 to produce the two lines.

Press F1 and the x and y coordinates will be displayed at the bottom of your screen. Use the arrow keys to move the cursor (which may not be in view) towards the intersection point of the lines. The calculator *may* not be able to find the exact intersection point but all the answers in this exercise are integers. For question **1** the intersection point may be displayed as $x = 1.0256$, $y = 2.0256$. If this happens, bring up the V-Window and press F1 (INIT) to enable the solution $x = 1, y = 2$.

When you have finished each question press [SHIFT] [F3] [EXE] to return to the GRAPH mode. Delete your equations one by one by using the arrow keys to select the equations and pressing the [F2] key followed by the [F1] key.

1 Draw the two lines $y = x + 1$ and $y = 3 - x$, to use your calculator to solve the simultaneous equations:

$y = x + 1$
$y = 3 - x$

Use your calculator to solve the following equations:

2 $y = 2x - 1$
$y = 2 - x$

3 $y = \frac{1}{2}x + 3$
$y = x + 2$

> Press [0] [.] [5] for $\frac{1}{2}$

4 $y = 3x + 2$
$y = 7 - 2x$

> You can also solve simultaneous equations using a computer software package like *Omnigraph*.

5 $y = x^2 + 1$
$y = -3x - 1$

> Press [X, T] [x²] for x^2

19.5 Finding Pythagorean triples

Exercise 19E Scientific calculator

1 In Chapter 13 you saw that Pythagorean triples can be generated using the expressions

$$2nm, \quad n^2 - m^2, \quad n^2 + m^2$$

where m and n are positive integers and $n > m$.

> There is more on Pythagorean triples on page 275.

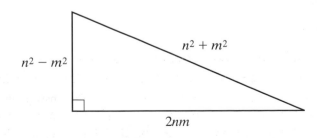

Every Pythagorean triple generates a *family* of triples, created by multiplying each number by an integer:

There is more on similar triangles on page 307.

$$[3, 4, 5], [6, 8, 10], [9, 12, 15], [12, 16, 20] \ldots$$

is a family of Pythagorean triples. These triples create similar triangles.

There are 15 other families of Pythagorean triples containing integers less than 100. Substitute values of n and m into the expressions on page 387 to find them.

You can just write down the simplest triple from each family.

2   In the following sequence:

- you add the numerator and denominator of any fraction to obtain the denominator of the *next* fraction,
- you **double** the denominator and add the numerator of any fraction to obtain the numerator of the next fraction.

$$= 2 \times 2 + 3$$

$$\frac{1}{1}, \frac{3}{2}, \frac{7}{5}, \frac{17}{12}, \ldots$$

$$= 3 + 2$$

(a) Find the next 10 terms of the sequence.

For the term $\frac{7}{5}$, you can split the numerator into the sum of two consecutive integers: $\frac{7}{5} = \frac{3+4}{5}$. This reveals the Pythagorean triple [3, 4, 5]. Every second term after $\frac{7}{5}$ also hides a Pythagorean triple.

(b) Find the next 5 triples hidden in the sequence.

19.6 Handling data

You can use a spreadsheet to create line graphs, pie charts, scatter graphs and lines of best fit.

Exercise 19F Spreadsheet

1   The temperature of a patient, Allan, was recorded twice a day whilst he was recovering in hospital from a fever.

Date	Temperature in degrees Celsius
Monday am	39.2
Monday pm	38.7
Tuesday am	38.3
Tuesday pm	38.1
Wednesday am	37.9
Wednesday pm	37.6
Thursday am	37.6
Thursday pm	37.5
Friday am	37.3
Friday pm	37.3
Saturday am	37.2
Saturday pm	37.1
Sunday am	37.0
Sunday pm	37.1
Monday am	37.0
Monday pm	37.0
Tuesday am	37.0

- Enter all the data into columns A and B of a spreadsheet.
- Highlight all the data and use the chart wizard to create a line graph. Make sure you add appropriate labels to your chart at step 3 of the wizard.

- Choose this chart type:

- Add labels to your chart at step 3
- At the last step of the wizard choose the option to place the chart as a new sheet.
- Print out a hard copy of your line graph.

2   The number of ice creams sold by Jules in her shop during one week in July are shown in the following frequency table:

Day of the week	Number of ice creams sold
Monday	62
Tuesday	65
Wednesday	78
Thursday	36
Friday	58
Saturday	91
Sunday	70

- Enter the data into cells A1 to A8 and B1 to B8 of your spreadsheet.

- Use the chart wizard to create a pie chart of your data and place the chart as a new sheet at the last step of the wizard.

- Give two reasons why you think the sales might have been so low on the Thursday.

- Enter the formula =AVERAGE(B2:B8) in cell B9 to calculate the mean number of sales.

- Enter the formula =MEDIAN(B2:B8) in cell B10 to calculate the median number of sales.

There is more on averages in Chapter 4.

3 The data in this table shows the number of goals scored, goals conceded and points total for the 24 football clubs in the Nationwide Division One 1999/2000 season.

(a) Enter the frequency table headings and all the data into columns A, B and C of a new spreadsheet. using the rows 1 to 25.

(b) Enter the heading "Goal difference" in cell D1.

(c) Enter the formula =A2-B2 in cell D2 and copy it down to cell D25.

(d) Use the chart wizard to create the following 3 scatter graphs – remember to place each graph as a new sheet at the final step of the wizard:

> goals scored against points total
> goals conceded against points total
> goal difference against points total

> Hold down the Ctrl key on your keyboard to highlight any columns not next to each other.

(e) For each scatter graph describe the type of correlation.

(f) On each graph click Chart on the menu bar and Add Trendline. (In *Excel* a line of best fit is called a trendline.)

(g) Enter the formula =AVERAGE(A2:A25) in cell A26 and copy it *across* to cell C26 to calculate the mean for columns A, B and C.

(h) Enter the formula =MEDIAN(A2:A25) in cell A27 and copy it *across* to cell C27 to calculate the median for columns A, B and C.

(i) Enter the formula =MODE(A2:A25) in cell A28 and copy it across to cell C28 to calculate the mode for columns A, B and C.

	A	B	C
1	Goals scored	Goals conceded	Points total
2	79	45	91
3	78	40	89
4	71	42	87
5	88	67	82
6	65	44	77
7	69	50	76
8	64	48	74
9	62	49	74
10	49	41	67
11	62	53	66
12	55	51	62
13	45	50	57
14	57	68	57
15	53	55	56
16	57	67	54
17	59	71	54
18	55	67	54
19	55	66	51
20	46	67	51
21	41	67	51
22	43	60	49
23	52	77	46
24	48	69	36
25	38	77	36

19.7 Powers, factors, primes and perfect numbers

Exercise 19G Scientific calculator and the Internet

Investigation

Finding perfect numbers:

A number is said to be 'perfect' if all its factors, apart from the number itself, add up to the number.

For example, the factors of 6 are 1, 2, 3 and 6:

$$1 + 2 + 3 = 6$$

So 6 is a perfect number.

There is more on factors and powers in Chapter 1.

- Find the next perfect number after 6
- Complete the following table to help you find the next *four* perfect numbers.

Hint:
The next perfect number is between 20 and 30.

n	$2^n - 1$	Is $2^n - 1$ a prime number?	2^{n-1}	$(2^n - 1) \times 2^{n-1}$	Is $(2^n - 1) \times 2^{n-1}$ a perfect number?
2	3	Yes	2	6	Yes
3	7	Yes	4	28	
4	15	No	8		
5					
6					
7					
8					
9					
10					

If $n = 4$, press:

[2] [x^y] [4] [−] [1] [=]

to give 15

If $n = 4$, press:

[2] [x^y] [3] [=]

to give 8 $n - 1$

- Visit www.heinemann.co.uk/hotlinks (express code: PRIME) to check for prime numbers.
- Visit www.heinemann.co.uk/hotlinks (express code: PERFECT) to check for perfect numbers.
- When is $(2^n - 1) \times 2^{n-1}$ a perfect number?
- List the perfect numbers you have found as the sum of their factors apart from the number itself.

E 19.8 Fruitful fractions

There is no pattern in the frequency of occurrence of prime numbers and so there can be no formula that will generate them all. However, the following sequence of fractions will generate all the prime numbers... if you had an infinite amount of time! This sequence of *fruitful fractions*, was created by John Conway, Professor of Mathematics at Princeton University in the USA. The fourteen fractions are:

$$\frac{17}{91}, \frac{78}{85}, \frac{19}{51}, \frac{23}{38}, \frac{29}{33}, \frac{77}{29}, \frac{95}{23}, \frac{77}{19}, \frac{1}{17}, \frac{11}{13}, \frac{13}{11}, \frac{15}{14}, \frac{15}{2}, \frac{55}{1}$$

You can use them to find primes like this:

- Start with the number 2.
- Multiply 2 by the first fraction in the sequence that gives a whole number. The fraction is $\frac{15}{2}$, since

$$2 \times \frac{15}{2} = 15$$

- Multiply 15 by the first fraction in the sequence that gives a whole number. The fraction is $\frac{55}{1}$, since

$$15 \times \frac{55}{1} = 825$$

- The next multiplication is $825 \times \frac{29}{33} = 725$

- Followed by $725 \times \frac{77}{29} = 1925$

Notes:
- You must always go back to the start of the sequence of fruitful fractions after each whole number is found.
- You may use a fraction more than once.
- Breaking down each answer into its prime factors may help you choose the next fraction:

$15 = 5 \times 3$
$825 = 3 \times 5^2 \times 11$
– contains '33'
$725 = 5^2 \times 29$
— contains '29'

You can continue this process forever. Every time the sequence reaches a power of 2, the power is the next prime number. After *fifteen* multiplications the sequence reaches $4 = 2^2$. 2 is a prime number.

After *fifty* more multiplications the sequence reaches $8 = 2^3$. 3 is a prime number. The sequence will never reach $16 = 2^4$ because 4 is not prime.

Exercise 19H Fruitful fractions

1 What is the next power of 2 the sequence will reach after 8?

2 Find the values of the sequence up to $4 = 2^2$. The first five are listed below:

$$2, 15, 825, 725, 1925, \ldots 4$$

If you are confident with programming a graphical calculator or computer you could write a program to find prime numbers using fruitful fractions. Use your program to work out how many multiplications will be needed to reach $128 = 2^7$.

E 19.9 Quadratic curves, translations and reflections

Exercise 19I Graphical calculator

You can use your graphical calculator to study transformations of the curve $y = x^2$. If necessary, use the instructions on page 386 to set both the x and y axes of your calculator to run from -5 to $+5$ and set the scale for both axes to 1 unit.

In questions **1** to **10** use your graphical calculator to help you describe the transformation, or transformations, from the first curve to the second curve. Describe the translation using distance across and up and give the equations of any lines of reflection.

There is more on quadratic curves in Chapter 7 and more on transformations in Chapter 15.

To begin question **1**, press [X, T] [X²] [EXE] to store the equation $Y1 = X^2$.

Then press [X, T] [X²] [+] [2] [EXE] to store the equation $Y2 = X^2 + 2$.

Press [F4] to produce the two curves.

When you have finished each question press [SHIFT] [F3] [EXE] to return to the GRAPH mode. Delete your equations one by one by using the arrow keys to select the equations and then the [F2] key followed by the [F1] key to delete your equations.

In question **3** press [(] [X, T] [+] [2] [)] [X²] [EXE] to enter $(x + 2)^2$.

1 $y = x^2$ and $y = x^2 + 2$
2 $y = x^2$ and $y = x^2 - 3$
3 $y = x^2$ and $y = (x + 2)^2$
4 $y = x^2$ and $y = (x - 3)^2$
5 $y = x^2$ and $y = -x^2$
6 $y = x^2$ and $y = (x + 3)^2 + 2$
7 $y = x^2$ and $y = (x - 4)^2 - 2$
8 $y = x^2$ and $y = (x + 4)^2 - 2$
9 $y = (x + 4)^2$ and $y = -(x + 4)^2$
10 $y = (x - 2)^2$ and $y = (x - 2)^2 + 4$

For each of questions **11** to **14**, sketch the two graphs on paper and describe the transformation.

11 $y = x^2$ and $y = x^2 + a$, where $a > 0$
12 $y = x^2$ and $y = (x + b)^2$, where $b > 0$
13 $y = x^2$ and $y = x^2 - c$, where $c > 0$
14 $y = x^2$ and $y = (x - d)^2$, where $d > 0$

Index